Constructing Global Order

For a long time, international relations scholars have adopted a narrow view of what is global order, who are its makers and managers, and what means they employ to realize their goals. Amitav Acharya argues that the nature and scope of agency in the global order – who creates it and how – needs to be redefined and broadened. Order is built not by material power alone, but also by ideas and norms. While the West designed the post-war order, the non-Western countries were not passive. They contested and redefined Western ideas and norms, and contributed new ones of their own making. This book examines such acts of agency, especially the redefinitions of sovereignty and security, shaping contemporary world politics. With the decline of the Western dominance, ideas and agency from the Rest may make it possible to imagine and build a truly global order.

Amitav Acharya is Distinguished Professor of International Relations and the UNESCO Chair in Transnational Challenges and Governance at the School of International Service, American University, Washington, DC. His recent books include: *The End of American World Order* (2014); *Rethinking Power, Institutions and Ideas in World Politics: Whose IR?* (2014); *Whose Ideas Matter? Agency and Power in Asian Regionalism* (2009); and *Why Govern? Rethinking Demand and Progress in Global Governance* (edited, 2016). He is the first non-Western scholar to be elected as the President of the International Studies Association (ISA).

Constructing Global Order

Agency and Change in World Politics

Amitav Acharya

American University, Washington, DC

CAMBRIDGE
UNIVERSITY PRESS

CAMBRIDGE
UNIVERSITY PRESS

University Printing House, Cambridge CB2 8BS, United Kingdom

One Liberty Plaza, 20th Floor, New York, NY 10006, USA

477 Williamstown Road, Port Melbourne, VIC 3207, Australia

314–321, 3rd Floor, Plot 3, Splendor Forum, Jasola District Centre,
New Delhi – 110025, India

79 Anson Road, #06-04/06, Singapore 079906

Cambridge University Press is part of the University of Cambridge.

It furthers the University's mission by disseminating knowledge in the pursuit
of education, learning, and research at the highest international levels of
excellence.

www.cambridge.org
Information on this title: www.cambridge.org/9781107170711
DOI: 10.1017/9781316756768

First published 2018
Printed in the United Kingdom by Clays, St Ives plc

A catalogue record for this publication is available from the British Library.

Library of Congress Cataloging-in-Publication Data

Names: Acharya, Amitav, author.
Title: Constructing global order : agency and change in world politics /
    Amitav Acharya.
Description: Cambridge, United Kingdom ; New York, NY : Cambridge
    University Press, 2018. | Includes bibliographical references and index.
Identifiers: LCCN 2017058321| ISBN 9781107170711 (hardback) | ISBN
    9781316621783 (paperback)
Subjects: LCSH: International organization. | East and West. | Agent
    (Philosophy) | Nonwestern countries.
Classification: LCC JZ1318 .A275 2018 | DDC 341.2 – dc23 LC record
available at https://lccn.loc.gov/2017058321

ISBN 978-1-107-17071-1 Hardback

ISBN 978-1-316-62178-3 Paperback

Contents

Figures

Figures

Tables

Acknowledgements

My greatest debt is to John Haslam, for keeping faith with the project through the prolonged review process and many delays on my part. I thank Goueun Lee, Di Wu, Ji Young Kwon, and Sahil Mathur, all graduate students at American University, for their excellent research and editorial assistance, Robert Judkins of Cambridge University Press for his production management, and Carol Fellingham-Webb for her editorial work.

Some of the thinking behind this book has been stimulated by the work of Mohammed Ayoob, Barry Buzan, Andrew Hurrell, Louise Fawcett, Ramesh Thakur, Michael Barnett, Robert Cox, Randolph Persaud, Thomas Weiss, Thomas Risse, Jack Snyder, Yaqing Qin, Keith Krause, Peter Katzenstein, Kathryn Sikkink, Martha Finnemore, Lisbeth Zimmermann, Alan Bloomfield, and David Capie. However, I take sole responsibility for the views expressed here.

A special thanks to the two anonymous reviewers for their detailed, trenchant yet constructive comments on earlier drafts of the manuscript.

I am always thankful to colleagues at the School of International Service, American University, for providing a warm and intellectually vibrant environment for my work, and I am especially grateful to former Dean Jim Goldgeier for his unfailing support for my work related to this book. Visiting professorships at St Gallen University and the Schwarzman College, Tsinghua University, allowed much needed time for reflection and writing to complete the project.

Amitav Acharya
Washington, DC,
3 December 2017

A Note on the Text

This book brings together a number of ideas that I have developed over the past two decades. Hence, some of the material presented in the book draws from my previous writings.

Parts of Chapters 2, 3, and 4 are drawn from "How Ideas Spread, Whose Norms Matter: Norm Localization and Institutional Change in Asian Regionalism," *International Organization* 58, no. 2 (Spring 2004), 239–275; "Norm Subsidiarity and Regional Orders: Sovereignty, Regionalism and Rule Making in the Third World," *International Studies Quarterly* 55, no. 1 (2011), 95–123; and *Whose Ideas Matter: Agency and Power in Asian Regionalism* (Cornell University Press, 2009); *East of India: South of China: Sino-Indian Encounters in Southeast Asia* (Oxford University Press, 2017); "R2P and Theory of Norm Diffusion: Towards a Framework of Norm Circulation," *Global Responsibility to Protect* 5, no. 4 (2013), 466–479.

Chapter 4 relies on "R2P and a Theory of Norm Circulation," in Ramesh Thakur and William Maley, eds., *Theorising the Responsibility to Protect* (Cambridge University Press, 2015); and "'Idea-shift': How Ideas from the Rest Are Reshaping Global Order," *Third World Quarterly* 37, no. 7 (2016), 1156–1170.

Chapter 5 draws from "The Periphery as the Core: The Third World and Security Studies," in Keith Krause and Michael Williams, eds., *Critical Security Studies* (Minneapolis: University of Minnesota Press, 1996), 299–327; "Human Security," in John Baylis, Steve Smith, and Patricia Owens, eds., *The Globalisation of World Politics* (Oxford University Press, 2005, 2017); and "Beyond Anarchy: Third World Instability and International Order After the Cold War," in Stephanie Neumann, ed., *International Relations Theory and the Third World* (New York: St Martin's Press, 1997), 159–211.

Chapter 6 borrows from "Regionalism Beyond EU Centrism," in Tanja A. Börzel and Thomas. Risse, eds., *Oxford Handbook of Comparative Regionalism* (Oxford University Press, 2016); and "Comparative Regionalism: A Field Whose Time Has Come?" *International Spectator* 47, no. 1 (2012), 3–15.

1   Introduction: Rethinking Agency and Change in Global Order

What is order in world politics? Who are the makers and managers of that order? Which means do they employ to realize their goals? These questions are of course hardly new. Indeed, they have preoccupied international relations scholars for a long time. But answers to them have remained contested and unsettled.

In this book, I address these questions. And in so doing, I focus on the issue of agency in world politics. This book argues that the nature and scope of agency need to be further recast, redefined, and broadened. While some of this broadening has already taken place, recent theoretical work in international relations, especially concerning norm diffusion, and developments in world politics, such as the global power shift, require us to take a fresh look at agency in global order. The main arguments of the book are:

1. The existing global order is traditionally conceptualized, first, as an extension of the European state system, and subsequently, as the by-product of an American-led liberal hegemonic order. Yet, such characterizations obscure the role of other actors, including non-Western states and societies in the building of global order.
2. Many governing ideas and institutions of the post-war global order, despite originating from specific European and American milieux, are assumed to have a universal quality, in the sense of applying to all. Yet, in reality, they have been and continue to be contested. This is especially the case with sovereignty and security, the two core themes of this book. For example, while sovereignty at its origin was a European (Westphalian) construct, security, especially the prevailing idea of national security, is American in origin. IR scholars and policymakers take them to be universal, but the meaning and practice of both have been marked by significant variations around the world.
3. These contestations open the space for other actors, including non-Western actors, to put forward alternative, sometimes localized, ideas and institutions that also support order-building. To understand

and analyze these multiple and diverse foundations of contemporary global order, we need a broader conception of agency.

4. Agency can be material as well as ideational or normative. When it comes to normative agency, the role of non-Western actors is not simply a matter of passive acceptance of Western principles and approaches to sovereignty and security. For example, the global sovereignty regime, the foundation of the modern world polity, came about not just through the passive inheritance of Westphalian principles by newly decolonized states. The latter also actively constructed these principles and translated the abstract notion of sovereignty into rules of conduct. The process was marked by local initiative and adaptations in various parts of the world. The same can be said about the idea of security, the meaning of which has changed through distinctive constructions in non-Western contexts that have wider global relevance and applicability.

5. Such contestations, variations, and constructions of order-building ideas and institutions are often overlooked by mainstream IR theories. But they are among the fundamental mechanisms and building blocks of global order today. They produce a diversity that challenges the orthodox conceptions of a universal order of humankind. Universality, the sense of one set of standards or principles "applying to all," is neither possible nor in many cases desirable. True universality lies in recognizing the essential diversity of states, societies, and regions, and finding common ground among them.

6. Hence, we do not live in a world of seamless globality that simply erases or subsumes the local. Despite some homogenization through international institutions and norms, local or regionally specific understandings and approaches to international order remain a vital aspect of global order-building. Regional institutions offer crucial sites for the creation and diffusion of these understandings and approaches, and variations in regionalisms are a major factor shaping global order. At the same time, the world is not being divided into regions and neither are regions and regionalism becoming the sole driving forces of global order. Rather, what we see is a world of growing complexity and overlapping diversity where local and regional constructions of concepts and approaches to order assume greater significance than they are assigned by much of traditional international relations.

7. This diversity may actually be a necessary and critical factor in managing world politics as the hitherto Western-dominated order fades and gives way to a more pluralistic or "Multiplex" World. The emerging

global order will not be a hegemonic construction, in the sense of being constituted by the principles, institutions, and modes of managing stability that are dominated by a single power or a concert of powers. Instead, it will be constructed through the broader and more diffuse forms of agency and leadership that are outlined in the book.

These arguments are developed in this book in seven chapters. Chapter 1 examines the varied conceptions of order in world politics, differentiating between situational and normative conceptions of global order. It then reviews the meaning of agency in building global order, taking stock of attempts to expand its meaning, and offers a further redefinition and broadening of the concept. Chapter 2 discusses the interplay between power, interest, and ideas in order-building, and specifies different forms of normative agency employed by actors in building order in world politics. Overall, Chapter 2 highlights the normative behaviors and agency of non-Western countries, a neglected aspect of the literature on norm dynamics, in the construction of regional and global order.

Chapter 3 examines the agency in the contestations about, and reinterpretations and extensions of, Westphalian sovereignty, especially the norm of non-intervention, in different regions in the early post-war world. Chapter 4 brings the discussion of redefining sovereignty to the more contemporary period, especially locating agency in the transformation of humanitarian intervention to Responsibility to Protect (R2P).

Chapter 5 shifts the focus of the book to the concept of security, tracing agency in the changing understanding of security from national security to human security. Chapter 6 looks at regionalism, a major site of agency in world politics, in redefining sovereignty and security. A major theme of this chapter is to analyze the shift from a Eurocentric conception of regionalism to a more inclusive and pluralistic notion that captures diverse patterns of regional interactions around the world.

Chapter 7, the conclusion, not only sums up the main findings of the previous chapters, but also looks ahead by outlining the shift from a Western-dominated hegemonic or quasi-hegemonic order to a more complex, diverse, and decentered (post-hegemonic) world politics. The pluralization of agency outlined conceptually in Chapters 1 and 2, and illustrated through the discussions of sovereignty and security in the subsequent chapters, has driven and will continue to drive the transformation of global order. It is opening the door to a multi-agentic, pluralistic or Multiplex World, which also portends the narrowing, if not the end, of the West–Rest divide and makes it feasible to imagine the possibility of a truly global order.

This introductory chapter has three objectives. The first is to examine the concept of world or global order in its multiple meanings,[1] but especially highlighting the conflation and tension between its descriptive and normative aspects. The second is to analyze the concept of agency, including the actors and the forms of action that constitute agency in global order-building. Here, key is the outline of a broader conception of agency that goes beyond the rationalist-materialist conception that has dominated the traditional literature of international relations. Third, the chapter presents the outline of an emerging global order that, while retaining some key features of the Western- and American-dominated world order of the present, would be more diverse and pluralistic: a Multiplex World.

Defining Order

The meaning of order in world politics is a matter of much contention. As Alagappa notes, order is a "slippery" concept in international relations, and can be used in "multiple ways."[2] Some definitions of order are situational or descriptive, while others are normative, although it is commonplace to see a conflation of the two.[3] The *Macmillan English*

---

[1] The terms "international order," "world order," and "global order" are often conflated. Bull made a distinction between "international order" and "world order." While the former applies mainly to the relationships between states, the latter applies to "social life among mankind as a whole." Hedley Bull, *The Anarchical Society*, 3rd edition (Basingstoke: Macmillan, 2002), 19. In this book, I use "world order" and "global order" interchangeably, but am mindful that global order is a more recent and expansive notion associated with growing interdependence and globalization. I accept Bull's view that world order (in my case, global order) involves all humankind. But while Bull may have considered the position of non-Western countries in world order, I do not think he gave due recognition to their positive contribution, or agency, in building that order. Hurrell defines "global political order" as a "world made up of separate, sovereign states which are, in turn, linked through various kinds of political practices and institutionalized structures." Andrew Hurrell, *On Global Order: Power, Values, and the Constitution of International Society* (Oxford University Press, 2007), 3. While I accept Hurrell's association of global order with linkages forged through political practices and institutions, this book gives more play to ideas and norms that shape those practices and institutions. But above all, this book develops and employs a broader notion of the agency through which global order is produced and managed, comprising both Western and non-Western actors, than is available from any previous work on the subject.

[2] Muthiah Alagappa, "The Study of International Order," in *Asian Security Order: Instrumental and Normative Features*, ed. Muthiah Alagappa (Stanford University Press, 2003), 34.

[3] For example, Stanley Hoffmann summarized Raymond Aron's five meanings of world order with the following words:

> order as an arrangement of reality,
> order as the relations between parts,

Dictionary offers a purely descriptive notion of world order as "the political, economic, or social situation in the world at a particular time and the effect that this has on relationships between different countries."[4] Order in this sense is "a description of a particular status quo."[5] This can imply an existing distribution of power or an institutional arrangement, irrespective of its consequences for peace or conflict. Weston and Falk also define world order in situational terms. It "refers to the aggregation of norms, procedures and institutions that give shape and structure to international society at any given time."[6] Using the same definition, Falk elsewhere argues that the concept of world order does not necessarily mean a condition that "prohibits the recourse to war, or is successful as a peace system, although it may accomplish either of these things."[7]

A normative conception of order stresses some desirable objectives, such as increased stability, predictability, if not peace per se, in international relations. In the literature on international relations, the normative conceptions of order have varied widely. Some are mainly goal-oriented to a minimalist conception of stability, while others are more expansively tied to upholding morality, justice, and "good-life." The *Oxford Living Dictionary* defines world order as "a system controlling events in the world, especially a set of arrangements established intentionally for preserving global political stability."[8] In a particularly influential formulation, Bull defines international order as "a pattern of activity that sustains the elementary or primary goals of the society of states, or international society."[9] He identifies several such goals: preservation of the state system, maintaining the sovereignty or independence of states, relative peace or absence of war as normal condition among states, limitation of violence,

---

order as the minimum condition for existence,
order as the minimum condition for co-existence,
order as the condition for the good life.

According to Hoffman, the first two of the above are purely descriptive, the next two are partly descriptive and partly normative, and the last one is purely normative. Cited by Richard A. Falk, "Contending Approaches to World Order," in *Peace and World Order Studies: A Curriculum Guide*, ed. Barbara J. Wien, 3rd edition (New York: Institute for World Order, 1981), 30.

[4] *Macmillan English Dictionary*, 2nd edition (Oxford: Macmillan Education, 2010).
[5] Mohammed Ayoob, "Regional Security and the Third World", in *Regional Security in the Third World*, ed. Mohammed Ayoob (London: Croom Helm, 1986), 4.
[6] Burns H. Weston, "Peace and World Order Education: An Optimal Design," in *Peace and World Order Studies*, ed. Wien, 59.
[7] Richard A. Falk, *A Global Approach to National Policy* (Cambridge, MA: Harvard University Press, 1975), 198.
[8] *Oxford Living Dictionary*, https://en.oxforddictionaries.com/definition/world_order.
[9] Hedley Bull, *The Anarchical Society*, 2nd edition (Basingstoke: Macmillan, 1999), 8.

keeping of promises, and protection of property rights.[10] Hurrell follows
Bull in associating global political order with relative peace and stability.
Hence his notion of "global political order" is to be understood in terms
of the extent to which the political practices of and institutional linkages
among states "have reduced conflict and facilitated some degree of cooperation and stability."[11]

Although Bull's definition goes beyond a purely descriptive or situational understanding of order, it has been accused of not being normative enough, and of giving priority to stability over equity and justice.
Falk sees in it a "hostility towards 'normative' conceptions of world order
that stress the pursuit of valued goals as the object of inquiry."[12] Hence,
at its most extreme normative end, world order involves considerations
of morality, inclusiveness, and justice, which seek "to replace the system
of states with a universal community of mankind."[13]

In international relations theory, a normative understanding of order
has been popular with constructivists.[14] For realists generally speaking,
order involves a balance of power produced and managed through military
and economic capabilities. Liberals stress economic interdependence

---

[10] Ibid., 16–19.
[11] Hurrell, *On Global Order*, 3. Deutsch and Singer define stability, a key element of order
for Bull and Hurrell, in terms of the absence of system-destroying conflict, or "war of
survival," rather than absence of competition and conflict among nations per se. As they
put it, stability for individual nations refers to "the probability that the system retains
all of its essential characteristics; that no single nation becomes dominant; that most of
its members continue to survive; and that large-scale war does not occur. And from the
more limited perspective of the individual nations, stability would refer to the probability
of their continued political independence and territorial integrity without any significant
probability of becoming engaged in a 'war for survival.'" Karl W. Deutsch and J. David
Singer, "Multipolar Power Systems and International Stability," *World Politics* 16, no. 3
(1964), 390–391.
[12] Falk, "Contending Approaches to World Order," 31.
[13] Alagappa, "The Study of International Order," 36. Here, Alagappa argues that while
Bull's conception of order conflates international order with "international society,"
which assumes the existence of common interests and values, rather than a Hobbesian
world, it excludes the Kantian conception of a universal community.
[14] Sorensen distinguishes between four understandings of order: "(a) the realist concern
of the politico-military balance of power; (b) the liberal concern of the make-up of
international institutions and the emergence of global governance; (c) the constructivist
concern of the realm of ideas and ideology, with a focus on the existence or not of common values on a global scale; and (d) the IPE (International Political Economy) concern of the economic realm of production, finance, and distribution." Georg Sorensen,
"What Kind of World Order? The International System in the New Millennium," Paper
presented at the annual meeting of the American Political Science Association, Hilton
Chicago and the Palmer House Hilton, Chicago, IL, September 2, 2004, http://www
.allacademic.com/meta/p59921_index.html.

and multilateral institutions. But constructivist scholarship gives a frontal place to ideas, norms, and legitimacy in conceptualizing order.[15]

There is of course abundant tension between the descriptive and normative elements of order. Since the former implies a given situation, or status quo, what if that status quo is not acceptable to everyone who is supposed to live within it and expected to support and sustain it? Here, a key question about the normative understanding of order is whether achieving it might require changing an existing or dominant situation of configuration of power, institutions, and norms in world politics. But who are the agents of that change? Traditional international relations literature often credits powerful actors, especially the established great powers, with order-creation, maintenance, and change. But as Barnett puts it, "World orders are created and sustained not only by great power preferences but also by changing understandings of what constitutes a legitimate international order."[16]

Hence the key to any normative understanding of order is its legitimacy. For this book, the legitimacy of international or global order depends on representation and participation,[17] or the extent to which an order represents the wider segment of the international system, and whether it enjoys the support and participation not just of the established powers, but also of other actors, including the weaker ones, newcomers, and the emerging regional and global players, who may have a different understanding of what constitutes a legitimate and effective world order. In fact, it is the latter who are likely to drive the impetus for change, and constructing a global order means accommodating their initiative, support, and commitment.

---

[15] Constructivism is not the only theoretical position to consider the ideational dimensions of order. Cox, a Gramscian Marxist, argues that "material relations and ideas are inextricably intertwined to co-produce world orders." "Robert Cox on World Orders, Historical Change, and the Purpose of Theory in International Relations," Robert Cox, "Theory Talk," 37, accessed December 25, 2012, www.theory-talks.org/2010/03/theory-talk-37.html; Robert W. Cox, "Social Forces, States, and World Orders," in Cox with Timothy J. Sinclair, *Approaches to World Order* (Cambridge University Press, 1996). Yet with transnational production conditioning political, ideological, and military relations, it is difficult to discern how much autonomy ideational forces might enjoy in the Coxian formulation.

[16] Michael Barnett, "Social Constructivism," in *The Globalisation of World Politics*, ed. John Baylis, Steve Smith and Patricia Owens, 4th edition (Oxford University Press, 2008), 168.

[17] Abram Chayes and Antonia Chayes point out that legitimacy depends on "the degree of international consensus" and "participation." Chayes and Chayes, *The New Sovereignty: Compliance with International Regulatory Agreements* (Cambridge, MA: Harvard University Press, 1995), 41, 128. Chapter 2 provides further discussion of legitimacy through representation and participation, which are key to building the subsidiary norms of world order.

This is especially challenging because the key rules, institutions, and context of the post-World War II international order were based on the European state system, albeit modified if not fundamentally transformed by the power and purpose of the United States. For example, the idea and rules of Westphalian sovereignty were European in origin, while the dominant post-war idea of security, "national security," was a distinctively American contribution. But turning an *international* order based on these ideas, despite their utility and resilience, into a true *global* order could not be possible, or would remain incomplete, without the consent and participation of actors other than the core group of Western nations, especially the postcolonial states. And securing their support means accommodating their challenges and proposed changes to the status quo of the distribution of power, institutional arrangement, and normative structure of world politics, and developing more inclusive ideas and interactions. This process is crucial to the transformation of the Europe-derived international order into a global order, although it remains a work-in-progress. It is the theme of this book, and informs its reconceptualization and broadening of what constitutes agency in world politics.

A few clarifications about this book's conceptual approach are necessary. First, it is both analytical and normative. While analyzing what world order is or has been, I also pay attention to what should have been and ought to be. I realize that the line between the two can be blurred; this is not uncommon in any work inspired by constructivism. To the extent that this book offers a critique of the existing world order, and the orthodox view of agency that underpins the analysis of that order, it is bound to take on a normative tone. But at the same time, a great deal of the criticism of the order in the book concerns the demonstrated practical limitations of that order. In this book, I look at non-intervention, humanitarian intervention, human security, and regionalism in both analytical and normative terms. My analysis in each of these areas is analytical in the sense that it captures the limitations and failures of the existing notions of sovereignty and security in ensuring global order. At the same time, I take a normative position by siding with the demands for redefinition and broadening of sovereignty and security that I consider to be more progressive and emancipatory. I hope this is a defensible approach. As Jack Snyder has argued,

the relationship between normative and empirical arguments is considerably more complex than the usual view taken by most empirical social scientists, who stick strictly to the "is" and leave the "ought" to political theorists, op-ed writers, and non-governmental organization (NGO) activists ... this division is unhealthy and unnecessary. Empirical social science has a great deal to contribute to contemporary debates on multiculturalism, human rights and virtually every other normative question of international relations.[18]

In this book, I extend the blended analytical/empirical and normative approach to investigate the changing norms of sovereignty, intervention, security, and regionalism in the making of global order.

Second, world or global order does not necessarily exclude the consideration of regional orders. Indeed, ideas about world order often have their origin within a specific region or civilization. Here, Kissinger's definition of world order is especially relevant:

World order describes the concept held by a region or civilization about the nature of just arrangements and the distribution of power thought to be applicable to the entire world. An international order is the practical application of these concepts to a substantial part of the globe – large enough to affect the global balance of power. Regional orders involve the same principles applied to a defined geographical area.[19]

One merit of Kissinger's definition is that it stresses the importance of regions and regionally held and applied conceptions of order. In other words, it brings regions into the discussion of global order. Hence, "No truly global 'world order' has ever existed."[20] A global or world order may emerge through the application of concepts and approaches initially held regionally or even nationally but which its proponents see relevant for, and seek to apply to, the whole world, or at least "to a substantial part of the globe." I agree with Kissinger that different regions or civilizations have their own ideas about how the world works, and what are the requisite elements of stability and cooperation not only for their regions but also for the world as a whole. Unlike Kissinger though, I believe such local or regional conceptions can affect not just the global balance of power, but also global interdependence, normative structures, and insti-

---

[18] Jack Snyder, "'Is' and 'Ought': Evaluating Empirical Aspects of Normative Research," in *Progress in International Relations Theory: Appraising the Field*, ed. Colin Elman and Miriam Fendius Elman (Cambridge, MA: MIT Press, 2003), 377. Snyder offers several examples of such work, including Finnemore and Sikkink's work on norm diffusion. Part of their research program "is aimed at discovering 'if, then' laws about the effects of given constraints on normative outcomes," while another part is "transformational ..., which seeks to understand how activists can overcome such constraints" (ibid., 371–372). Other examples Snyder cites include the work of Risse, Ropp, and Sikkink on human rights, which not only analyzes how and why human rights violations occur, but also "what tactics are most effective at what stage of the process of normative persuasion" (372). Another example offered by Snyder is J. S. Mill's analysis of the advantages of free speech in terms of normative claims and arguments about "how society *ought* to be organized or how people *ought* to behave" (350).

[19] Henry Kissinger, *World Order* (New York: Penguin, 2014), 9.

[20] Ibid., 2.

tutions of cooperation. Just as the post-World War II order was conceived initially by Europe and then the United States, one finds ideas about world order emanating from China (such as its *Tianxia*, or "all under heaven" cultural concept), India, and regions such as East Asia.

If this view is accepted, it follows that global order can be affected by regional ideas and actions. In the international system, actors, especially weaker ones such as the developing countries, usually find regional action necessary and useful in developing a collective voice in international affairs and addressing global challenges that they cannot address on their own or at the more crowded and complex global level. Stronger countries and rising powers may view regions as a springboard while seeking global status and leadership. National and regional conceptions of order may filter and modify the effects of global interdependence, ideas, norms, institutions, and distribution of power. Hence regionalism and regional norm dynamics are important factors shaping global order.

A third clarification about the concept of global order is that it is not the same as global governance. As discussed earlier, global order in its descriptive sense refers to the institutions, norms, and distribution of power, etc. that exist at a given time. Global governance, on the other hand, is about addressing cross-border issues such as trade or climate change that affect the world or a significant part of it.[21] To be sure, by managing and solving common problems, global governance can facilitate the realization of a stable and just global order, but it is not the same as global order itself.

To sum up some of the key points about the idea of global order employed in this book: while taking into account both the descriptive and normative conceptions of global order, it aligns more with a normative understanding. It does not assume that global order already exists or is possible, or that there is already a progressive pathway to global order unfolding before us. Rather, this book argues that efforts at achieving global order should produce a situation of "reduced conflict," and "some degree of cooperation and stability" (Hurrell), including the absence

---

[21] Global governance is the "formal or informal management of cross-border issues affecting a significant proportion of the international system by states, international institutions and non-state actors, through power, functional cooperation, laws, regimes, and norms." Amitav Acharya, "Rethinking Demand, Purpose and Progress in Global Governance: An Introduction," in *Why Govern?: Rethinking Demand and Progress in Global Governance*, ed. Amitav Acharya (Cambridge University Press, 2016), 6. Another definition of global governance sees it "as the sum of laws, norms, policies, and institutions that define, constitute, and mediate trans-border relations between states, cultures, citizens, intergovernmental and nongovernmental organizations, and the market." UN Intellectual History Project, "The UN's Role in Global Governance," Briefing Note no. 15 (August 2009), www.unhistory.org/briefing/15GlobalGov.pdf.

of a "war for survival" (Deutsch and Singer) or system-destroying war. But going beyond such a minimalist normative view of order, this book holds that *global* order depends on ensuring the representation and participation of the broadest possible segment of humankind (in keeping with Bull's notion of *world* order). The attainment of global order, as Barnett emphasizes, cannot be separated from its legitimacy, which in turn depends critically on broadening representation and participation in it.

To this end, and in keeping with the book's constructivist framework, it stresses the role of ideas and norms in global order, rather than viewing it as the by-product of material forces (military and economic) alone, which would privilege the role of great or established powers. Order, as Alagappa puts it, is about "rule-governed interaction" among states in "pursuit of [their] individual and collective goals." The existence of order depends on "whether interstate interactions conform to accepted rules."[22] For this book, the foundations of global order include a set of ideas and norms pertaining to sovereignty, security, development, human rights, environmental protection, etc., that help to limit conflict, induce cooperation and stability, and expand legitimacy through representation and participation. And unlike some traditional conceptions of *international* order which see its creation mainly in terms of the role of a hegemonic power, or a select group of established powers and the institutions they have created and dominated, *global* order depends on the extent to which its core ideas, rules, and contexts are created and shared by the widest segment of humankind. In the contemporary international system, founded as it was upon the expansion of the European state system, constructing global order means securing and expanding the participation of postcolonial actors, and acknowledging and accommodating their ideas, norms, and practices. This may require challenging and changing the existing configuration of power, institutions, and norms in world politics, and developing a more inclusive and participatory approach by drawing upon the ideas and practices of previously neglected or marginalized actors. It may also mean accepting, as Kissinger has argued, ideas about world or global order that are regionally or locally conceived, including from outside the Western core. This may lead to differences over how order is understood and managed in different parts of the world. Hence constructing global order ultimately depends on reconciling or finding common ground among, if not entirely overcoming, these differences to ensure stability and cooperation in a pluralistic world.

---

[22] Alagappa, "The Study of International Order," 39.

From the foregoing, it emerges that this book's central question is not just about what global order is, or should be, but more importantly about who makes it and how. Hence, we now turn to the question of agency in global order.

Redefining Agency

In analyzing the construction of global order, the question of agency is of fundamental importance. Here, IR scholarship faces huge challenges. As Colin Wight notes, "IR has not grappled, in a systematic manner, with the concept of agency ... Rarely is it clear what agency is, what it means to exercise agency, or who and what might do so."[23] But what is clear is that traditional notions of agency in international relations tend to privilege power, especially material power.[24] In its dictionary meaning, agency is defined as "the capacity, condition, or state of acting or of exerting power."[25] Buzan defines agency as the "faculty or state of acting or exerting power."[26] The traditional conception of agency also stresses "instrumentality," or rational or instrumental action.[27]

Moreover, some definitions of agency, including positivist and constructivist perspectives, adopt an anthropomorphist understanding of the state-as-a-person. Wendt's view that "states are collectivities of individuals that through their practices constitute each other as 'persons' having interests, fears, and so on"[28] has been interpreted by other scholars as suggesting that (1) "agency is a category that applies only to persons,"

---

[23] Colin Wight, *Agents, Structures and International Relations: Politics as Ontology* (Cambridge University Press, 2006), 178.

[24] Although the concept of power is no longer viewed primarily in material terms, but has been expanded to include ideational, normative, and cultural elements, its material sources continue to dominate the traditional conception of agency. On the pluralization of power, see Michael Barnett and Raymond Duvall, eds., *Power in Global Governance* (Cambridge University Press, 2005); Joseph S. Nye, *Soft Power: The Means to Success in World Politics* (New York: PublicAffairs, 2004). I believe the Barnett and Duvall effort dilutes the meaning of power to the extent that it loses some of its analytical utility. I find the original constructivist distinction between power (defined mainly as material power) and ideas/norms more meaningful analytically. Nye's concept of soft power is US-centric and can be viewed as an adjunct to the material or "hard" power of the United States in maintaining its global primacy. While both efforts to expand the meaning of power are useful, neither goes as far as this book's framework in pluralizing the notion of agency and capturing the role of non-Western agency.

[25] "Agency," merriam-webster.com, www.merriam-webster.com/dictionary/agency.

[26] Barry Buzan, Charles Jones and Richard Little, *The Logic of Anarchy* (New York: Columbia University Press, 1993), 103.

[27] *Kernerman Webster's College Dictionary* (New York: Random House, 2010).

[28] Alexander Wendt, "Anarchy is What States Make of It: The Social Construction of Power Politics," *International Organization* 46, no. 2 (Spring 1992), 397, footnote 21. See also Wendt, "The State as Person in International Theory," *Review of International Studies* 30,

and (2) that "states are individuals writ large."[29] Challenging this notion, Wight calls for a "multi-layered view of agency, wherein agency refers to both individual and social predicates."[30] In his view, agency reflects and combines the "'freedom of subjectivity'" of individuals, the "sociocultural system into which persons are born and develop," and their role as "the social actor" or "'positioned-practice places'" which individual agents inhabit.[31] While I adopt Wight's concept of agency, I also stress Bhaskar's association of agency with the ability to foster change: an agent must be "capable of bringing about a change in something (including self)."[32] This relates to the previous point about the normative conception of order, which can mean rejecting or transforming the prevailing status of power and institutional arrangements of a given time by those who seek to inject greater legitimacy to world order. And here, normative agency assumes critical importance, especially for those who lack the material capacity to reshape world order.

The framework of this book is informed by a further pluralization of agency, which is at the core of the emerging "Global IR" idea.[33] A key element of Global IR is the "recognition of multiple forms of agency, including the agency of non-Western actors."[34] To elaborate:

In Global IR, agency is ideational as well as material. It goes beyond military power and wealth and avoids privileging transnational norm entrepreneurship ... agency involves resistance and rejection, and not just the strengthening of the status quo in world politics. An agent-oriented narrative in Global IR should tell us how actors (state and nonstate), through their material, ideational, and interaction capabilities, construct, reject, reconstitute, and transform global and

---

no. 2 (2004), 289–316; Wendt, "How Not to Argue against State Personhood: A Reply to Lomas," *Review of International Studies* 31, no. 2 (April 2005), 357–360.

[29] Wight, *Agents, Structures and International Relations*, 180–182.

[30] Ibid., 210. He critiques both positivists', as well as early constructivist Wendt's, view of agency which he associates with anthropomorphism.

[31] Ibid., 213.

[32] Roy Bhaskar, *A Realist Theory of Science*, 2nd edition (Brighton, Sussex: Harvester Press, 1978), 109.

[33] On the Global IR approach, see: Amitav Acharya, "Global International Relations (IR) and Regional Worlds: A New Agenda for International Studies," *International Studies Quarterly* 58, no. 4 (2014), 647–659; Special issue on "Global International Relations and Regional Worlds," *International Studies Review* 18, no. 1 (March 2016); Ingo Peters and Wiebke Wemheuer-Vogelaar, eds., *Globalizing International Relations: Scholarship amidst Divides and Diversity* (London: Palgrave Macmillan, 2016).

[34] The main elements of a Global IR approach are: "A commitment to pluralistic universalism (one that does not impose any particular idea or approach on others but respects diversity while seeking common ground), grounding in world history, theoretical pluralism, a close nexus with the study of regions, regionalisms and area studies, avoidance of cultural exceptionalism, and recognition of multiple forms of agency, including the agency of non-Western actors." Amitav Acharya, "Advancing Global IR: Challenges, Contentions and Contributions," *International Studies Review* 18, no. 1 (March 2016), 5.

regional orders ... [A]gency is not the prerogative of the strong. It can manifest as the weapon of the weak. Agency can be exercised in global transnational space as well as at regional and local levels. Agency ... can describe ... localization of global norms and institutions ... Agency also means constructing new rules and institutions at the local level to support and strengthen global order against great-power hypocrisy and dominance ... Agency involves conceptualizing and implementing new approaches to development, security, and ecological justice ... Some of these acts of agency – which have involved rejecting attempts by the major Western powers to create privileged space for their interests as well as collaborating with them to organize and manage global governance – are not just for specific regions or for the Global South itself, but are important to the world order as a whole.[35]

Drawing from the above, I outline and discuss below six dimensions of the pluralization of agency that are especially relevant to this book.

First, agency often begins with challenge, or resistance, to and contestation about an existing order and its core norms, institutions, and practices. Contestation has various meanings, such as "a contentious speech act,"[36] "to compete or strive for," "a struggle for superiority or victory between rivals," and "to call into question and take an active stand against; dispute or challenge."[37] Contestations can be of different kinds and occur at different levels. Some are within the bounds of the existing world order (for example, within the liberal international order). Using a term that Robert Cox developed, one might call these "problem-solving" contestations,[38] in the sense that despite some differences among the parties, they accept the "parameters of the present order." There can be meaningful debate between status-quo and reformist positions over global order within the problem-solving approaches. Antje Wiener's important work on norm contestation deals primarily

---

[35] Acharya, "Global International Relations (IR) and Regional Worlds," 651–652.

[36] Contestation. (n.d.) WordNet 3.0, Farlex clipart collection. (2003–2008). Retrieved March 15, 2011 from www.thefreedictionary.com/Contestation.

[37] *The American Heritage® Dictionary of the English Language*, Fourth Edition. S.v. "Contestation." Retrieved March 15, 2011 from www.thefreedictionary.com/Contestation.

[38] Robert W. Cox, "Social Forces, States and World Order: Beyond International Relations Theory," in Robert O. Keohane, ed., *Neorealism and its Critics* (New York: Columbia University Press, 1986). Cox juxtaposes problem-solving with "critical." While problem-solving approaches help "legitimate an unjust and deeply iniquitous system," the latter "attempts to challenge the prevailing order by seeking out, analyzing, and where possible, assisting social processes that can potentially lead to emancipatory change." Stephen Hobden and Richard Wyn Jones, "Marxist Theories of International Relations," in Baylis, Smith and Owens, eds. *Globalization of World Politics*, 7th edition (Oxford University Press, 2017), 136.

with contested compliance *within* a given "normative community,"[39] or contestation among the "involved stakeholders."[40] But another type of contestation could be *between* different normative systems. This is akin to Cox's "critical theory," which "attempts to challenge the prevailing order by seeking out, analyzing, and where possible, assisting social processes that can potentially lead to emancipatory change."[41] While there are many examples of such contestation, in this book I apply this second type of contestation primarily to North–South relations, especially their disagreements over sovereignty and security, although there can be examples of such contestations within each camp as well.

For example, since the 1980s, there has been considerable debate over the meaning of security, and the merits and pitfalls of broadening the concept. But as discussed in Chapter 5, such redefinitions of security were mainly about extending the concept of *national security* in the West. They did not engage security issues in the Third World, or the idea of human security, which came later thanks to the contribution of a different group of scholars from the Third World reflecting on its distinctive

---

[39] Matthew J. Hoffman, "Norms and Social Constructivism in International Relations," in *The International Studies Encyclopedia*, ed., Robert A. Denemark (Malden, MA: Blackwell Reference, 2010), www.isacompendium.com.

[40] Antje Wiener, *A Theory of Contestation* (Heidelberg: Springer, 2014), 74–77. Wiener has analyzed the puzzle of why the fundamental norms of international relations are contested even by their presumed followers. Wiener contends such contestations occur over interpretation, which is "derived from the social practice of enacting meaning that is used in a specific context." Antje Wiener, *The Invisible Constitution of Politics: Contested Norms and International Encounters* (Cambridge University Press, 2008), 4. See also Wiener, "Contested Compliance: Interventions on the Normative Structure of World Politics," *European Journal of International Relations* 10, no. 2 (2004), 189–234. While Wiener's analysis is illuminating and informs my position, my concept of resistance and contestation goes beyond Wiener's theory. As Bloomfield and Scott point out, "the aspect of Acharya's work that distinguishes him most from Wiener" is that "his local actors do not share the same normative understandings; they are not from the same *community* as the norm entrepreneurs." Alan Bloomfield and Shirley V. Scott, "Norm Antipreneurs in World Politics," in *Norm Antipreneurs and the Politics of Resistance to Global Normative Change*, ed. Alan Bloomfield and Shirley V. Scott (London: Routledge, 2017), 8. See also: Matthew J. Hoffman, "Norms and Social Constructivism in International Relations," in *The International Studies Encyclopedia*, ed. Denemark. My work gives the contestation literature a wider framing by focusing on the contestation about global ordering between the North and the South, and between universal (or global) and regional (or local) actors. Moreover, while Wiener's framework focuses on contestation at the level of compliance, my approach as presented in this book and in my earlier work highlights contestation at all levels, including the creation and diffusion of norms. And the empirical referents in this book are different. While Wiener's work focuses on human rights, democracy, and rule of law and citizenship, the focus of this book is on security (including human security) and sovereignty. And this book is concerned with more than normative contestation per se. It is primarily interested in linking contestations with the agency of those who are on the weaker side of the normative divide.

[41] Hobden and Wyn Jones, "Marxist Theories of International Relations," 136.

security predicament. I see these latter contestations as more transform-ative or "critical" in the Coxian sense.

But two important clarifications about this contestation are needed here. First, in this book, by "non-Western," or "South," I mean the members of what used to be called, and is still recognized by many as, the "Third World," albeit acknowledging it as a more differentiated entity today than the conventional understanding of the term implied.[42] Second, categories such as "West" and "the Rest" (or "non-Western") are not fixed or homogeneous categories, and the relationship between them is neither unchanging nor defined by an immutable dichotomy. Many of the contestations about global order, including those over sover-eignty, security, and identity, have taken place as much *within* categories such as North and South, Western and non-Western, as *between* them.

The dichotomy between the West and Rest has always been problem-atic, because of the differences among postcolonial leaders. Some, like India's Jawaharlal Nehru, were essentially liberal internationalists similar to many Western leaders, while others, such as Sukarno, were not. But the situation was more complex. Hence some postcolonial advocates like Nehru were framing diversity or the difference between the West and the Third World in liberal terms, while also opposing liberalism in other areas, like economic development, where Nehru went socialist. A liberal international position is a very broad tent, which can accommodate lots of different positions. Nehru also challenged the West's economic model in significant respects. But what was common to most leaders was that they wanted to enhance Southern agency in the making of the post-war international system and give more voice to the Third World. Hence, despite their ideological differences, they came together in gatherings such as the Bandung Conference and its offshoot, the Non-Aligned Movement (as discussed in Chapter 3). Many leaders were also localizers (discussed in Chapter 2); while accepting liberal norms, they wanted to reinterpret them to fit the postcolonial context of Asia and other parts of the developing world.

Hence the discussion of the West and the Rest in this book is more nuanced and qualified than has been the case with much of the postcolonial literature in international relations theory. Indeed, the "Global IR" per-spective underpinning this book "regards 'non-Western' or 'post-Western' as part of a broader challenge of reimagining IR as a global discipline ... [and] transcends the distinction between West and non-West – or any

---

[42] See Chapter 5 for further discussion of the analytical relevance of the concept "Third World."

similar binary and mutually exclusive categories."[43] Yet, it is also true that the contestation between the West and the non-West over the meaning of and approaches to order has in the early postcolonial era produced some of the most serious points of contention in global order-building, residues of which continue to inform, at least to some extent, the positions of the emerging powers like China, India, Brazil, and South Africa. As Ramesh Thakur notes, "differences within both camps notwithstanding, the global North/South divide is the most significant point of contention for 'the international community'."[44] Indeed, the blurring of the North–South divide is not due to some inevitable structural forces; rather it is being (re)negotiated, especially through the debates about and agentic constructions of global order discussed in this book.

A key element of contestation is resistance. Here, James Scott's conceptualization of resistance is especially useful. In his *Weapons of the Weak*, Scott outlines the notion of "everyday forms" of resistance, albeit in a vastly different context. Scott observes that some forms of resistance "require little or no coordination or planning; they often represent a form of individual self-help; and they typically avoid any direct symbolic confrontation with authority or with elite norms."[45] Instead, "ordinary weapons of relatively powerless groups" might include "foot dragging, dissimulation, false compliance, pilfering, feigned ignorance, slander, arson, sabotage, and so on."[46] "Where everyday resistance most strikingly departs from other forms of resistance is in its implicit disavowal of public and symbolic goals. Where institutionalized politics is formal, overt, concerned with systematic, de jure change, everyday resistance is informal, often covert, and concerned largely with immediate, de facto gains."[47] One important implication of Scott's formulation is that contestations about, and resistance to, ideas and practices that are seen as deficient on grounds of justice, morality, or functionality can be the starting point of order-building. In this book, Chapter 3 examines the postcolonial countries' resistance to Cold War alliances, whereas Chapter 4 discusses their contestation and rejection of some aspects of the humanitarian intervention idea and its offshoot, the R2P norm. Subsequently, Chapter 5 deals with resistance to the idea of national security, and Chapter 6 highlights disagreements over EU-centric ideas about regionalism.

---

[43] Acharya, "Global International Relations (IR) and Regional Worlds," 649.
[44] Ramesh Thakur, *The Responsibility to Protect: Norms, Laws and the Use of Force in International Politics* (London: Routledge, 2011), 159.
[45] James C. Scott, *Weapons of the Weak: Everyday Forms of Peasant Resistance* (New Haven and London: Yale University Press, 1985), 29.
[46] Ibid., 29.
[47] Ibid., 33.

This leads to a second element of the pluralization of agency: attention to its subjective and inter-subjective elements. For Spivak, the key element of agency is "freedom of subjectivity." As she put it: "The idea of agency comes from the principle of accountable reasons, that one acts with responsibility that one has to assume the possibility of intention, one has to assume even the freedom of subjectivity."[48] Hence agency comprises three key elements: accountability, intentionality, and subjectivity. Constructivists have especially stressed the ideational, inter-subjective elements of agency – captured in the diffusion of ideas and norms in world politics. Thus, Price and Reus-Smit reject Wendt's state-as-agent perspective in favor of inter-subjective meanings, "since constructivists generally define the state as an administrative and institutional structure, not an actor." Instead, they define agency primarily in terms of how "intersubjective meanings, operating at the levels of domestic and international society, license and define sovereign, territorial political units, and how the definition of such units constitutes and empowers certain political actors, particularly governments."[49] Sikkink has called for an "agentic constructivism" that is "concerned with the role of human consciousness in international politics," but with a specific focus on "the role of human agency in struggles for the creation of new norms and new forms of governance that may lead to changes in global politics ... that may, over time create new understanding of the ways states and non-state actors ought to behave, and new understandings of the national interests of states."[50] Several chapters in this book illustrate inter-subjective agency in norm-making: Chapter 2 in laying out different forms of normative agency, especially localization, subsidiarity, and circulation, Chapter 3 in discussing non-intervention, Chapter 4 in tracing the origins of R2P, and Chapter 5 in discussing human security.

A third element of the pluralization of agency includes the agency of materially weaker actors. While some liberal scholars question the central position accorded to the United States in building the liberal

---

[48] Gayatri Chakravorty Spivak, "Subaltern Talk: Interview with the Editors (1993–94)," in *The Spivak Reader*, ed. Donna Landry and Gerald MacLean (New York: Routledge, 1996), 294.

[49] Richard Price and Christian Reus-Smit, "Dangerous Liaisons? Critical International Theory and Constructivism," *European Journal of International Relations* 4, no. 3 (September 1998), 286.

[50] Sikkink argues that agentic constructivism had already existed within constructivism, but did not have such a name and deserves greater recognition. Kathryn Sikkink, "What is Agentic Constructivism?" Paper presented to the colloquium: The Future of Constructivist Research in International Relations, Oxford University, April 30, 2013, 2–3. Note that Sikkink returns to "human agency" here, the very thing that Colin Wight had criticized and wanted to be broadened.

international order and point to the role of the Western middle powers such as Western European states, Australia, and Canada in building and sustaining the liberal order,[51] they leave out non-Western actors. Yet their agency remains neglected in the mainstream scholarship in international relations. This is not to say that existing IR theories ignore the non-Western world or have no or little relevance for understanding its position and role in world politics. As a Global IR approach recognizes, existing IR theories "are not monolithic or static in dealing with the non-Western world."[52] Some theories have been more sensitive to non-Western contexts and experiences than others. Thanks to its focus on culture and identity, constructivism has been especially useful in creating more space for scholarship on the non-Western world. The ongoing global power shift has seen realism paying more attention to the non-Western world, especially to the emerging powers such as China. Globalization (though uneven and non-linear), the proliferation of multilateral institutions, and democratic transitions since the end of the Cold War have rendered the non-Western world more amenable to liberal explanations of war and peace.

But recognizing the place or position of the non-Western countries is not the same as recognizing their *agency* in building global order. When it comes to the latter, traditional theories have tended to view the non-Western world more as "'objects' rather than 'subjects'" in international relations.[53] Even postcolonialism and feminism have arguably devoted far more attention and energy to highlighting the marginalization of the

---

[51] Miles Kahler, "Who is Liberal Now?: Rising Powers and Global Norms," in *Why Govern?*, ed. Acharya, 55–73.

[52] Acharya, "Global International Relations (IR) and Regional Worlds," 650; Amitav Acharya, *Rethinking Power, Institutions and Ideas in World Politics: Whose IR?* (New York: Routledge, 2013).

[53] Mohammed Ayoob, "Security in the Third World: The Worm about to Turn?", *International Affairs* 60, no. 1 (Winter 1983/4), 44. The neglect of non-Western agency can be observed not only of realism, liberalism, and constructivism, but also of non-mainstream or "critical" IR theories and postcolonialism. See Acharya, *Rethinking Power, Institutions and Ideas in World Politics*, introduction and chapter 1; Amitav Acharya, "Ethnocentrism and Emancipatory IR Theory," in *Displacing Security*, ed. Samantha Arnold and J. Marshall Bier (Toronto: Centre for International and Security Studies, York University, 2000); John M. Hobson, "Orientalism and the Poverty of Theory Three Decades on: Bringing Eastern and Subaltern Agency Back into Critical IR Theory," in *Critical Theory in International Relations and Security Studies*, ed. Shannon Brincat, Laura Lima and João Nunes (London: Routledge, 2012), 129–139; John M. Hobson and Alina Sajed, "Navigating Beyond the Eurofetishist Frontier of Critical IR Theory: Exploring the Complex Landscapes of Non-Western Agency," *International Studies Review* (2017), doi.org/10.1093/isr/vix013.

non-Western world,[54] than recognizing its positive agency.[55] Hence this book differs from both Western and postcolonial theories in expanding their investigations into the pluralization of agency in global order that is taking place. Here, normative agency, or agency through ideas and ideologies, becomes especially relevant. As Donald Puchala has argued, for "ThirdWorld countries, ideas and ideologies are far more important" than power or wealth, because "powerlessness" and "unequal distribution of the world's wealth" are "constants" for them. "Hence, they [ideas] drive world affairs."[56] This issue of the normative agency of non-Western actors is the central theme of Chapter 2. This volume also discusses various examples of non-Western agency: Chapter 3 (extending universal sovereignty), Chapter 4 (constructing R2P), Chapter 5 (redefining security), and Chapter 6 (building different forms of regionalisms).

Fourth, the question of agency cannot be divorced from the context out of which the agents operate. Wight calls for a view of agency that is "layered and differentiated and inextricably linked to social contexts ... in which it is embedded."[57] "The social groups and collectives that one is born into crucially affect the potential of agency."[58] Wight stresses the "power agents accumulate by virtue of their positioning in a social context."[59] An agent is a "'social actor' who is neither a passive puppet of social forces, nor a pre-social Cartesian self."[60]

An important part of the consideration of agency in global order lies in recognizing where and when its key ideas and norms came from. Many *global* ideas and norms are local in origin. They have a specific point of origin and are developed out of the particular context of a leading state or group of states. Hence, as noted earlier, sovereignty was developed out of the European context, and national security emerged from the postwar US context. Agency thus means building congruence between these

[54] See Anna M. Agathangelou and L. H. M. Ling, *Transforming World Politics: From Empire to Multiple Worlds* (London: Routledge, 2009); Geeta Chowdhry and Sheila Nair, eds., *Power, Postcolonialism, and International Relations: Reading Race, Gender, and Class* (London and New York: Routledge, 2004); L. H. M. Ling, "Said's Exile: Strategies for Postcolonial Feminists," *Millennium: Journal of International Studies* 36, no. 1 (2007), 135–145; L. H. M. Ling, *Postcolonial International Relations: Conquest and Desire between Asia and the West* (London: Palgrave Macmillan, 2002); Swati Parashar, "Feminist (In) securities and Camp Politics," *International Studies Perspectives* 13, no. 4 (2013), 440–443.
[55] Acharya, "Global International Relations and Regional Worlds."
[56] Donald J. Puchala, "ThirdWorldThinking and Contemporary Relations," in *International Relations Theory and the Third World*, ed. Stephanie Newman (New York: St Martin's Press, 1995), 150–151.
[57] Wight, *Agents, Structures and International Relations*, 213.
[58] Ibid.
[59] Ibid., 212.
[60] Ibid., 215.

ideas and norms and the distinctive or different contexts of other actors. It is to ensure that the key rules and norms represent and fit the context (social, political, economic) of all the actors in a global order. Hence redefining and broadening Westphalian sovereignty and national security to ensure that they capture the distinctive position and predicament of newcomers has been a major aspect of agency in global order.

Moreover, what matters in agency is not just the agent's persona (i.e. that of a norm entrepreneur), whether it is an individual or a group (like an NGO), but also the context from which the agent draws the norms. As a comprehensive review of ideas that underpin the United Nations (UN) system, appropriately titled *UN Ideas That Changed the World*, found, many ideas have multiple points of origin, and the "economic and social ideas at the UN cannot be properly understood when they are divorced from their historical and social context."[61] This proposition would be even more meaningful if the term "local" were used to qualify "historical and social context," since the origins and vantage points of the progenitors (especially from the developing world) of new ideas matter a great deal in many of the key UN ideas about development, security, and ecology. Some supposedly universal ideas and norms can have a regional context in terms of their origins or influences. One should not assume – as most norm scholars do – that regions merely adopt or adapt global norms; it can be the other way around.

It may be argued that many of the new ideas – and hence the agency – coming from the non-West are from individuals whose training and career have been in the West, and that their innovations were disseminated through Western think-tanks and global institutions dominated by the West. This was as true of *Satyagraha* of Mahatma Gandhi as of the Human Development Index (HDI) of Mahbub ul Haq, the Green Belt movement of Wangari Maathai, and the responsible sovereignty idea of Francis Deng. Hence, they cannot be taken as real examples of non-Western ideational agency. Yet this misses an important part of the picture. The main inspiration and source of the ideas and innovations of people trained in the West could be their upbringing, early education and the situation at home which they had to deal with even when sitting in Western locations. We cannot think of the genesis of new ideas without taking into consideration the personal circumstances and early struggle of those who create them. Many such ideas come from places of economic hardship and social-political conflict. It should not surprise anyone that the origins of some of the boldest ideas for development, security, and

---

[61] Richard Jolly, Louis Emmerji and Thomas G. Weiss, *UN Ideas That Changed the World* (Bloomington and Indianapolis, IN: Indiana University Press, 2009), 42.

ecology are from developing nations. These ideas are often shaped by the force of adversity and necessity that their proponents faced. The credit for these innovations cannot be solely given to Western institutions or governments that occasionally back these ideas and international agencies that market them. Chapter 4, in discussing humanitarian intervention and R2P, and Chapter 5, in discussing security in the Third World and the origins of human security, highlight the importance of the local context of agency in constructing order.

Fifth, agency can be at different levels. Regionalism is a major site of agency in constructing global order. There are important reasons for focusing on the regional level. Regionalism – formal and informal – has been a persistent phenomenon in world politics. Universalism and regionalism have been seen in the aftermath of World War II as alternative ways of organizing world order. Since then, whether regionalism is a "building block" or a "stumbling block" in developing the key norms and institutions of global order, including security, conflict management, and trade, has been a major point of contention in world politics. Hence the understanding of the role of regions and regionalisms is indispensable to any meaningful debate about and analysis of global order.

Both Western and non-Western actors have resorted to regional action to organize their security and economic well-being and develop a political identity that co-exists or even challenges the nation-state model. Whether as a form of resistance or as a stepping-stone to global order, or both, regionalism is one of the most important elements of the pluralistic conception of agency that this book develops. While local can mean many things in international relations, in this book I focus on studying locality primarily in terms of regions and regionalism. There are important reasons for focusing on the regional level of agency. First, regionalism has been a key channel for articulating the voices and concerns of weaker actors, including non-Western states. Second, regional interactions and institutions have been crucial to norm diffusion, in terms of both localizing global norms and globalizing locally developed norms. Third, regions are a site of resistance to powerful and hegemonic actors in global politics and important alternatives to the dominant theories and discourses about international relations which have privileged, falsely in my view, a universal framing. The importance of regionalism as a form of agency in building global order is the principal theme of Chapter 6, although other chapters also highlight this.

Finally, attention should be given not only to how and where agency originates, but also to how and where it works subsequently, including the challenges and redefinitions that it faces. The first mention of a new term or concept of a norm is important, but agency can also lie in by whom and how the norm in question is being promoted. Agency is never a *one-source, one-way,* or *one-step* process. Agency and its instruments – such as ideas, norms, and institutions – remain subject to continuous challenge and feedback following their creation (more on norm contestation in Chapter 2). This is true not only of the fundamental and "established" norms of international relations like sovereignty, non-intervention and equality of states, but also of newer norms such as the R2P. These have been continually contested over their meaning, interpretation, and application over time and space. Scholars and global policymakers concerned with creating and implementing new principles of collective action should take into account the diversity of sources, multiplicity of agents, and plurality of contexts. Only by developing a broader framework of agency, feedback, and accountability can one appreciate the complexity of agency in world politics. And employing such a broader framework of agency is crucial to the legitimacy of global order.

To sum up, the pluralistic conception of agency that informs this book pays particular attention to non-Western agency, although not in exclusive terms. Rather, it seeks to correct the general neglect of weaker actors, including non-Western ones, in the mainstream literature on global order with a view to showing the role of both Western and non-Western agents in constructing global order. Building on previous debates over agency, the purpose of the book is to show how actors through their material, ideational, and interaction capabilities construct, reject, reconstitute, and otherwise influence a prevailing order with a view to accommodating their interests and identities.

While the above discussion of the pluralization of agency permeates this book, in Chapter 2 I conceptualize and elaborate on the specific processes through which these forms of agency actually work. There, I discuss two key processes, "localization" and "subsidiarity," and an extension of them, which I term as norm "circulation." The rest of the book uses these processes to understand the redefinition of sovereignty and security in world politics. The rationale for this focus may be briefly outlined.

Sovereignty and Security

The ideas and norms underpinning sovereignty and security tell us much about what kind of global order we live in and the directions in which any change may occur. It is fairly obvious that some of the most fundamental shifts of the past decades which would have a lasting impact on global order in the twenty-first century concern the changing meanings of and approaches to sovereignty and security, especially from the norm of non-intervention to humanitarian intervention and R2P, and from national security to human security. These are the empirical core of this book.

Sovereignty is the fundamental or constitutive principle, the *grund-norm*, of international relations. Theoretical writings on the origins and impact of sovereignty are mainly derived from the European experience. The natural law conceptions of sovereignty, identified with writers like Hugo Grotius, did not exclude non-Western states. This changed with the rising power of European nations. European superiority in science, technology, warfare, among other areas, and European subjugation of non-Western territory required a new justification that could not be found in natural law conceptions of sovereignty under which non-Western states could be considered to have sovereignty. Hence a new body of international law emerged. The positive international law regime speci-fies that sovereign statehood requires a "delimited territory, a stable pop-ulation, and most importantly, a reliable government with the will and capacity to carry out international obligations" that were perceived to be absent in many non-Western states.[62] The constitutive recognition prin-ciple that resulted from this reflected both rising Western power and an "instrument of European dominance" used to exclude not just colonies but also independent entities such as China.[63]

With decolonization, the Westphalian model was assumed to have become the universal model of the sovereign state system. Yet, when con-fronted with a serious disjuncture between Westphalian sovereignty and the realities of state-building in the Third World, some Western scholars came up with a distinction between juridical and empirical statehood, and the idea of "negative sovereignty," focusing mainly on the non-intervention principle.[64] The idea of negative sovereignty assumes that the principle of non-intervention is an instrument of state survival and regime security of Third World states, rather than the pursuit of positive and normative concerns.

These assumptions can be questioned. If positive sovereignty meant an ability to engage in the high politics of international affairs (i.e. questions of order, stability, and justice, as well as power politics), then there can be many examples of Third World states playing the positive sovereignty game. In the 1950s, China, India, and the Colombo Powers played such roles;

---

[62] Robert H. Jackson, *Quasi-States: Sovereignty, International Relations and the Third World* (Cambridge University Press, 1990), 61.

[63] Ibid.

[64] Robert H. Jackson and Carl G. Rosberg, "Why Africa's Weak States Persist: The Empirical and the Juridical in Statehood," *World Politics* 35, no. 1 (1982), 259–282; Jackson, *Quasi-States*.

while many of them suffered from contested boundaries, they did have "a stable population, and most importantly, a reliable government with the will and capacity to carry out international obligations."[65] Moral concerns, such as decolonization and resistance to superpower intervention, played an important part in their effort to universalize sovereignty. Hence, it would be wrong to assert that the sovereignty game in the non-Western world was primarily one of negative sovereignty. These states were concerned with building *universal sovereignty* rather than with regime survival.

This construction of sovereignty demonstrating the agency of non-Western actors in the postcolonial world is the principal theme of Chapter 3. It offers a historical perspective to highlight the role of the newly independent states in developing norms of international conduct that would have a significant global impact. This chapter discusses how regional actors, with Asia acting as the hub in the crucial early postcolonial era, extended the meaning of sovereignty to make it more universal. They did so to assert their autonomy and compensate for their marginalization in global norm-making processes, as well as the violation of the so-called universal norms by powerful actors and the incapacity of global institutions embodying these norms to prevent such violation. Asia's newly independent states were under-represented in the UN. During the post-war period, many Asian nationalist leaders saw the two superpowers violating the norm of non-intervention, especially through their rivalry over Indo-China. Yet, the UN seemed to be too paralyzed by the Cold War to address their security concerns. Hence, developing a local norm against collective defense pacts was seen as a necessary way not only of countering superpower interventionism, but also of compensating for the deficiencies of the UN. Moreover, while non-intervention was supposedly a "universal" norm, in reality its European application had not been unexceptional, allowing intervention to maintain the balance of power. In Latin America, the doctrine and practice of non-intervention did not rule out membership in great power-led collective defense arrangements. Yet, in post-war Asia, and later Africa, local conditions, especially the new-found independence of Asian states which had to be safeguarded and the preexisting ideas of nationalist leaders such as Nehru or Aung San rejecting great power spheres of influence, provided the basis for reformulating the norm of non-intervention with a view to delegitimizing great power-led military pacts as a new form of intervention. As such, the scope of non-intervention was broadened to include rejection of multilateral defense pacts within great power orbits.

---

[65] Jackson, *Quasi-States*, 61.

Who constructed sovereignty is not the only contentious aspect of the global sovereignty regime. Equally important is the debate over how it is being transformed. Although disagreements persist as to whether there has actually been an "end" to sovereignty, there is far less doubt that sovereignty is at least a changing notion. But the literature on this issue leaves several questions inadequately addressed. The fact that sovereignty is changing does not tell us much about how and where (at what level) such change is taking place. Grand theorizing with propositions such as "organized hypocrisy" (realists), the "end of sovereignty" (hyper-liberals) or the "social construction of sovereignty" (constructivists) fails to capture the wide variations in the addiction and approaches to sovereignty and its norms in various parts of the world.

The key question about sovereignty addressed in this book is how and in what different ways the norms of sovereignty are being reconstructed and reformulated at both the global and regional levels. There have been several transitions in the ideas and norms about sovereignty and its corollary, non-intervention. One occurred after the end of the Cold War, and involved a shift from geopolitical to humanitarian intervention. Another occurred after the 9/11 attacks, producing a sort of reversal from the humanitarian to the geopolitical as the George W. Bush administration waged its global war on terror and adopted the policy of preemption. But the most important normative shift in the thinking about sovereignty remains the further evolution of humanitarian intervention to the R2P norm. And it is here that a surprising and little noticed aspect of the genesis of the R2P norm could be noted: the role of non-Western advocates, especially from Africa, in promoting humanitarian intervention and the idea of "responsible sovereignty." Their role and the African context of the norm, discussed in Chapter 4, was a primary basis of the emergence of the R2P norm.

The redefinition of security paralleled those of sovereignty, although here the debate took slightly different forms and sequence. One aspect of the debate about security involved the concept of national security, a state-centric and military-focused notion which reflected the concerns and evolutionary experiences of Western states, and especially the post-World War preoccupations of the United States. National security meant security against external threats. But by the 1970s, the international situation took a turn that would expose the limitations of this concept. The oil crisis of 1973 led to calls for redefining security in economic terms, and by the 1980s, concerns about global ecological health had sparked initial ideas about environmental security. The proponents of redefining security were not, however, calling for a radical shift in the focus from state security; they were rather concerned with extending the state's capacity, and role into areas previously left out of the security domain. Such redefinition of security thus smacked of a problem-solving agenda, rather than a fundamental rethinking of security as a statist enterprise.

The other debate was over security in the Third World, or what during the Cold War came to be known as "regional security issues." During the Cold War, there was a widespread tendency to draw a sharp distinction between systemic conflicts (or the central balance conflict) and regional conflicts, many of which occurred in the Third World, and to view the latter through the prism of the former. This tendency had practical consequences, leading to policy (mis)calculations that might have aggravated and intensified Third World conflicts by viewing them as sideshows to the great power games and as "safety valves" for the release of superpower tensions. The end of the Cold War highlighted the need and case for viewing regional conflicts on their own terms. But a more fundamental change to the traditional thinking on security was from national to human security, the theme of Chapter 5. This change also highlights the agency of non-Western actors, because the idea of human security has strong Asian roots. An interesting parallel here is the African agency behind the R2P norm. Human security is not simply "new wine in old bottles." It represents a significant broadening of the notion of national security to "comprehensive security," which privileged regime security, and "cooperative security," which did not address the possible tension between individual and state security.

In this book's analytic framework (Table 1.1), while Chapters 3 to 5 discuss the pluralization of agency in sovereignty and security, Chapter 6 examines the specific role of regional institutions. These are a critical building block of the pluralization of agency. Questions about both sovereignty and security featured very prominently in one of the foundational debates over the post-war order-building that pitted the "universalists" against the "regionalists." The liberal internationalists led by the United States viewed regionalism and universalism as competitive forces, and rejected the former in favor of the latter; others, including the Latin American and Middle Eastern countries, saw regionalism as a critical ingredient of global order which would also complement universalism. The debate has continued till now. While some scholars and policymakers see regionalism as a recipe for global fragmentation and chaos, others take a more positive view of regionalism and advocate a more regionalized approach to global order-building. The European Union (EU) has done much to dispel the traditional geopolitical view of regionalism, and has inspired other regions to follow its example. But other regions of the world have also developed their unique approaches to regionalism, which have made important contributions to their own

Table 1.1. *The analytic framework*

Chapters	Challenge	Agency	Outcome
Chapter 3	Localizing and expanding sovereignty to advance decolonization and limit outside (great power) intervention	Latin America's Calvo and Drago Doctrines; the Bandung injunction against Cold War pacts; postcolonial leaders in Asia (e.g. Nehru, Sukarno), Middle East (Nasser) and Africa (Nkrumah)	Building subsidiary norms in Asia, Africa, Latin America, and the Arab World; related but differing regional conceptions of sovereignty and non-intervention
Chapter 4	Transforming sovereignty to address humanitarian crises without inviting great power geopolitical intervention	African context, leaders, and diplomats (Nelson Mandela, Francis Deng, Kofi Annan, Mohamed Sahnoun); Brazil's "responsibility while protecting"	Contributing to the norms of humanitarian intervention and R2P; initial North–South disagreements over humanitarian intervention, but greater convergence on the R2P norm
Chapter 5	Redefining security to make it relevant to the security predicament of Third World countries where security of people is often threatened by governments	Development economists (Mahbub ul Haq, Amartya Sen), Third World (especially South Asian) context	Shaping the redefinition and broadening of "national security"; proposing ideas of "human development" and "human security"
Chapter 6	Ensuring a role for regionalism in the universal collective security system and developing a mode of regionalism relevant to stability and development (not the same of integration)	Latin American and Arab representatives at the San Francisco Conference; regionalist advocates and ideologies (pan-Americanism, pan-Africanism, pan-Arabism)	Challenging the exclusive role of the UN in conflict resolution, and the primacy of the EU model of economic integration; conceiving and diffusing other forms of regional institution-building

areas' peace and security and hence to global order. Any consideration of regionalism must capture the diversity of these regionalist constructions.

A Pluralistic or Multiplex Global Order?

What does a pluralized conception of agency mean for the emerging global order? We live in a moment of history in which both the challenges and approaches to global order are undergoing fundamental transformation. On the challenge side are momentous events like the end of the Cold War, the 9/11 attacks, the growing prominence of transnational threats, and perhaps most importantly, the rise of new powers and the "relative" but unmistakable and possibly permanent decline of the United States as *the* sole global superpower. On the response side are the doctrine and practice of humanitarian intervention, the war on terror led by the United States, and a fundamental redefinition of North–South relations, and the emergence of new categories and institutions like the BRICS and G20, spurred in part by the rise of new powers like China and India. While the relative decline of the United States can no longer be in doubt, what is more debatable is what sort of order is replacing the unipolar moment. Most people had earlier assumed that it would be multipolarity (although some foresee Sino-US bipolarity) and debated whether multipolarity would prove more or less destabilizing. Latterly, public intellectuals have come up with some fashionable sound-bites: "apolar," "non-polar," "post-American," or "neo-polar."[66]

Yet, a more accurate description of the emerging pluralistic world order is captured in the notion of a "Multiplex World."[67] The idea of the

---

[66] "A Worrying New World Order," *The Economist*, September 11, 2008, www.economist.com/node/12203018; Fareed Zakaria, *The Post-American World* (New York: W. W. Norton, 2008); Richard Haass, "The Age of Nonpolarity," *Foreign Affairs* (May–June 2008).

[67] The idea of a pluralistic world order has resonance with the English School's debate between "pluralist" and "solidarist" views of international society. Briefly stated, the pluralists stress the resilience of sovereignty, non-interference, and state (national) security, the prior importance of order over justice, and the difficulty of achieving consensus over values and norms at the global level. The solidarists claim the possibility of universal values such as human rights and limits to sovereignty, and hold that the realization of order is contingent upon the fulfillment of justice. Jackson and Wheeler are usually presented as belonging to the "pluralist" and "solidarist" camps respectively. On the "pluralist–solidarist" debate within the English School, see: Hedley Bull, "The Grotian Conception of International Society," in *Diplomatic Investigations: Essays in the Theory of International Politics*, ed. Martin Wight and Hubert Butterfield (London: Allen and Unwin, 1966); Hedley Bull, *The Anarchical Society* (London: Macmillan, 1977), 157; Barry Buzan, *From International to World Society: English School Theory and the Social Structure of Globalization* (Cambridge University Press, 2004); Andrew Hurrell, *On Global Order: Power, Value, and the Constitution of International Society* (Oxford University Press, 2007); Robert Jackson, *The Global Covenant: Human Conduct in a World of States* (Oxford University Press, 2000); Nicholas Wheeler, *Saving Strangers: Humanitarian Intervention in International Society* (Oxford University Press, 2000); Andrew Linklater, *The Transformation of Political Community* (London: Macmillan, 1998). But this book's conception of a pluralistic global order is more agent-centric, while a key inspiration of the English School, as outlined in Bull and Watson's classic work, is structural, i.e. the worldwide "expansion" of European international rules and institutions due to colonialism and decolonization. Hedley Bull and Adam Watson, eds., *The Expansion of International Society* (Oxford: Clarendon Press, 1984). The early English School has been criticized for its ethnocentrism, for not sufficiently acknowledging the coercive

Multiplex World was initially developed in this author's 2014 book *The End of American World Order*.[68] But the discussion of agency in that book was brief and meant mainly as a contribution to the policy debates over the unipolar moment and the decline of US-centric international order. In this book, I introduce a significant historical and theoretical dimension to the emergence of such a pluralistic world, with specific focus on the normative agency of non-Western actors.

In essence, a Multiplex World is culturally and politically diverse but deeply interconnected and interdependent. Such a world is "decentered" in the sense that there is no global hegemony,[69] but multiple, overlapping layers of governance, at global, regional, and local levels. The rules and institutions of global order are not dominated by any single power or a small group of like-minded powers (e.g. the "West"). Instead, the sources of ideas and approaches to order are diffuse and shared among actors with differential material capabilities. The distinction between the West and the Rest is increasingly blurry. The absence of a global hegemony gives more play to regionalisms, which play an important, if not always successful, role in order-building. In short, the idea of a Multiplex World is a metaphor for multiple, diverse but cross-cutting forms of agency in global order-building.

The dominant conception of the current international order sees it as having been constituted by the universalization of the principles and institutions of the European international society and the hegemonic role of the United States. While there is much truth to this assertion, it needs to be qualified. First, it obscures the role of the newcomers to the international system in both challenging, upholding, and modifying their inheritance. Second, as the countries that have been hitherto viewed as part of the Third World or Global South develop vis-à-vis the dominant Western actors, thereby strengthening their agency further, the existing global order becomes more pluralistic. While the prevailing liberal international order dominated by the West does not disappear, it has to negotiate accommodation with the Rest.

---

aspect of the "expansion" and the agency of non-Western societies in international relations. See Acharya, *Rethinking Power, Institutions and Ideas in World Politics*, chapter 1. My conception of a pluralistic global order (or a Multiplex World) shares aspects of the "pluralist" English School's emphasis on sovereignty and non-intervention, but goes beyond it by stressing the contribution of the Global South in promoting humanitarian intervention, human security, and regionalism. Hence, a pluralistic global order occupies a middle ground in the English School's "pluralist–solidarist" divide.

[68] Amitav Acharya, *The End of American World Order* (Cambridge, UK: Polity Press, 2014).

[69] A similar view is offered by Richard Ned Lebow and Simon Reich, *Good-Bye Hegemony!: Power and Influence in the Global System* (Princeton University Press, 2014).

At the same time, a Multiplex World is not a post-Western world. It retains key features of the existing liberal international order. But it is more diverse and less US- and Western-centric than the hitherto liberal international order, which was essentially a club of like-minded Western nations. It is also both more global and more diverse in scope.[70] More elaboration of this order, and how the changing ideas and norms of sovereignty and security are contributing to it, can be found in Chapter 7 which draws on the empirical chapters of this book.

While it is too early to say how Trump's policies might unfold and whether they will endure, the election of Donald Trump as the US President complicates any predictions about the future of global order. Normative concerns (whether Trump and the values and policies he represents are bad for global cooperation) aside, they are unlikely to reverse or arrest the broadening of agency discussed in this book, which is already set in motion by long-term developments in world politics. As I shall discuss in the concluding chapter, the emerging powers of the Global South, especially China and India, are unlikely to abandon globalism or globalization. Instead they may take up a greater share of promoting it, albeit differently from the United States and the West. The new globalization may be based more on South–South linkages (which are already expanding) than traditional North–North and North–South linkages. Due to the prominence of China and other emerging powers, it could be more mindful and respectful of the sovereignty and security problems and concerns of the developing countries. All this will accentuate the complexity of the twenty-first-century global order, and the advent of a Multiplex World (see Table 1.2).

---

[70] One of the most prominent advocates of the liberal order, Joseph Nye, agrees with my assessment of the limited scope of that order. See Joseph S. Nye, "Review of *The End of American World Order*, by Amitav Acharya," *International Affairs* 90, no. 5 (2014), 1246–1247.

Table 1.2. *A pluralistic ("multiplex") global order?*

	Hegemonic or quasi-hegemonic (international order)	Pluralistic or Multiplex World (global order)
Makers of order	Imperial powers, superpowers, great powers defined by material capabilities, international and regional institutions designed and dominated by great powers (including elements of the UN multilateral system)	Absence of global hegemony, new and emerging global and regional-level players, individual idea-shifters and norm entrepreneurs (Chapters 3, 4 and 5), transnational civil society (Chapter 6), fragmented global governance with regional and "parallel" institutions (G20, AIIB) and other actors
Concepts and practices of sovereignty	"Standards of civilization," unequal treaties, "selective sovereignty" (Chapter 4), great power intervention (Chapter 3), "humanitarian intervention" to effect regime change (Chapter 4)	Anti-colonial struggles, "moral sovereignty," "non-alignment," and non-participation in Cold War alliances (Chapter 3), "responsible sovereignty" (Chapter 4), humanitarian intervention against genocide with multilateral and regional authority
Concepts and practices of security	Collective defense and alliances (Chapter 3), national security (Chapter 5)	Common and cooperative security, human security as both "freedom from fear" and "freedom from want" (Chapter 5)
Diffusion of ideas/norms	Coercion, strategic interaction, proselytism (Chapter 2)	"Constitutive localization," "norm subsidiarity," circulation, vernacularization, "translation" (Chapter 2)
Types of order	Liberal hegemony, unipolar, bipolar, multipolar (Chapters 1 and 7)	Pluralistic or "Multiplex World" (Chapters 1 and 7)

2   Theorizing Normative Change

In Chapter 1, I argued that a key form of agency in global order-building is ideational and normative.[1] Hence, the study of how ideas and norms travel is of central concern to this book. In this chapter I examine different understandings of the relationship between power and ideas in the literature on international relations. I then outline different but interrelated processes in norm-building and global order-building. The main ideas of this chapter are as follows: first, norm creation in world politics is not the prerogative of materially powerful actors. Second, nor is it a matter of the wholesale adoption of foreign norms by local actors. Third, the process of norm creation and diffusion is seldom a single, one-step process with a dose of finality. Rather it involves continuous resistance, feedback, and circulation.

Interest, Power, and Ideas

International relations theory tells us about three main pathways of how ideas and norms spread: through strategic interaction; through power and hegemonic socialization; and through social construction (see Table 2.1).

Strategic Interaction

As dominant approaches to international relations in the 1980s, realism and institutionalism had both neglected the impact of ideas on policy.[2]

---

[1] In this book, the terms "ideas" and "norms" are used interchangeably, while recognizing that ideas can be held privately, and may or may not have behavioral implications, while norms are always collective and behavioral. Judith Goldstein, *Ideas, Interests, and American Trade Policy* (Ithaca: Cornell University Press, 1993). I use norm to mean "standard of appropriate behavior for actors with a given identity." Martha Finnemore and Kathryn Sikkink. "International Norm Dynamics and Political Change," *International Organization* 52, no. 4 (1998), 891.

[2] As Goldstein and Keohane note, "The most widely accepted systemic approaches to the study of international relations, realism and liberal institutionalism, take rationalist models as their starting points. Both realism and institutionalism assume that self-interested actors maximize their utility, subject to constraints. In such models, actors' preferences

Table 2.1. *Three ways of ideas*

	Strategic interaction	Hegemonic socialization	Social construction
Who	Rational unit level actors: e.g. states/ multinational corporations	Hegemonic/colonial powers	Epistemic communities/ transnational norm entrepreneurs
What for	Utility/efficiency	Legitimation of hegemonic orders; civilizing mission ("white man's burden")	Universal moral purpose/standards of appropriateness
How	Strategic interaction	Conquest/coercion/ reward	Symbolic interaction
When	Moments of opportunity for mutual gain	"After victory" (Ikenberry)	Ending (mid-point or end-point of) major rivalry or war, emerging or escalating transnational challenges
Which ideas (mainly)	Causal ideas	World views/causal ideas	Principled ideas
Impact of ideas	Constraining/ regulatory	Constraining	Constitutive

Keohane and Goldstein have blamed this on the influence of economics, which treats ideas as epiphenomena, or at best as "hooks" that could be used to propagate and legitimize the policies of elites.[3] But challenged by the so-called "reflectivists" in the 1990s, rationalist scholars began to accept a causal role of ideas. As Keohane and Goldstein put it: "even if we accept the rationality premise, actions taken by human beings depend on the substantive quality of available ideas, since such ideas help to clarify principles and conceptions of causal relationships, and to coordinate individual behavior. Once institutionalized, furthermore, ideas continue to guide action in the absence of costly innovation."[4] International institutions thus play a key role in the transmission of ideas. Ideas can make

---

and causal beliefs are given, and attention focuses on the variation in the constraints faced by actors." Judith Goldstein and Robert O. Keohane, "Ideas and Foreign Policy: An Analytical Framework," in *Ideas and Foreign Policy: Beliefs, Institutions, and Political Change*, ed. Goldstein and Keohane (Ithaca: Cornell University Press, 1993), 4.

[3] Ibid.

[4] Ibid., 5.

institutions more efficient, and help parties to them to realize more utility. Despite this concession to reflectivism (including constructivism), the treatment of ideas by neoliberal scholars remained within the broad parameters of rationalism.[5] Their main concern was "to show that ideas matter for policy, even when human beings behave rationally to achieve their ends."[6] This implies that ideas serve the ends of rational behavior. Ideas are important because they "affect strategic interactions, helping or hindering joint efforts to attain 'more efficient' outcomes."[7] The three core elements of strategic interaction processes apply: (1) utility and efficiency are the key goals; (2) interests and identities remain fundamentally unchanged; (3) power remains an important determinant of the acceptance or rejection of new ideas.

Moreover, contractualist theories stress power variables. For contractual theories, cooperation and institution-building are viewed as being conditioned heavily by the preferences of hegemons or a small group of relatively powerful states. Keohane and Martin concede that the efficacy of international regimes and institutions is subject to the prevailing distribution of power.[8] While conceding that weak powers can develop and use regimes to pursue their interests and advantage, regime theorists have tended to underestimate the extent to which weak powers may use international institutions to bring about more fundamental transformation. To be sure, international regimes can still be maintained "after hegemony."[9] Snidal argues that a small group of rising powers may sustain regimes and assume responsibility for cooperation and provision of collective good in a post-hegemonic setting.[10] But this solves the problem

---

[5] Despite having contributors from constructivism (Sikkink) and the English School (Jackson), the Keohane and Goldstein volume was rationalist. It was dedicated to two goals: to demonstrate the reflectivist shortcoming of inattention to empirical work and to address whether ideas matter in the positive; hence their null hypothesis: "that variation in policy across countries, or over time, is entirely accounted for by changes in factors *other than* ideas." Goldstein and Keohane, "Ideas and Foreign Policy: An Analytical Framework," 6. This was therefore more of an effort to answer whether ideas matter than how they matter.

[6] Goldstein and Keohane, "Ideas and Foreign Policy: An Analytical Framework," 5.

[7] Ibid., 12.

[8] Robert O. Keohane and Lisa Martin, "The Promise of Institutionalist Theory," *International Security* 20, no. 1 (Summer 1995), 39–51.

[9] Robert Keohane, "Hegemonic Leadership and US Foreign Economic Policy in the 'Long Decade' of the 1950s," in *America in a Changing World Economy*, ed. William P. Avery and David P. Rapkin (New York: Longman, 1982), 49–97, 50–52; Robert O. Keohane, *After Hegemony: Cooperation and Discord in the World Political Economy* (Princeton University Press, 1984).

[10] Duncan Snidal, "The Limits of Hegemonic Stability Theory," *International Organization*, 39, no. 4 (Autumn 1985), 579–614.

of regime maintenance, rather than regime creation.[11] The creation of regimes and institutions that could spread ideas for the sake of efficiency and utility is contingent on the role of powerful actors. Rapkin contends that "states lacking structural power can exercise entrepreneurial and/ or intellectual leadership to activate – by establishing settings, framing issues and forming coalitions – cooperation that induces the structural leadership of those that possess it."[12] But the "pluralization of leadership" in institution-building stops at the level of the middle powers and seldom extends to coalitions in the Third World.

Hegemonic Socialization

Theories of hegemonic socialization see norm diffusion and change as the function of a leading state propagating some preferred values to lesser states. The agency role of lesser actors is minimal, although their acceptance of the hegemon's ideas creates legitimacy for the hegemon's authority. This by itself is not a single or coherent perspective. At least three main variants can be identified: structural realism; Gramscian theory; and the "institutional-binding" perspective.

Realists argue that the diffusion of norms depends critically on powerful actors. Thus Krasner argues that the relative power of states was central to the spread of four norms: religious toleration, abolition of the slave trade, protection of minorities in Central Europe, and promotion of individual rights. Religious toleration became an accepted principle in seventeenth-century Europe because those local rulers resisting it were materially too weak. The slave trade could be abolished because of the vigorous monitoring and enforcement efforts of the major European powers, especially Britain, whereas efforts to promote minority rights failed because of the absence of a similar commitment by the dominant European powers. And the acceptance of individual human rights was possible because of the power, resources, and political will of the major Western powers led by the United States.[13] As the liberal theorist Andrew Moravcsik sums up, the realist position is that "governments accept

---

[11] Donald Crone, "Does Hegemony Matter? The Reorganization of the Pacific Political Economy," *World Politics* 45, no. 4 (July 1993), 503. It should also be noted that Snidal's reference does not specifically distinguish between middle and weak powers. He speaks of rising powers and not weak powers.

[12] David P. Rapkin, "Leadership and Cooperative Institutions in the Asia-Pacific," in *Pacific Cooperation: Building Economic and Security Regimes in the Asia-Pacific Region*, ed. Andrew Mack and John Ravenhill (St. Leonards, NSW: Allen and Unwin, 1994), 109.

[13] Stephen D. Krasner, "Sovereignty and Intervention," in *Beyond Westphalia?: State Sovereignty and International Intervention*, ed. Gene M. Lyons and Michael Mastanduno (Baltimore: The Johns Hopkins University Press, 1995), 228–249.

formal human rights enforcement regimes because they are compelled to do so by great powers, who externalize their ideology – a view shared by the theory of hegemonic stability and conventional realist bargaining theory."[14] The message is clear: to be successfully propagated, principled ideas have to be "imposed" by a hegemon. Where the hegemonic power lacks the political will or simply lacks the resources to impose new ideas, their diffusion fails.

Cox's neo-Gramscian theory also stresses the role of power. His notion of hegemony differs from traditional Marxism (historical materialism) by paying attention to both its material and ideational aspects.[15] While the core features of a hegemonic order are material, especially interconnectivity of production structures among countries and alliances among their dominant social classes, the creation of a hegemonic order also presupposes shared "mutual interests and ideological perspectives of social classes in different countries."[16] Hegemony is thus viewed less as a matter of coercion than as one of consent.[17] Consent is generated through ideological consensus in which the hegemon's preferred ideas legitimize "the continuing supremacy of the leading state or states and leading social classes but at the same time offer some measure or prospect of satisfaction to the less powerful."[18] These ideas are institutionalized through global and regional institutions, which "legitimate prevailing norms, co-opt elites from peripheral countries and absorb counter-hegemonic ideas."[19] The diffusion of the social, economic, and political ideas and practices of the hegemon to the weak peripheries occurs through a "process of *passive revolution*."[20] Once such institutions are created, they continue even after the material power of hegemony has declined, because of the ideological consensus already in place.[21]

[14] Andrew Moravcsik, *Explaining the Emergence of Human Rights Regimes: Liberal Democracy and Political Uncertainty in Postwar Europe*, Working Paper Series 98, December 17, 1998, Weatherhead Center for International Affairs Harvard University, www.princeton.edu/~amoravcs/library/emergence.pdf.
[15] Robert Cox, "Gramsci, Hegemony and International Relations: An Essay in Method," *Millennium* 12, no. 2 (1983), 162–175; Keohane, "Hegemonic Leadership and US Foreign Economic Policy in the 'Long Decade' of the 1950s"; Robert Baldwin and Anne Krueger, *The Structure and Evolution of Recent US Trade Policy* (University of Chicago Press, 1984).
[16] Robert Cox, *Production, Power, and World Order: Social Forces in the Making of History* (New York: Columbia University Press, 1987), 7.
[17] Ibid.
[18] Ibid., 7.
[19] Jane Ford, *A Social Theory of the WTO: Trading Cultures* (New York: Palgrave Macmillan, 2003), 25; see Cox, "Gramsci, Hegemony and International Relations," 168, 172.
[20] Ford, *A Social Theory of the WTO*, 22.
[21] Gramscian and neo-Marxist perspectives speak to the possibility of a counter-hegemonic spread of ideas. These are ideas in direct juxtaposition to those of the hegemon. The goal

The theory of hegemonic socialization, developed by Ikenberry and Kupchan, is another body of work that emphasizes the role of power in norm diffusion. It covers both material and ideological or normative instruments of socialization. The former include "military capabilities, control over raw materials, markets, and capital and competitive advantages in highly valued goods."[22] The latter rest on ideology, which a hegemon uses to develop a normative order that justifies its rule. While the two are complementary, the "rule of might" is prior to the "rule based on right." But the "[r]ule based on might is enhanced by rule based on right."[23] In his later work, Ikenberry lays less emphasis on the role of crude material power, and gives more play to a process of "institutional-binding" which relies heavily on "agreed-upon legal and political institutions that operate to allocate rights and limit the exercise of [the hegemon's] power."[24] In Ikenberry's perspective, ideas and norms are transmitted and institutionalized through the creation of "constitutional orders" that tame the power of a hegemon "after victory" in a major war with a view to legitimizing its authority and prolonging its rule. The core feature of constitutional orders is an act of "strategic restraint" and a framework of "institutional self-binding" by the hegemon. But Ikenberry remains wedded to the basic premise that socialization in international relations requires a hegemon's initiative, and a hegemon's "self-binding" act. The weaker states "accept the deal"[25] in the hope that this will mitigate their fear of domination or abandonment, especially if the hegemon offers credible commitments to refrain from exploitation and domination. The agency role of weaker states in initiating and maintaining international regimes to manage their relationship with stronger powers is at best obscured.

Social Construction

The third perspective on the spread of ideas and norms has come from social constructivism.[26] While rationalists stress utility maximization,

---

of counter-hegemonic movements is not to localize hegemonic norms, but to provide a complete alternative. The main agents of this process are social movements.

[22] Johanna Mohring, "International Institutions and State Socialization: NATO and the 'Enlargement' of the Western Community of Values," Paper Prepared for the International Studies Association Annual Convention, February 16–20, 1999, Washington, DC.

[23] John Ikenberry and Charles A. Kupchan, "Socialization and Hegemonic Power," *International Organization* 44, no. 3 (Summer 1990), 286.

[24] John Ikenberry, *After Victory: Institutions, Strategic Restraint, and the Rebuilding of Order after Major Wars* (Princeton University Press, 2001), 29.

[25] Ibid., 56.

[26] Peter Katzenstein, Robert Keohane, and Stephen Krasner, eds., *Exploration and Contestation in the Study of World Politics* (Cambridge, MA: MIT Press, 1999).

many, if not all, constructivists emphasize a moral purpose.[27] Actors accept ideas, build institutions around them, and behave accordingly not because ideas act as tools of utility and efficiency in a strategic interaction setting, but because these ideas and the behavior they shape are understood to be good, desirable, and appropriate. While the rationalist perspective on ideas stresses coercion, bargaining, and compromises, the constructivist perspective on norms centers on socialization, compliance, and positive transformation through the diffusion of norms.

But in conceptualizing the process through which such ideas and norms spread, constructivists earlier tended to privilege universal moral entrepreneurship and understate the importance of local dynamics and cultural feedback. This was especially true of the early literature on norms. A good deal of the foundational constructivist narrative on norms focuses on what Ethan Nadelmann has called the "moral proselytism" of "transnational moral entrepreneurs."[28] Influenced by sociological institutionalism, constructivists have tended to reproduce its assumptions of a "world social structure"[29] that acts as a wellspring of good and universal

[27] Constructivists disagree on the importance of moral purpose, especially those who tend to see rationalism and constructivism as complementary, rather than mutually exclusive. See James Fearon and Alexander Wendt, "Rationalism vs. Constructivism: A Skeptical View," in *Handbook of International Relations*, ed. Walter Carlines, Thomas Risse, and Beth Simmons (Thousand Oaks, CA: Sage, 2002), 52–72. In this respect, Wendt's position is more "conventional" than that of "critical" constructivists. Ted Hopf, "The Promise of Constructivism in International Relations Theory," *International Security* 23, no. 1 (1998), 171–200. For moral-leaning constructivism, see: Finnemore and Sikkink, "International Norms and Political Change"; Margaret E. Keck and Kathryn Sikkink, *Activists beyond Borders: Advocacy Networks in International Politics* (Ithaca: Cornell University Press, 1998). Recent work has criticized the constructivist neglect of superficial or "bad" norms and the role of those "antipreneurs" who promote bad norms over good. See Alan Bloomfield and Shirley V. Scott, eds., *Norm Antipreneurs and the Politics of Resistance to Global Normative Change* (New York: Routledge, 2017); Clifford Bob, *The Global Right Wing and the Clash of World Politics* (Cambridge University Press, 2012). The "goodness" of ideas and norms can vary and change over time. Bloomfield and Scott show how the idea of sovereignty and the associated norm of non-intervention, once considered to be a moral norm by postcolonial states, acquired the status of a bad norm when states invoked non-intervention to shield themselves from human rights abuses, leading to the idea of humanitarian intervention and the norm of R2P.
[28] Ethan Nadelmann, "Global Prohibition Regimes: The Evolution of Norms in International Society," *International Organization* 44, no. 4 (1990), 479–526.
[29] Martha Finnemore, "Norms, Culture and World Politics: Insights from Sociology's Institutionalism," *International Organization* 50, no. 2 (1996), 343. On sociological institutionalism, see: John W. Meyer, "The World Polity and the Authority of the Nation-State," in *Studies of the Modern World-System*, ed. A. Bergesen (New York: Academic Press, 1980); John W. Meyer, John Boli, George M. Thomas, and Francisco O. Ramirez, "World Society and the Nation-State," *American Journal of Sociology* 103, no. 1 (July 1997), 144–181; George M. Thomas, John W. Meyer, Francisco O. Ramirez, and John Boli, *Institutional Structure: Constituting State, Society, and the Individual* (Newbury Park, CA: Sage, 1987). Even the more recent constructivist scholarship, which stresses the

normative ideas and standards. Norms which make a universalistic claim about what is good are seen as more likely to spread than norms which are localized or particularistic.[30] The staple of early constructivist writings on norms attests to this; it focuses on the propagation of certain "good" universal norms concerning land mines, protection of whales, struggle against racism, intervention against genocide, and promotion of human rights.[31] This strong ethos of normative universalism predisposes constructivist norm theorists, much like their sociological institutionalist predecessors, against the expansive appeal and feedback potential of regional or localized norms.

Moreover, an ambiguity marks the constructivist view on the relationship between material power and norms. Some constructivists believe that normative change does not require the backing of powerful actors. Some constructivists reject hegemonic socialization, and hold that norms can spread through a process of social and cultural interaction without the backing of physically or materially powerful nations. Finnemore and Sikkink show that consent of a materially powerful state is not a necessary

---

importance of domestic structures and the interaction between domestic and international actors on receptivity to emerging norms, hardly addresses the issue of feedback. See: Thomas Risse and Kathryn Sikkink, "The Socialization of International Human Rights Norms into Domestic Practices: Introduction," in *The Power of Human Rights: International Norms and Domestic Change*, ed. Thomas Risse, Stephen C. Ropp and Kathryn Sikkink (Cambridge University Press, 1999), 1–38.

[30] Thomas et al., *Institutional Structure: Constituting State, Society, and the Individual*; Martha Finnemore and Kathryn Sikkink, "International Norm Dynamics and Political Change," in *Exploration and Contestation in the Study of World Politics*, ed. Peter Katzenstein, Robert Keohane, and Stephen Krasner (Cambridge, MA: MIT Press, 1999), 267.

[31] See, for example, Richard Price, *The Chemical Weapons Taboo* (Ithaca: Cornell University Press, 1998); "Reversing the Gun Sights: Transnational Civil Society Targets Land Mines," *International Organization* 52, no. 3 (1997), 613–644; Kathryn Sikkink, "Human Rights, Principled Issue Networks and Sovereignty in Latin America," *International Organization* 47, no. 3 (1993), 411–441; M. J. Peterson, "Whales, Cetologists, Environmentalists and the International Management of Whaling," *International Organization* 46, no. 1 (1992), 147–186; Karen Litfin, *Ozone Discourses: Science and Politics in Global Environmental Cooperation* (New York: Columbia University Press, 1994); Audie Klotz, "Norms Reconstituting Interests: Global Racial Equality and US Sanctions against South Africa," *International Organization* 49, no. 3 (1995), 451–478. Summarizing the literature on norms, Keith Krause points to the overwhelming dominance of "environmental or human rights issues, with case studies of such topics as international whaling, human rights in Latin America and Western Europe, the abolition of apartheid, protection of the Ozone Layer or the world's forests, or the creation and activities of international institutions such as the ICRC or UNESCO." Studies of norms in "high" security issues have been far fewer and that too from a "peace research perspective"; these include the International Campaign to Ban Land Mines and the more recent work on the proliferation of small arms and light weapons. Keith Krause, *Norm-Building in Security Spaces: The Emergence of the Light Weapons Problematic*, Working Paper 11, Research Group in International Security, Joint Program of the Université de Montreal and McGill University, Montreal, 2001, 6–7.

condition for norm cascades.[32] Norms can themselves be empowering. Through norms, states with less material power can "influence [international] regime change and cultural transformation," by focusing on "discursive, deliberative and persuasive" mechanisms."[33] Moreover, powerful states do not always make good norm entrepreneurs. As contemporary debates about human rights, humanitarian intervention, and democracy promotion show, ideas and norms peddled by powerful states (e.g. superpowers, great powers) easily invite suspicion and resistance, including perceptions of cultural bias, double standards, and ulterior motives. But other constructivists assume that normative agency is contingent upon material power. Florini points out that norms held by powerful actors "have many more opportunities to reproduce through the greater number of opportunities afforded to powerful states to persuade others of the rightness of their views."[34] In Wendt's theory of socialization, power relations play "a crucial role" in the direction and success of social interactions leading to structural (which is mainly ideational) change.[35] Ideas matter in socialization, but social processes that produce structural change, such as symbolic interaction processes, are "weighted" by considerations of power and dependence.[36]

Challenging this view, I have argued that ideas and norms constitute an important tool for the agency of weaker actors in world politics. Moreover a good deal of this agency happens at the "local" level, signifying the agency of the norm-takers, rather than the norm-givers. In my

---

[32] Finnemore and Sikkink, "International Norm Dynamics and Political Change," 900–901.

[33] Ford, *A Social Theory of the WTO: Trading Cultures*, 39. Also see Jeffrey T. Checkel, "The Constructivist Turn in International Relations Theory (A Review Essay)," *World Politics* 50, no. 2 (1998), 326; Friedrich Kratochwil, "Contracts and Regimes: Do Issue Specificity and Variations of Formality Matter?" in *Regime Theory and International Relations*, ed. Volker Rittberger (Oxford: Clarendon Press, 1993).

[34] Ann Florini, "The Evolution of International Norms," *International Studies Quarterly* 40, no. 3 (1996), 363–389, 375.

[35] Here, power is defined softly, in non-coercive terms. Power in this sense means the ability to "get the other side to see things its way." This is done by rewarding compliant behavior and punishing deviant behavior. Power is context-dependent, its meaning depends on their definitions of the situation, but in general, "where there is an imbalance of relevant material capability social acts will tend to evolve in the direction favored by the more powerful." Alexander Wendt, *Social Theory of International Politics* (Cambridge University Press, 1999), 331.

[36] This is an implicit factor in Wendt's social interactionist model: "The interactionist model of how identities are learned centers on the mechanism of reflected appraisals. Actors learn to see themselves as a reflection of how they are appraised by significant Others. The key variable here is how the Other treats or 'casts' the Self, weighted by power and dependency relations." See: Wendt, *Social Theory of International Politics*, 341.

earlier work, I have conceptualized two processes through which local actors construct norms.

Processes of Norm Diffusion

Norm Localization

"Localization" is "the active construction (through discourse, framing, grafting, and cultural selection) of foreign ideas by local actors, which results in the former developing significant congruence with local beliefs and practices."[37] When such processes significantly change the identity and behavior of the local actors, they may be called "constitutive localization."

The idea of localization (or "constitutive localization") was initially derived from Southeast Asian historiography, which holds that Southeast Asian societies were not passive recipients of foreign (Indian and Chinese) cultural and political ideas, but active borrowers and modifiers.[38] Localization describes a process of idea transmission in which Southeast Asians borrowed foreign ideas about authority and legitimacy and fitted them into indigenous traditions and practices. Ideas which could be constructed to fit indigenous traditions and thereby enhance local beliefs and practices were better received than those that did not have such potential. O. W. Wolters, a leading proponent of localization in Southeast Asian studies, defines it as a "local statement ... into which foreign elements have retreated."[39]

The theory of constitutive localization holds that the initial global prominence or reputational power of a norm and the commitment of "outside proponents" (transnational norm entrepreneurs) are necessary but not sufficient conditions to secure its acceptance and institutionalization in

---

[37] This section draws heavily from my earlier work. Amitav Acharya, "How Ideas Spread: Whose Norms Matter? Norm Localization and Institutional Change in Asian Regionalism," *International Organization* 58, no. 2 (Spring 2004), 239–275 (quotation from p. 245); Acharya, *Whose Ideas Matter? Agency and Power in Asian Regionalism* (Ithaca: Cornell University Press, 2009); Acharya, "Norm Subsidiarity and Regional Orders: Sovereignty, Regionalism and Rule Making in the Third World," *International Studies Quarterly* 55, no. 1 (2011), 95–123.

[38] See O. W. Wolters, *History, Culture and Region in Southeast Asian Perspectives* (Singapore: Institute of Southeast Asian Studies, 1982); O. W. Wolters, *History, Culture and Region in Southeast Asian Perspectives*, rev edn (Ithaca: Cornell University Southeast Asian Studies Program and Singapore: Institute of Southeast Asian Studies, 1999). For a summary of the literature, see: I. W. Mabbett, "The 'Indianization' of Southeast Asia: Reflections on the Prehistoric Sources," *Journal of Southeast Asian Studies* 8, no. 1 (1976), 1–14; I. W. Mabbett, "The 'Indianization' of Southeast Asia: Reflections on the Historical Sources," *Journal of Southeast Asian Studies* 8, no. 2 (1976), 143–161.

[39] Wolters, *History, Culture and Region in Southeast Asian Perspectives*, 57.

the absence of their congruence with local norms and practices and the advocacy role of inside proponents. Emerging norms that make universal claims are more likely to succeed in a regional setting if they can be grafted onto a prior local norm (including a previously legitimized foreign norm) or policy discourse. Norms which can be thus modified to fit a local tradition, or complex and malleable norms, may actually spread more easily and faster than "simple and clear" (morally unambiguous) and less inflexible norms.[40] Normative discourse which gives a universal frame to local principles is likely to fare better than norm entrepreneurship which simply seeks to supplant local principles. Foreign norms which seek to displace existing beliefs and practices are more likely to be accepted if the local beliefs and practices are already discredited domestically/locally than if they still enjoy legitimacy and support.

The theory of localization addresses three key questions: its motivations, the processes through which localization occurs, and its outcome. The main driving force of localization is the localizer's desire for legitimation and empowerment. This may entail some degree of utilitarian calculations, but it goes beyond the purely "strategic" intent of acquiring great material power. Ideas are borrowed because they enhance the prestige and authority of the recipient by making its behavior conform to a foreign universal standard. There are strong parallels here with constructivist norm theory. Cottrell and Davis have shown how domestic actors borrow international rules to justify their own actions and call into question the legitimacy of others.[41] Keck and Sikkink's study of the anti-foot-binding campaign in China during 1874–1911 and the anti-circumcision campaign in Kenya in 1923–1931 establishes that the fate of these campaigns was decided by whether the norm legitimized or conflicted with the local nationalists' agenda.[42] Diffusion occurred when the foreign norm sought to replace a local norm internally discredited, but failed when it competed with a still-legitimate local norm.

The idea of constitutive localization presented here places an even greater emphasis on local agency and its acts of legitimation. The process of localization involves three types of acts. The first is termed "local initiative." Ideas are not imposed through force or purchased through commerce; instead local actors proactively seek out foreign ideas that they

---

[40] Hence, among the "intrinsic characteristics" of norms that determine the prospects of their acceptance may not be the "clarity or specificity" stressed by Finnemore and Sikkink as a key condition for successful norm diffusion. Finnemore and Sikkink, *Activists beyond Borders*, 906.

[41] Andrew P. Cottrell and James W. Davis, "How do International Institutions Matter?" *International Studies Quarterly*, 40, no. 4 (December 1996), 453.

[42] Keck and Sikkink, *Activists beyond Borders*, 63.

find morally appealing or politically empowering.[43] In normative change, this perspective would stress the agency role not just of "outsider proponents" – the standard definition of a norm entrepreneur – pursuing a universal moral agenda, but also of "insider proponents" seeking to legitimize a local identity.[44] Outside proponents are more likely to advance their cause if they act through local agents, rather than coming independently at it. Successful diffusion of emerging norms depends on the degree to which they can be said to build upon and supplement, rather than supplant, existing ideas and norms. One example can be found in Wiseman's analysis of the non-provocative defense norm in the Soviet Union, which demonstrates the crucial role of insider proponents within the Soviet military who worked "by resurrecting a defensive 'tradition' in Soviet history," and thereby "sought to reassure domestic critics that they were operating historically within the Soviet paradigm and to avoid the impression that they were simply borrowing Western ideas."[45]

A second act of localization is the use of foreign ideas as a frame to express local beliefs and practices.[46] The formal shape (name or structure) of the foreign idea may remain intact, but its contents are infused with local beliefs and practices. Norm-takers may resort to infusion to validate existing beliefs, demonstrate the broader relevance and appeal of local beliefs and practices, and sell "homegrown" ideas to a larger market.[47] Moreover, in accepting the outsiders' normative ideas, local actors may see an opportunity to ensure that the former too learn from local

---

[43] This meaning of localization derives from the work of Jacob Van Leur, a Dutch economic historian. Advancing what has since been called the "Idea of Local Initiative," Van Leur described the transmission of Indian ideas into Southeast Asia as a matter of active borrowing, rather than imposition or passive acceptance. It was the Southeast Asian rulers who, in an "attempt at legitimizing their interest ... and organizing and domesticating their states and subjects ... called Indian civilization to the east." Jacob C. Van Leur, "On Early Asian Trade," in *Indonesian Trade and Society: Essays in Asian Social and Economic History*, ed. Van Leur (The Hague: W. van Hoeve, 1955), 98.

[44] Geoffrey Wiseman, *Concepts of Non-Provocative Defence: Ideas and Practices in International Security* (London: Palgrave, 2002).

[45] Ibid., 104.

[46] The clearest example here is the Code of Manu (Manusrmiti), the most important Indian source of legal and moral conduct in classical Southeast Asia. This Hindu Manual of Laws identifies eighteen points of litigation. In Java, where the code was widely used, some of its laws were modified to accommodate Javanese customary law, but without altering the number. Wolters, *History, Culture and Region in Southeast Asian Perspectives*, 42.

[47] Such validation happens where foreign ideas appear to resonate with new or emerging local practices. For example, Krasner's analysis of the diffusion of Westphalian sovereignty shows that the principles and practices of sovereignty had existed for some time before 1648, and that the main contribution of Westphalia was to validate existing practices and not create an entirely new institutional form. Stephen S. Krasner, "Westphalia and All That," in *Ideas and Foreign Policy*, ed. Goldstein and Keohane, 235–264.

practices. Such acts of "amplifying," "signifying," and "universalizing" local beliefs and practices[48] help us develop an understanding of idea transmission as a two-way dialogue.

A third act of localization involves changing the formal shape and content of foreign ideas on the basis of the recipient's own prior beliefs and practices. This might involve borrowing only those ideas which are, or can be made, congruent with local beliefs and which may enhance the prestige of the borrower. It could also involve pruning outside ideas to get rid of their undesirable elements, especially those which challenge established beliefs and practices, while finding a fit between the desirable elements and existing local beliefs and practices.[49]

Thus defined, constitutive localization is different from *mimicking, teaching, persuasion,* and *adaptation,* concepts popular with norm theorists. *Mimicking* leaves the original norm more or less intact. This seldom happens in the real world. *Teaching*[50] is a top-down process, while localization connotes a bottom-up dynamic initiated by the norm-taker. It assumes a greater equality of status and knowledge between the norm-maker and norm-taker than is the case with a teacher–student relationship. *Persuasion* is a form of non-coercive socialization through which a communicator attempts to change the beliefs, attitudes, and behavior of others. This process allows those being persuaded some degree of choice.[51] But unlike localization, persuasion mostly implies changes at the norm-taker's end, while bracketing the persuader's beliefs and preferences. Similarly, *adaptation* "shirk[s] the crucial question of where, how and why foreign elements began to fit into a local culture," and obscures "the initiative of local elements responsible for the process and the end

---

[48] Wolters asserts that Hindu ideas did not supplant many indigenous Southeast Asian political beliefs and practices; they merely "amplified" the authority of the ruler by bringing "ancient and persisting indigenous beliefs into sharper focus." Wolters, *History, Culture and Region in Southeast Asian Perspectives,* 9. The term "universalization" can be found in Thomas Kirsch's explanation of the interaction between Thai animism and imported Indian Buddhism. The advent of Buddhist religious ideas and practices in Thailand did not lead Thais to abandon their existing practice of worshipping local spirits. Rather Thai shrines placed Buddhist deities alongside local spirits. This transformed the status of both religious practices, resulting in the simultaneous "parochialization" of Indian Buddhism and "universalization" of indigenous and preexisting animism, adding civilizational complexity to Thai religion and society. Thomas A. Kirsch, "Complexity in the Thai Religious System," *Journal of Asian Studies* 36, no. 2 (1977), 241–266, 263.

[49] An important example of existing tradition can be found in M. B. Hooker's analysis of how Indian legal–moral frameworks were adjusted to fit indigenous beliefs and practices in Indonesia. M. B. Hooker, *A Concise Legal History of South-East Asia* (Oxford: Clarendon Press, 1978), 35–36.

[50] On the teaching of norms, see: Finnemore, "Norms, Culture and World Politics."

[51] Alastair I. Johnston, "Treating International Institutions as Social Environments," *International Studies Quarterly* 45, no. 4 (2001), 487–515.

product."[52] Furthermore, while adaptation, especially in its biological sense, describes how norm-takers *adapt to* outside ideas (stimuli) by adjusting indigenous beliefs and practices,[53] in constitutive localization, norm-takers also *adapt from* outside ideas, selecting and integrating into the local milieu those elements which fit within existing beliefs, practices, and structures. This helps resolve the tension between the norm-takers' desire to preserve an existing identity, and the lure of new ideas that offer the promise of greater legitimacy and authority. What results is a two-way dialogue involving the localization of universal ideas and universalization of local normative and social frameworks.

With respect to the outcome, localization produces changes to the interests and identities of the localizers. But the nature of that change differs from some understandings of "constitutive" change in constructivist theory. There, constitutive is understood to occur when the identity and behavior of local agents change fundamentally under the influence of new ideas.[54] This definition of constitutive seems one-sided. It describes how foreign ideas constitute local structures, but not how local structures reconstitute foreign agents. The foreign ideas remain dominant, even in the local context, supplanting preexisting local normative structures and redefining the interests and identities of the local actors. The change produced by constitutive localization is different in three respects. First, the outside norms are themselves open to redefinition and change, at least in the local context, on the basis of the local actors' own preferences and identities.[55] In Southeast Asian discourses on localization, Wolters has discussed "long periods of time when both local and foreign elements were changing."[56] Second, constitutive localization does not produce dramatic one-step change in the norm-takers' identity and behavior, which has been common to some of the early constructivist work on normative change (the fall of communism, the end of apartheid, etc.). Rather it often leads to evolutionary forms of change, what I have called "everyday forms of normative change." Third, the effect of change is not to extinguish the identity of the local actors, but to produce a creative synthesis between it and that of foreign ideas and norms. In this process,

---

[52] Wolters, *History, Culture and Region in Southeast Asian Perspectives*, 56.

[53] Florini, "The Evolution of International Norms."

[54] Alexander Wendt, "Constructing International Politics," *International Security* 20, no. 1 (Summer 1995), 72; Fearon and Wendt, "Rationalism vs. Constructivism: A Skeptical View."

[55] As Checkel suggests, constructivists have rarely paid attention to this, concentrating instead on changes at the "receiving end." Jeffrey C. Checkel, "Why Comply? Social Learning and European Identity Change," *International Organization* 55, no. 3 (Summer 2001), 579.

[56] Wolters, *History, Culture and Region in Southeast Asian Perspectives*, 56.

the cognitive priors of the norm-taker remain salient, at least initially, in deciding the shape and content of the modified external norm. In other words, in constitutive localization, local and foreign elements are in a truly mutually constitutive relationship, but the resulting behavior of the recipient can be understood more in terms of the former than the latter, although it can only be fully understood in terms of both.

Norm Subsidiarity

Subsidiarity may be viewed as the opposite of localization. It is understood as a "process whereby local actors create rules with a view to preserve their autonomy from dominance, neglect, violation, or abuse by more powerful central actors."[57] The concept derives from the general notion of subsidiarity, "a principle of locating governance at the lowest possible level – that closest to the individuals and groups affected by the rules and decisions adopted and enforced."[58] Subsidiarity is a key principle of the EU's institutions,[59] but has a prior local as well as universal basis. Its origins can be traced to Pius XI's papal encyclicals of 1931.[60] In international relations, it defined the relationship between universalism

---

[57] This definition is taken from Amitav Acharya, "Norm Subsidiarity and Regional Orders: Sovereignty, Regionalism and Rule Making in the Third World," *International Studies Quarterly* 55, no. 1 (2011), 95–123. That essay discusses the multiple origins and meanings of subsidiarity. While the common understanding of subsidiarity in Europe/the EU suggests a rather consensual division of labor among the various levels of governance, there are other potential applications that are not always consensual, but imply resistance and contestation. In my view, the demand for subsidiarity starts with resistance to the tyranny of higher authority of governance. While borrowing from the traditional understanding of subsidiarity, I use the term as a principle which can originate from resistance, but can lead to a consensus over the relationship between local and global norms. I am grateful to an anonymous reviewer of the manuscript of this book for helping me clarify my position relative to other meanings of subsidiarity.

[58] Anne-Marie Slaughter, *A New World Order* (Princeton University Press, 2004), 30.

[59] Andrew Moravcsik, *The Choice for Europe* (Ithaca: Cornell University Press, 1998), 455; "Protocol on the Application of the Principles of Subsidiarity and Proportionality," *Official Journal of the European Union* C 310/207 (December 16, 2004); Gráinne De Búrca, "The Principle of Subsidiarity and the Court of Justice as an Institutional Actor," *Journal of Common Market Studies* 36, no. 2 (1998), 217–235; Sean Pager, "Strictness and Subsidiarity: An Institutional Perspective on Affirmative Action at the European Court of Justice," *International and Comparative Law Review* 35 (2003); Edward Swaine, "Subsidiarity and Self-interest: Federalism at the European Court of Justice," *Harvard International Law Journal* 4, no. 1 (2000), http://scholarship.law.gwu.edu/cgi/viewcontent .cgi?article=1001&context=faculty_publications.

[60] Steering Committee on Local and Regional Authorities in Europe, "Definition and Limits of the Principle of Subsidiarity," draft study (Strasbourg: Council of Europe, November 9, 1993).

and regionalism at the time of the UN's birth in 1945.[61] With the dramatic expansion of US peace operations in the post-Cold War period, subsidiarity has been invoked as a principle around which a division of labor can be constructed between an overstretched UN and regional organizations.[62]

Slaughter proposes subsidiarity and proportionality as "vertical norms" of contemporary world order, "dictated by considerations of practicability rather than a preordained distribution of power," alongside the "horizontal norms of global deliberative equality, legitimate difference, and positive comity."[63] Others see subsidiarity as a fundamentally normative obligation (rather than a matter of practicality alone), for example as an element of "panarchy," i.e. "rule of all by all for all."[64]

As a form of behavior in relation to a higher authority, subsidiarity by local actors can be "challenging/resisting" or "supportive/subordinating."[65] The former implies active efforts on the part of local players to deal with their own issues without intervention by a higher authority. The latter implies their willingness to serve higher institutions. To elaborate, "challenging/resisting" implies the desirability of non-intervention by a higher authority which is allowed to perform "only those tasks which

---

[61] Minerva Etzioni, *The Majority of One: Towards a Theory of Regional Compatibility* (Beverly Hills: Sage, 1970); Norman J. Padelford, "Regional Organizations and the United Nations," *International Organization* 8, no. 2 (1954), 203–216; Ernst Haas, "Regionalism, Functionalism and Universal Organization," *World Politics* 8, no. 2 (January 1956), 238–263; Joseph S. Nye, *Peace in Parts: Integration and Conflict in Regional Organization* (Boston: Little Brown and Company, 1971).

[62] Resolution 1631 (2005) SC/8526, Security Council (United Nations, Department of Public Information, 2005); W. Andy Knight, "Towards a Subsidiarity Model for Peacekeeping and Preventive Diplomacy: Making Chapter VIII of the UN Charter Operational," *Third World Quarterly* 17, no. 1 (1996), 31–52; David O'Brien, "The Search for Subsidiarity: The UN, African Regional Organizations and Humanitarian Action," *International Peacekeeping* 7, no. 3 (Autumn 2000), 57–83; Sorpong Peou, "The Subsidiarity Model of Global Governance in the UN–ASEAN Context," *Global Governance* 4 (1998), 439–459; Connie Peck, "The Role of Regional Organizations in Preventing and Resolving Conflict," in *Turbulent Peace: The Challenge of Managing International Conflict*, ed. C. Crocker, F. O. Hampson, and P. Aall (Washington, DC: USIP Press, 2001). For its application to other international organizations, see: The Director-General's Programme of Work and Budget 2006–07, Supplement to (Reform proposals) C 2005/3/Sup.1 August 2005 (Rome: Food and Agriculture Organization of the United Nations, 2005), www.fao.org/docrep/meeting/009/j5800e/j5800e_sup1/j5800e03_sup1.htm.

[63] Slaughter, *A New World Order*, 29.

[64] James P. Sewell and Mark B. Salter, "Panarchy and Other Norms for Global Governance: Boutros-Ghali, Rosenau and Beyond," *Global Governance* 1, no. 2 (1995), 156–169; Knight, "Towards a Subsidiarity Model for Peacekeeping and Preventive Diplomacy."

[65] The distinction between these meanings of subsidiarity can be found in Steering Committee on Local and Regional Authorities in Europe, "Definition and Limits of the Principle of Subsidiarity," 10–11.

cannot be performed effectively at a more immediate or local level."[66] A conflict between local/national and supranational norms/legislation should be resolved in favor of the former if the lower authority is able to address the issue on its own. The supportive/subordinating meaning of subsidiarity is consistent with the dictionary meaning of the term subsidiary: "serving to assist."[67] This notion of subsidiarity presumes a more cooperative relationship between the central and local authorities, which "encourages and authorises [local] autonomy."[68] This concept of subsidiarity harks back to the early post-war view of regional organizations as "stepping-stones" to global order, or as US Senator Arthur Vandenberg put it at the San Francisco Conference of 1945 that drafted the UN Charter, "regional king-links into the global chain" of order-building principles and institutions.[69]

The concept of subsidiarity is relevant to the relationship between universal and regional actors. As a coalition on UN reform argues, "subsidiarity is a concept that can be applied globally. Regional organizations embody regional norms. As such, they can play a role in interpreting and coordinating implementation of global conventions, which, by political necessity, must be abstractly defined."[70] In this sense, *subsidiary norms* could be region-specific interpretations and extensions or reconstructions of "meta norms," such as non-intervention or equality of states, or new principles that preserve or extend meta norms or limit exceptions to them in the regional context.

Why do local or regional actors engage in norm subsidiarity? Three major motivations may be identified. The first is when local actors are excluded from or marginalized in global norm-making and institution-building. Subsidiarity could be a response to the potential "tyranny" of higher-level institutions and greater powers. During the

---

[66] John Barnes et al., *Federal Britain: No Longer Unthinkable?* (London: Centre for Policy Studies, 1998), 34; Explanatory Memorandum on the EU Constitutional Treaty (01/12/04), "Treaty establishing a Constitution for Europe including the Protocols and Annexes, and Final Act with Declarations," Command Paper Number: Cm 6429, Presented to Parliament: December 2004 (London: Foreign and Commonwealth Office, 2004).

[67] *Concise Oxford Dictionary* (Oxford University Press, 1976), 1150.

[68] Steering Committee on Local and Regional Authorities in Europe, "Definition and Limits of the Principle of Subsidiarity," 11.

[69] Senator Arthur Vandenberg, *Documents of the United Nations Conference on International Organization, San Francisco, 1945*, vol. VI (London and New York: United Nations Information Organizations, 1945), 5.

[70] *A Fork in the Road: Conversations on the Work of the High Level Panel on Threats, Challenges and Change*, Report of the March 12–13 and 26–27 ambassadorial discussion meetings convened by the Permanent Missions to the United Nations of Australia, Mexico, the Netherlands, Singapore and South Africa, through the International Peace Academy, 10.

drafting of the UN Charter, representatives of regional organizations argued that investing the sole authority for handling global peace and security issues in the UN Security Council would result in the loss of autonomy of regional bodies.[71] Newly independent states looked to regional action as a "regional solution to regional problems" because their UN membership was yet to be assured. Norm subsidiarity was thus a means for regional autonomy, a condition in which intra-regional "actions and responses predominate over external influences,"[72] and which allows regional groups to "keep outsiders from defining the issues that constitute the local agenda."[73] Regional norm-setting is justified on the ground that regional bodies may have better information about local problems and hence may be better able to devise solutions than global bodies.[74]

Second, regional actors may resort to norm subsidiarity if they see violation of their cherished meta norms by powerful actors and if global institutions embodying these norms seem incapable of preventing such violations. These subsidiary norms may limit the scope for great power caprice or unilateralism at least in the regional context. The global superpower competition and intervention during the Cold War, and the consequent paralysis of the UN in preserving the norm of non-intervention, created the imperative for subsidiary norms against intervention in different regions and globally through the Non-Aligned Movement. Later, Europeans responded to American unilateralism during the presidency of George W. Bush not by balancing against US power (as would be predicted by realists) but by seeking to bind the United States to the norms, institutional structures, and processes of multilateralism.[75]

A third trigger for norm subsidiarity is the regional actors' desire to fit the more "abstractly defined" meta norms to local ideas, identities, and practices. This could mean applying global rules to the local context, especially rules which are most relevant to local/regional conditions. This motivation

---

[71] Etzioni, *The Majority of One*; Inis Claude, *Swords into Ploughshares* (New York: Random House, 1964), chapter 6.

[72] I. William Zartman, "Africa as a Subordinate State System in International Relations," in *Regional Politics and World Order*, ed. Richard A. Falk and Saul H. Mendlovitz (San Francisco: W. H. Freeman, 1973), 386.

[73] Thomas P. Thornton, *The Challenge to US Policy in the Third World* (Boulder, CO: Westview Press, 1986), 25.

[74] Nye, *Peace in Parts*.

[75] Thomas Risse, "Beyond Iraq: Challenges to the Transatlantic Community," Paper presented at the American Institute for Contemporary German Studies, January 24, 2003; Steven Everts, "A Question of Norms: Transatlantic Divergences in Foreign Policy," *The International Spectator* 36, no. 2 (April–June 2001), www.iai.it/pdf/articles/everts_2.pdf.

is best understood within the framework of "norm localization," which identifies such triggers of idea borrowing as the desire for legitimation, a sense of uniqueness of the local actors' values and identities, and a general cultural trait to localize.[76] Regional actors may reject some aspects of the global norms and retain others, or modify some aspects to suit local context and need, in accordance with preexisting beliefs and practices.

How do subsidiary norms make their impact? Drawing upon the literature on institutions, I argue that they constitute an ideational structure that can shape the legitimacy of hegemonic institutions, or institutions created by hegemonic actors with a view to offer public goods, including protection, to weaker states. Hence, Keohane has drawn attention to the importance of analyzing the "legitimacy of hegemonic regimes."[77] Chayes and Chayes maintain that international institutions derive their legitimacy from "the degree of international consensus" and "participation."[78] And Ikenberry and Kupchan point out that in a hegemonic configuration, the legitimacy of power instruments depends on the "common acceptance of a consensual normative order that binds ruler and ruled."[79] Since a hegemon is expected to possess the required resources to offer sufficient material incentives (including security protection and economic aid) to lure weak states into its ambit, its failure to attract the desired level of weak state representation in a hegemonic system would indicate non-material variables at work, including normative forces. Constructivists have pointed to the effects of norms in legitimation and delegitimation of specific types of behavior, including power politics.[80] Subsidiary norms developed by regional actors could thus determine whether a "consensual normative order" binding the ruler and the ruled within hegemonic systems would be possible.

A good indicator of normative consensus in hegemonic or great power-led institutions would be the willing participation of the "ruled" or the less powerful actors. When a great power fails to obtain such participation, despite its expressed wishes, the outcome is a legitimacy deficit capable of crippling its alliance framework. Hence, the legitimacy of institutions created and maintained by powerful actors can be affected by subsidiary norms developed at the local level.

[76] Acharya, "How Ideas Spread."
[77] Keohane, *After Hegemony*, 39.
[78] Abram Chayes and Antonia Chayes, *The New Sovereignty: Compliance with International Regulatory Agreements* (Cambridge, MA: Harvard University Press, 1995), 41, 128.
[79] Ikenberry and Kupchan, "Socialization and Hegemonic Power," 289; more fully developed in Ikenberry, *After Victory*.
[80] Finnemore and Sikkink, "International Norms and Political Change."

Comparing Subsidiarity with Localization

The concept of subsidiarity shares with "localization" the assumption that local actors are not passive recipients of outside ideas or norms, but active borrowers and interpreters.[81] But there are key differences. First, the localization process assumes the prior existence of a regional normative framework, which norm entrepreneurs use to construct a fit with new outside norms. Subsidiarity is basically about the creation of new norms, with or without basing them on a prior normative framework. In this sense, localization is only one of the motive forces for norm subsidiarity; the latter subsumes the former. Second, localization involves the redefinition of global norms in the local context only, whereas subsidiarity may have an effect at the systemic level, helping to strengthen the meta norm or maybe even diffusing to other regions. Finally, while the dependent variable of norm localization was institutional change, norm subsidiarity may occur even in the absence of formal institutions and institutional change.

Although both concepts stress the primacy of local agency, there are differences between them:

1. Localization is *inward-looking*. It involves making foreign ideas and norms consistent with a local cognitive prior.[82] Subsidiarity is outward-looking. Its main focus is on relations between local actors and external powers, in terms of the former's fear of domination by the latter.[83]
2. In localization, local actors are always norm-takers. In contrast, in subsidiarity, local actors can be norm-rejecters and/or norm-makers.
3. In localization, foreign norms are *imported* for *local usage only*.[84] In subsidiarity, local actors may *export* or "*universalize*" locally constructed norms. (Compare Figures 2.1 and 2.2.) This may involve using locally constructed norms to support or amplify existing global norms against the parochial ideas of powerful actors.
4. In localization, local agents redefine foreign norms which they take as generally good and desirable, but not fully consistent with their

---

[81] Acharya, "How Ideas Spread."
[82] Wolters, *History, Culture and Region in Southeast Asian Perspectives*; Acharya, *Whose Ideas Matter?*, 21. Here, cognitive prior is defined as an "existing set of ideas, belief systems, and norms, which determine and condition an individual or social group's receptivity to new norms." For the notion of cognitive prior in Europe, see Jeffrey Checkel, "*Going Native" in Europe? Theorizing Social Interaction in European Institutions*, ARENA Working Papers, WP 01/23 (Copenhagen, Denmark: Advanced Research on the Europeanization of the Nation-State, University of Oslo, 2003).
[83] Hiro Katsumata suggested this distinction.
[84] Acharya "How Ideas Spread," 252. "[L]ocalization reshapes both existing beliefs and practices and foreign ideas *in their local context*" (emphasis added).

Independent variable   Transnational (global) norms

Intervening variable   Local agents (cognitive priors)

Dependent variable

          Resistance/Rejection   Localization   Norm Displacement

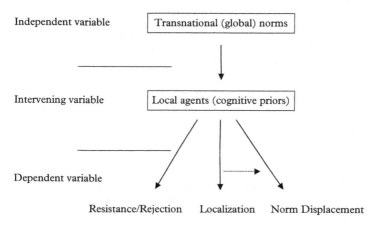

Figure 2.1 Localization
Source: Acharya, "How Ideas Spread."

Dependent variable   Challenging/resisting of   Supportive/strengthening
                       powerful actors/ideas   of transnational
                                                                norms

Intervening variable   Subsidiary norms

Independent variable   Local agents (cognitive priors)

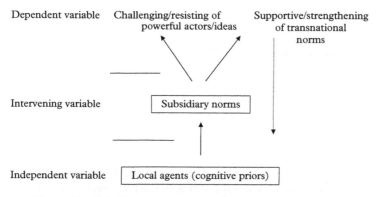

Figure 2.2 Subsidiarity
Note: The lower and middle layers do not necessarily comprise a single or coherent set of norms, but rather distinctive, similar, overlapping, and mutually reinforcing subsidiary norms developed by different regions. Subsidiary norms may be seen as mediating/intervening between global and local norms.

existing cognitive prior. In subsidiarity, local agents reject outside ideas (of powerful central actors, but not universal principles) which they do not view as worthy of selection, borrowing, or adoption in any form.

5. Hence, localization is generic to all actors, big or small, powerful or weak. Subsidiarity is specific to peripheral (smaller and/or weaker) actors, because by definition it's their autonomy which is more likely

to be challenged. "Norm localisation, or the process of adapting global norms to local ideas, identities, and practices ... occurs any time a global norm intersects with local/regional ideas/identities/practices; it happens in almost all instances where global norms need to be justified to domestic audiences."[85] It requires neither a sense of exclusion or a perception of big power hypocrisy, nor a perception of dominance, neglect, violation, or abuse. The latter are the triggers of norm subsidiarity, and they are more likely to be found among smaller, weaker, and peripheral actors.

Subsidiarity and localization can be complementary, much like two sides of the same coin, and run in tandem. Their motivators may occasionally overlap. There is no reason why actors cannot engage in both types of normative behavior. In fact, the creation of a single norm may involve both processes, whereby a global norm is redefined while a local norm is infused into a global common. Third World countries often do both. Together, they offer a comprehensive framework for understanding and explaining norm dynamics and diffusion in world politics. Hence, both processes have been at work in the Third World. The Asian response to the Cold War superpower rivalry involved the localization of universal norms of sovereignty while at the same time creating new norms concerning great power dominance and military alliances for export and universalization. Taken together, localization and subsidiarity help to capture the role of non-Western actors in constructing global order, especially security and sovereignty, at both global and regional levels.

This book's empirical chapters can be summarized in terms of the agent's objective of:

- interpreting global norms of sovereignty, such as non-intervention, and their adaptation and application to the local and regional contexts (Chapters 2 and 6);
- resisting and countering great power dominance in ideas and institutions of sovereignty and security (Chapters 2, 3, 5, and 6);
- constructing local rules of sovereignty to support and strengthen global rules and institutions, especially when these rules are being challenged or undermined by their original formulators to serve their own changing interests (Chapters 2, 4, 5, and 6);

---

[85] Acharya, "Norm Subsidiarity and Regional Orders," 98–99. I am grateful to an anonymous reviewer for *International Studies Quarterly*, where this section first appeared, for suggesting this distinction between localization and subsidiarity.

- conceptualizing and operationalizing new pathways to security, which reflect the distinctive predicament and concerns of the victims of insecurity (Chapter 5); and
- creating and maintaining regional institutions and orders that serve the set goals of sovereignty and security and offer a framework of conflict reduction and management in different regions. This has led to the qualified emulation of the EU model of regional institutionalization (Chapter 6).

Norm Circulation

What happens if a norm already accepted by all parties develops weaknesses or shortcomings at the level of compliance? Agency does not end after a norm is initially accepted. It also extends to monitoring, evaluation, modification, and reconstruction. This may involve sending non-performing norms back to the drawing board. If actors, after having signed on to a given norm, recognize its limitations or failures, they can revise it or add new injunctions based on the feedback they receive on the norm's application. I call this "norm circulation."[86] I do not consider circulation as a wholly distinct process by itself, but as an extension of localization and subsidiarity, because it involves monitoring compliance with norms that have been created through localization and subsidiarity.

Circulation attests to norm creation and diffusion as a two-way process. Here, global norms offered by transnational moral actors are contested and localized to fit the cognitive priors of local actors (localization), while this local feedback is repatriated back to the wider global context. This feedback, along with other locally constructed norms (created through subsidiarity), works to modify, defend, and strengthen the global norm in question. Norm circulation follows the logic of localization and subsidiarity but extends it to cover compliance and feedback. It can be presented with the help of Figures 2.3 and 2.4.

Most global norms go through a period of contestation, leading to their localization. This might create a feedback/repatriation effect which

---

[86] Arjun Appadurai's anthropological perspective helps to illuminate circulation as three related processes: how local communities are "inflected" by global ideas; how global ideas are indigenized and the resulting local forms are subsequently "repatriated" back to the outside world; and how local forms (such as Hinduism) are globalized. The framework is applicable to a very broad range of issues, ranging from cultural ideas to ethnic violence, militarization, and conflict. Note the similarities between this and the concept of localization in Southeast Asian historiographical literature. Arjun Appadurai, *Modernity at Large: Cultural Dimensions of Globalization* (Minneapolis: University of Minnesota Press, 1996).

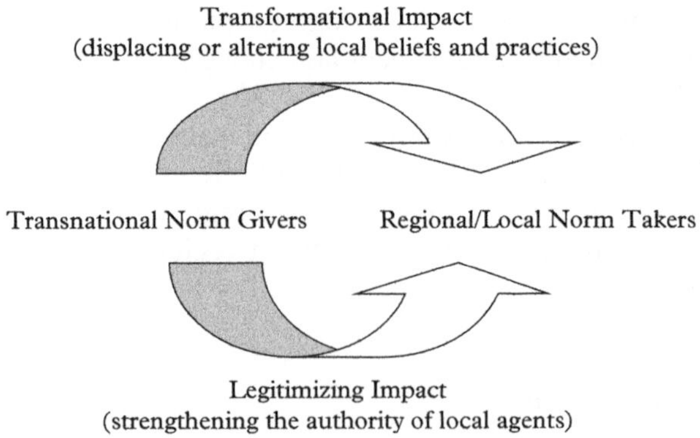

Transformational Impact
(displacing or altering local beliefs and practices)

Transnational Norm Givers   Regional/Local Norm Takers

Legitimizing Impact
(strengthening the authority of local agents)

Figure 2.3   Norm internalization and localization

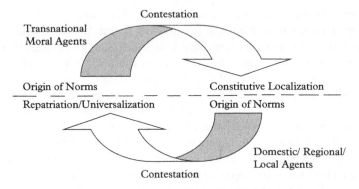

Figure 2.4   Norm circulation

might travel back to the point of origin of the norm in the transnational space and lead to its modification or qualification. At the same time, locally constructed norms in similar issue areas (including those in the West or non-West) might be exported to the transnational space and acquire a global resonance, thereby modifying the definition or promotion of the more globally prominent norm/s in similar issue areas. This multiple-agency, two-way, multi-step process of norm diffusion, based on resistance, feedback, and repatriation, is the essence of the idea of norm circulation. Such circulation does not imply the weakening of the norm in question. Instead, it can lead to its strengthening and enhance the prospects for its application and compliance.

The idea of norm circulation clarifies and extends the earlier concepts of localization and subsidiarity. First, norms come from a variety of sources, involving multiple actors, issues, and contexts. Second, in identifying the origins of norms and ideas, one should look not only at where individuals or groups championing them are trained or located, but also at the context to which they speak and from which they derive their inspiration. Some ideas and norms being propagated from New York or London by an individual trained and working there may be inspired by or directed at the situation in his/her village, country, or region. The discussion of R2P in Chapter 4 illustrates original contexts and feedback aspects of norm circulation.

Critique, Clarifications, and Extensions

The ideas of norm localization and subsidiarity have generated debate, and there remain some areas where the earlier literature, including my own work, needs clarification, extension, and revision. Let me discuss these briefly.

The Primacy of the Local?

The first concerns the primacy of the local which is central to the localization, subsidiarity, and circulation processes (the L-S-C framework). But the local as an autonomous sphere is not absolute. The main contribution of concepts is to show the interaction and mutual constitution between the local and the global (and *grundnorms*[87]), rather than treat them as autonomous spheres. Grundnorms apply at the global level, while local norms are mainly influential in a limited context. Local norms are not always new. Localization involves reinterpretation of existing norms. Subsidiarity creates new norms but with reference to some preexisting universal idea or principle. But during these processes, some preexisting global norms or reference points are modified, sometimes quite significantly, to fit a local context and to serve the needs of local actors. This can lead to new norms that either are applicable only in the local context or can travel outside, but without necessarily being adopted at the entire global level. My chapters on sovereignty and security provide examples of how localization and subsidiarity can lead to new norms. Chapter 3 discusses how the norm against superpower alliances is new; such a norm did not exist in Europe even if the idea of sovereignty

---

[87] *Grundnorms* have universal or global applicability, while local norms are specific to a region or a subset of the international system. For example, non-intervention is a *grundnorm* whereas non-participation in alliances, which was an extension of the non-intervention norm, was a local norm specific to parts of Asia.

and non-intervention did. Chapter 4 shows that the norm of R2P had a "distinctively" African origin, but it became enmeshed in other discourses and efforts to develop humanitarian intervention.

Some scholars prefer the term "vernacularization" to describe the transmission of ideas and norms from one context to another.[88] According to Goldstein, vernacularization is "a process of reception and transformation, a dialectic in which transnational conceptions are made meaningful within, or rejected on the basis of, local realities – themselves always already conditioned by their broader inclusion within transnational frameworks of economics, politics, and culture."[89] I consider vernacularization to be similar to constitutive localization.

Another concept is norm "translation."[90] Although variously conceptualized, norm translation entails "the multitude of changes a norm undergoes by moving from one normative context to another, be it from one state to another, from one international organization to another, from a specific international forum to a specific state, from a state back to the international level etc."[91] This might mean translation is a broader concept, able to explain both vertical and horizontal transmission of ideas and norms. But the L-S-C framework can also explain both vertical and horizontal transmission and do so more specifically. Here, "local" implies, first and foremost, norm recipients and "insider proponents"

---

[88] Sally Engle Merry, "Transnational Human Rights and Local Activism: Mapping the Middle," *American Anthropologist* 108, no. 1 (2006), 38–51. See also Sheldon Pollock, "The Sanskrit Cosmopolis, 300–1300: Transculturation, Vernacularization, and the Question of Ideology," in *Ideology and Status of Sanskrit*, ed. Jan E. M Houben (Leiden: E. J. Brill, 1996), 197–249; Siddharth Mallavarapu, "Development of International Relations Theory in India: Traditions, Contemporary Perspectives and Trajectories," *International Studies* 46, nos. 1–2 (2009), 165–183.

[89] Daniel M. Goldstein, *Outlawed: Between Security and Rights in a Bolivian City* (Durham, NC: Duke University Press, 2012), 210.

[90] Aaron P. Boesenecker and Leslie Vinjamuri, "Lost in Translation? Civil Society, Faith-Based Organizations and the Negotiation of International Norms," *International Journal of Transitional Justice* 5, no. 3 (2011), 345–365; Benjamin Brake and Peter J. Katzenstein, "Lost in Translation? Non-State Actors and the Transnational Movement of Procedural Law," *International Organization* 67, no. 4 (October 2013), 725–757; Susanne Zwingel, *Translating International Women's Rights: The CEDAW Convention in Context* (London: Palgrave, 2016); Lisbeth Zimmermann, "Same Same or Different? Norm Diffusion between Resistance, Compliance, and Localization in Post-conflict States," *International Studies Perspectives* 17, no. 1 (2016), 98–115.

[91] Email from Lisbeth Zimmermann to Amitav Acharya, October 11, 2016. I am grateful to Lisbeth for clarifying the differences between "localization" and "translation." As she notes in this correspondence, "'translation theory' as a coherent branch of theory in IR does not really exist and researchers differ on which agents they focus on in translation processes, though ... most focus on "meso-level" NGO or civil society actors who do the 'translation.'" In her view, the localization framework "broadens" the scope of translation by including "elite translators."

rather than a geographically "local" level of actors. This means local-ization and subsidiarity can explain not only a vertical (global–local) transfer of norms, but also horizontal diffusion from one local context (i.e. region) to another, and between groups of actors concerned with different issue areas, since in all such cases there would be both outsider and insider proponents as agents. I admit that this aspect of horizontal transmission was understated in my initial work on localization. But this dynamic of horizontal diffusion was evident in the diffusion of sovereignty norms constructed in Asia (the 1955 Asia–Africa conference in Bandung, as discussed in Chapter 3) to Africa (which was weakly repre-sented at Bandung), and to the Third World in general. It also captures the essence of the European Union's "interregionalism" approach (to be discussed in Chapter 6), which involves diffusing the norms and institu-tions of the EU to other regions.

Perhaps the main difference between "translation" and my approach lies in the latter being far more concerned about the relative agency of norm-takers and norm-givers. Any theory of norm diffusion must specify the identity of the agent, i.e. who is doing the vernacularization/transla-tion and on whose terms and under what conditions. I believe the L-S-C framework does this better. By specifying scope conditions of success or failure in norm diffusion, and explaining the result of localization as leading to the empowerment of the local actors and universalization of their identities, localization and subsidiarity models offer a clearer and more specific model of norm diffusion.

Norms and Practice

Unlike some constructivists, I do not make a sharp distinction between norms and practice. It is difficult to separate the two. I accept Wallace's perspective, as outlined in his book *Norms and Practices*, that norms are not practice-independent, and that "norms, including ethical norms, are fundamentally constituents of actual practices."[92] The case studies in this book differ in terms of their relative emphasis on norms and practices. But at the same time, each of them focuses on a norm (sovereignty and non-intervention in Chapter 3, humanitarian intervention and R2P in Chapter 4, human security in Chapter 5, and regionalism in Chapter 6) and discusses their enmeshment in practice.

This is a book more about norms than about practice. The main dif-ference between a norm and a practice may be that a practice is more

[92] James M. Wallace, *Norms and Practices* (Ithaca: Cornell University Press, 2008), 9, 55.

habitual, more settled, while a norm remains less so and is continually contested. As discussed in Chapter 1, Wiener's work on "contested compliance" shows that norms are disputed even after being accepted. My book also adopts a contestation perspective. Localization, subsidiarity, and circulation are essentially examples of contestations, reinterpretations, and reconstructions.

It is useful to make a distinction between "norms-as-ideal" and "norms-as-normal" and between norms and practice. Many norms originate as principled ideas with a strong aspirational element. But once accepted and institutionalized in practice, norms can specify what is considered to be normal practical behavior, although this takes time and involves contestations and complications. Once norms are accepted and internalized for some time, they became habit-forming, and thus turn into practices and eventually customs or conventions. This may reflect different evolutionary stages of progress of a norm. But this is not a linear process, and in some cases, they remain continually contested.

One way to recognize norms is to view them as "only those sets of clearly articulated principles and practices addressing a given set of issues."[93] This informs this book's selection of norms; while total clarity over the meaning and behavioral implication of norms is unattainable, the norms discussed in this book, such as non-intervention, R2P, human security, and regionalism, are reasonably clearly articulated to address a specific set of issues.

Subsidiarity or "Protagonism"?

Concerning the role of weaker actors in norm subsidiarity, Sikkink observes that while my works on subsidiarity are "important and persuasive," she would "prefer a simpler notion of 'norm protagonism'" instead of norm subsidiarity. As she put it, "Unlike subsidiarity, which refers specifically to norm promotion by weaker actors, norm protagonism can take place from any location in the global system."[94] In reality, Sikkink and I did not disagree that much. I originally conceptualized subsidiarity to specifically convey the normative agency of weaker actors. But I also specifically defined weaker actors to include those from the Third World or Global South. I resisted extending subsidiarity to weaker actors in the developed world on several grounds. First, the Third World countries have distinctive normative concerns which are not necessarily

---

[93] I owe this language and the preceding distinction between "norms-as-ideal" and "norms-as-normal" to an anonymous reviewer of this book manuscript.

[94] Kathryn Sikkink, "Human Rights," in *Why Govern?*, ed. Acharya, 123.

shared by the weaker countries of the Global North. The weak countries of Europe are not weak in terms of internal socio-political cohesion and regime legitimacy, but only in terms of independent material and military power.[95] Third World countries, on the other hand, tend to be weak both as states and as powers, especially the former (there are strong military powers in the Third World, like India). Moreover, although Western weak countries have reasons to be worried about great power hypocrisy, they are generally satisfied with the system status quo. As noted, Third World countries are more rebellious and feel more marginalized from global rule-making because they entered an international system that was European-created and dominated. While Western weak countries or middle powers may develop norms of their own, these norms are not motivated by an acute sense of marginalization or a security predicament where internal security concerns trump external ones. Because of these differences the normative behavior of weak actors in the South tends to be different from that of the weak states of the West.

But unlike Sikkink, whose idea of norm protagonism is not tied specifically to weaker states, and who states that it "can take place from any location in the global system," I associate subsidiarity with the agency of materially weaker actors. I still think it is useful to distinguish norm-making by weaker actors from that by great powers. A great deal more has been written about the normative behavior of powerful actors compared with that of the weak. The motivations and processes of the two are not identical. But as I hinted in my original work on the idea, the concept of subsidiarity is applicable to the normative behavior of all materially weaker actors, including those in the West (such as the Scandinavian countries), and not just the Third World. Norm subsidiarity is a response to the "tyranny" of higher-level institutions (including multilateral organizations or great power management[96]) in global rule-making.

It is noteworthy that the examples of norm protagonism cited by Sikkink are mainly from the Global South, a category that conjures up essentially weak actors in the global system. Thus, she cites Argentina's role as a "global human rights protagonist" in the area of transitional justice,[97] Jorge

[95] On the difference between weak states and weak powers, see: Mohammed Ayoob, *The Third World Security Predicament: State Making, Regional Conflict, and the International System* (Boulder, CO: Lynne Rienner, 1995); Barry Buzan, *People, States and Fear: An Agenda for International Security Studies in the Post-Cold War Era* (New York: Harvester Wheatsheaf, 1991); Joel Migdal, *Strong Societies and Weak States: State–Society Relations and State Capabilities in the Third World* (Princeton University Press, 1988).
[96] On great power management as an institution of international order, see: Hedley Bull, *The Anarchical Society*, 2nd edition (Basingstoke: Macmillan, 1975), chapter 9.
[97] Kathryn Sikkink, "From Pariah State to Global Protagonist: Argentina and the Struggle for International Human Rights," *Latin American Politics and Society* 50, no. 1 (2008),

Dominguez's work on the role of Latin American regional organizations as "international rule innovators" rather than simply "price takers,"[98] and Sally Engle Merry's work[99] on the role of civil society actors in the Global South as human rights intermediaries and vernacularizers of global human rights. But I do agree that the normative behavior implied in the concept of subsidiarity can be applied to relatively weaker actors in both the North and the South. Recent cases of norm creation show commonalities between the Global South countries and middle powers from the North, such as Canada, Japan, and the Scandinavian countries. This was evident in the crafting of R2P, as well as the idea of human security. These examples suggest that the middle powers of the North can be motivated by similar concerns about justice and fairness and redressing gaps in global rule-making that the Southern countries have. It is also evident in the development of the ideas and norms of regionalism, with the EU's interregional initiatives and the ASEAN Plus institutions such as the ASEAN Regional Forum (ARF) and the East Asia Summit (EAS).

Creating or Modifying Norms?

Another issue that merits clarification has to do with the question, do localization and subsidiarity involve the creation of new norms? This is an important aspect of the agency of weaker actors, especially from the Global South, in world politics. Are they norm creators or localizers? Can they create norms that have global resonance, as opposed to being mainly locally relevant? These questions deserve more clarification than has been provided in my own previous writings and those of others who have used these concepts.

I argue that both localization and subsidiarity do involve *norm creation*, although they specify the agency of local actors. To the extent perceptions matter, the variations and changes to an original norm produced by localization may seem distinctive enough to the localizers and presented as a new norm by them, even if it retains some similarities with the original outside norm. It is also *new* in the local context, which is what really matters in localization. In subsidiarity, it is worth noting that its definition, as noted earlier, begins with the words "a process whereby

---

1–29; Kathryn Sikkink, *The Justice Cascade: How Human Rights Prosecutions are Changing World Politics* (London: W. W. Norton and Company, 2011).

[98] Jorge I. Domínguez, "International Cooperation in Latin America: The Design of Regional Institutions by Slow Accretion," in *Crafting Cooperation: Regional International Institutions in Comparative Perspective*, ed. Amitav Acharya and Alastair I. Johnston (Cambridge University Press, 2008).

[99] Merry, "Transnational Human Rights and Local Activism."

local actors create rules." To be sure, the very term subsidiarity conveys the sense that these new rules are constructed with an outside point of reference, or some broader, universal idea/norm, which is supported and given added legitimacy against hypocrisy or violation by powerful actors. Such examples include the Calvo and Drago Doctrines, which were developed to defend the norm of non-intervention, which had already been developed in Europe, against the US Monroe Doctrine, and the idea of non-alignment introduced against superpower interventionism during the Cold War by India, Indonesia, Egypt, and Yugoslavia (the last not usually recognized as a member of the Third World or the Global South, which relates to my earlier point about extending subsidiarity to weaker actors outside the Global South).

In other words, just as in localization external or global norms are localized on the basis of a local cognitive prior, in subsidiarity local norms are conceived and externalized with reference to a global prior. While I did not take it as an absolute precondition, having a universal point of reference in norm subsidiarity is important for several reasons. First, norms are rarely wholly new or constructed out of nowhere. They are often developed with reference to some preexisting global cognitive prior. Latin American actors (used by Sikkink to illustrate her idea of norm protagonism) of course did not invent the idea of human rights, but they provided a regional anchor for a preexisting universal idea through their American Declaration. To me this fits well within the subsidiarity concept. As Sikkink puts it, "Southern protagonism arguably increases the global legitimacy of global governance projects including the human rights project."[100] Having a prior norm or idea to be defended against abuse by powerful actors or legitimized and strengthened through local support is central to the idea of subsidiarity.

But this leaves the question, can weaker actors, including those in the Global South, develop ideas and norms without a prior external or universal referent? This in my view is entirely possible. Actors create new norms in areas that have not simply been covered by existing norms. Such norms can be created for purely local usage and/or for export and wider application. I would still consider them as examples of norm subsidiarity. Some of this involves principled ideas, before they acquire broader support to become a norm. The proposal by India's first Prime Minister, Jawaharlal Nehru, for a universal moratorium on nuclear testing in 1954 is widely viewed as the germination of the norm against nuclear tests as enshrined in the Comprehensive Test Ban Treaty (CTBT). There are

---

[100] Sikkink, "Human Rights," 136.

likely to be more examples of such norm conception at local or regional levels. As an example, I would cite the principles of the ASEAN Way, especially the combination of informality, consensus, preference for non-legalistic and non-binding commitments and cooperation, and the practice of *Musyawarah* and *Mufakat* (which roughly translate as consultations and consensus). While not many norm conceivers have the capacity or will to promote a norm, whether locally or globally, their role should not be dismissed. To be sure, norm conception, of purely original norms, without reference to preexisting ideas, is rare. Just as localization requires a local cognitive prior, norm subsidiarity often requires a global cognitive prior or point of reference. Even the most original idea or norm can be linked to some preexisting universal values and standards. This attests to the analytical utility of the notion of subsidiarity. But it still leaves considerable room for creativity and innovation in developing specific ideas and norms to realize and support universal values and objectives, such as the ideas of human development, human security, and responsible sovereignty which are discussed in this book.

Outsiders and Insiders

Next, the role of outsiders in localization deserves more attention and clarification. Some argue that localization focuses too much on the agency of local actors and not enough on outsiders in producing the same result: an adjusted norm that fits the interests and identities of local actors. Hence, there have been calls for recognizing the role of external actors in localization. Some recent work on localization has argued that not just local, but also external actors can be important players in localization.[101] In other words, transnational norm entrepreneurs could themselves play an important role in localizing a given norm by taking into account the preexisting ideas and context of the regional actors and thus being able to mold the norm to fit the local circumstances. This raises the question, however, of the relative importance of local and outside actors and cognitive priors, as well as of on whose terms localization happens.

---

[101] Lisbeth Zimmermann, *Global Norms with a Local Face: Rule-of-Law Promotion and Norm-Translation* (Cambridge University Press, 2017); David Capie, "The Responsibility to Protect Norm in Southeast Asia: Framing, Resistance and the Localization Myth," *The Pacific Review* 25, no. 1 (2012), 75–93. Another important contribution is Tholens' "two-step localization" in which both international practitioners and domestic elites are involved in building congruence between external and local ideas and approaches. Simone Tholens, "Winning the Post-War: Norm Localisation and Small Arms Control in Kosovo and Cambodia," *Journal of International Relations and Development*, June 13, 2017, DOI: 10.1057/s41268-017-0098-9.

For myself, even when outside actors can engage in localization, the role of local actors matters more.

In another important contribution, Andrew Phillips examines how Westphalian sovereignty diffused in the Indian Ocean region. He challenges the notion that it was primarily due to its imposition through superior Western material power. Examining the historical interactions in the Indian Ocean between the Western colonizers and the indigenous societies, he finds that the Western powers had to negotiate and adjust to local realities to establish their colonial presence. Western imperial expansion required and was dependent upon constant negotiations and alliances with indigenous rulers, through a process he calls customization, by which outsiders adapt to local normative resources to support and strengthen themselves.[102] This act by outsiders in localizing European norms of sovereignty to fit the local context not only challenges traditional accounts of the spread of sovereignty, but also introduces a novel concept that has analytical utility well beyond that region.

The Role of Individuals and Civil Society

The last but not the least point concerns the role of individuals and non-state actors in normative agency. My earlier work on localization and subsidiarity, as some critics rightly point out, was state-centric.[103] I have subsequently tried to expand these concepts to examine the role

---

[102] Andrew Phillips, "Global IR Meets Global History: Sovereignty, Modernity and the International System's Expansion in the Indian Ocean Region," *International Studies Review* 18, no. 1 (March 2016), 62–77.

[103] For a postcolonial critique of the concepts of localization and subsidiarity, see: Charmaine Chua, "Against Localization: Rethinking Compliance and Antagonism in Norm Dynamics," in *Against International Relations Norms: Postcolonial Perspectives*, ed. Charlotte Epstein (New York: Routledge, 2017), 87–105. This entire volume is a welcome engagement by postcolonial scholars in norm scholarship which, despite its challenging tone, further advances my own broadening of agency in norm diffusion. Chua is right that my work, while overlapping with postcolonial theory, does not share all the main convictions and conventions of postcolonialism. But her critique is based on a reading of my initial two articles only, and does not cover my subsequent works, including this book, that speak to localization, norm creation, and idea-shifting roles of non-state actors or individuals such as Mahbub ul Haq on human security, Francis Deng on responsible sovereignty, or Wangari Maathai on sustainable development (see note 108). Another critique is that the concept of subsidiarity focuses on norm creation by nationalist leaders who accepted the sanctity of state sovereignty and were part of a privileged elite. But leaders such as Nehru, Sukarno, and Nkrumah did represent their people during the nationalist struggle and some such as Nehru were democratically elected after independence. But I agree that more research can be done on the role of the people and the local in the Global South in norm creation and diffusion, and indeed this is a challenge for postcolonial norm scholars.

of non-state actors, including civil society organizations and individuals, while not dismissing the role of states.[104]

A global *idea-shift* is taking place that may be as important for the future of global order as the *power-shift*, or the redistribution of material power.[105] This *idea-shift* comes from non-Western thinkers and practitioners, whom I call *idea-shifters*, a term similar to but broader than "norm entrepreneurs," in the sense that the former not only propagate new norms, but also challenge and alter existing ideas (not just principled ideas, but also causal ones) and devise and localize new ones. Ideas and idea-shifters from the postcolonial world have played an important role in developing new approaches to universal sovereignty, security, international development, and regionalism. In this book, I discuss the "responsible sovereignty" idea from Francis Deng and its African context (Chapter 4), and the "human development" and "human security" idea from Mahbub ul Haq and Amartya Sen and the South Asian context behind them (Chapter 5). Although these idea-shifters are often trained in the West, their ideas and innovations are deeply influenced by their place of origin and experience in their home country. Appreciating how much this local origin and context matters allows us to consider these as "ideas-from-below," and to enrich the existing literature on how ideas and norms spread. Chapter 6 highlights the role of Latin American leaders in challenging US-led universalism at the San Francisco Conference on the UN Charter and arguing the case for regionalism.

Just like states or individuals, civil society actors can engage in building norms through localization and subsidiarity. Local NGO communities in the Global South do not simply accept ideas and norms championed by their own governments or transnational civil society groups from rich donor countries from which they receive funding and various forms of material and political support. Local civil society groups do not end up passively accepting new norms, even when they have been accepted by local governments or regional organizations of which they are members, but actively constructing them. They do so if new norms are seen to privilege elite groups, undermine people's interests, or are primarily intended to serve the political and foreign policy objectives of foreign donors (states or NGOs). Another reason for civil society-led norm localization is to change the perception that they are simply the agents

---

[104] See Amitav Acharya, "Transnational Civil Society as Agents of Norm Diffusion," in *Reducing Armed Violence with NGO Governance*, ed. Rodney Bruce Hall (New York: Routledge, 2013), 97–113; Amitav Acharya, "'Idea-shift': How Ideas from the Rest are Reshaping Global Order," *Third World Quarterly* 37, no. 7 (2016), 1156–1170; Amitav Acharya, "R2P and Theory of Norm Diffusion: Towards a Framework of Norm Circulation," *Global Responsibility to Protect* 5, no. 4 (2013), 466–479.

[105] Acharya, "'Idea-shift.'"

of foreign influence. Local civil society actors may see new ideas as being too far removed from the local context and need. Hence they may strengthen and make a new norm more relevant and effective by adding new local dimensions to it. Finally, local civil society actors may contest and modify foreign norms or create parallel norms if they suspect selectivity, double standards, and hypocrisy on the part of the foreign norm entrepreneurs. Chapter 6 discusses the role of civil society in the official regionalisms of Mercosur/UNASUR, ASEAN, and the African Union (AU). I call this process "participatory regionalism,"[106] which comes about with the erosion of traditional sovereignty-mindedness of regional groups, and their adoption of a broader conception of security, such as human security, which in turn opens more space to normative agency by civil society groups.

Conclusion

The pluralization of agency discussed in Chapter 1, and the processes of localization, subsidiarity, and circulation and their extensions discussed in this chapter, substantially expand the nature and scope of normative agency in world politics. Normative agency can come from Western and non-Western states, global and local levels, and social movements. Norm initiation may happen in the transnational space where Western actors dominate or at a local level where the primary voice may be non-Western actors (as articulated through the idea of "norm subsidiarity").

The chapters that follow apply this framework to four case studies. Chapter 3 looks at the diffusion of sovereignty, where the key processes at play are localization and subsidiarity. Chapter 4 examines the emergence of humanitarian intervention and R2P, where the dynamics of norm subsidiarity are amply evident. The challenge to and redefinition of national security and the emergence of the human security idea discussed in Chapter 4 is also an example of subsidiarity. Finally, Chapter 5 examines the evolution of the ideas and norms of regionalism, as involving both subsidiarity and localization – the former in the context of UN-centered universalism that threatened to marginalize less powerful actors such as the Latin American and Arab states, and the latter entailing the issue of localization of the EU as a normative actor in world politics. These cases, though not exhaustive, tell us much about normative agency in world politics and global order.

---

[106] The term "participatory regionalism" was first coined in Amitav Acharya, "Democratisation and the Prospects for Participatory Regionalism in Southeast Asia," *Third World Quarterly* 24, no. 2 (2003), 375–390.

3   Provincializing Westphalia

On April 23, 1955, speaking before a session of the Political Committee of the Asian–African Conference in Bandung, Indonesia, Jawaharlal Nehru, the Prime Minister of India and a co-convener of the conference, launched into a bitter denunciation of regional defense arrangements of the kind being promoted by the USA in Asia and the Middle East. Membership in Cold War defense pacts such as the Southeast Asia Treaty Organization (SEATO) or the Central Treaty Organization (CENTO), argued Nehru, rendered a country a "camp follower" and deprived it of its "freedom and dignity." "It is an intolerable thought to me that the great countries of Asia and Africa should come out of bondage into freedom only to degrade themselves or humiliate themselves in this way."[1] The most eloquent response to the Indian Prime Minister's harsh words came the next day from Carlos Romulo, the lead delegate of the Philippines, which had just become a signatory to the Manila Pact. In a barely disguised dig at Nehru, Romulo urged his fellow leaders to be "realistic and not be starryeyed visionaries dreaming utopian dreams." He reminded Nehru that India was a big power, and the Philippines as a small nation could not follow its path in renouncing war or defense alliances to safeguard its newfound freedom. Defending this move as a necessary step against communist expansionism, he issued a prophetic warning: "May your India, Sir, never be caught by the encircling gloom."[2]

This exchange, other contestations occurring at the Bandung Conference, and the larger empirical and normative context in which they took place, should be of considerable importance to contemporary scholars of sovereignty in international relations. They challenge the view

---

[1] Speech by Jawaharlal Nehru, Proceedings of the Bandung Conference Political Committee, April 23, 1995 (original unpublished document in the author's personal collection).

[2] The text of Romulo's response can be found in Carlos Romulo, *The Meaning of Bandung* (Chapel Hill: University of North Carolina Press, 1956), 91.

that sovereignty has been an "essentially uncontested concept."[3] More importantly, they call for a more complex understanding of how the norms of sovereignty came to be transmitted and institutionalized in the Third World than is found in the available theoretical literature.

According to a generally accepted view, the "history of sovereignty is largely the history of Westphalia's geographic extension."[4] This extension was chiefly a by-product of decolonization; indeed, the latter was "the achievement of sovereignty by dependent states."[5] This view has largely been upheld by a more recent strand of scholarship which questions the earlier literature's emphasis on material forces (such as the physical exhaustion of the West due to two world wars or the militant struggles carried out by Third World national liberation struggles) in the expansion of sovereign statehood through decolonization, and stresses the role of ideas such as self-determination and equality in the normative delegitimation of imperialism and colonial rule and the achievement of sovereignty by dependent states.[6] Moreover, many traditional accounts of the geographical spread of sovereignty agree that having helped secure the liberation of dependent societies from colonial rule, sovereignty naturally formed the unquestioned core basis of the new international society that the newly liberated states sought to promote. The Third World states "took to Westphalian sovereignty like ducklings to water." Their approach to sovereignty after 1945 has been "overwhelmingly to protect rather than to subvert it."[7] The most important concern for Third World countries, argues Jackson, was to enjoy, develop, and defend their

---

[3] R. B. J. Walker, "Sovereignty, Identity, Community: Reflections on the Horizons of Contemporary Political Practice," in *Contending Sovereignties: Redefining Political Community*, ed. R. B. J Walker and Saul H. Mendlovitz (Boulder, CO: Lynne Rienner, 1990), 159.

[4] Daniel Philpott, "Westphalia, Authority and International Society," in *Sovereignty at the Millennium*, ed. Robert Jackson (Oxford: Blackwell, 1999), 160.

[5] Adam Watson, *The Evolution of International Society* (New York: Routledge, 1992), 317.

[6] Robert Jackson, "The Weight of Ideas in Decolonization: Normative Change in International Relations," in *Ideas and Foreign Policy: Beliefs, Institutions, and Political Change*, ed. Judith Goldstein and Robert O. Keohane (Ithaca: Cornell University Press, 1993), 111–138; Daniel Philpott, *Revolutions in Sovereignty: How Ideas Shaped Modern International Relations* (Princeton University Press, 2001). According to Philpott: "For protesting colonists, the ideas were nationalism and equality, which they translated into the demand for political independence, Westphalian statehood, for their colony. It was through their reflection upon these ideas that a small stratum of educated, elite Africans, Asians, and Latin Americans came to desire this statehood ... It was then these converts to revolutionary ideas who exercised the social power of protest ... Aside from their efforts, the [pro-independence] parties would never have formed, the campaigns never would have taken place, and so on" (191).

[7] Christopher Clapham, "Sovereignty and the Third World State," in *Sovereignty at the Millennium*, ed. Robert Jackson (Oxford: Blackwell, 1999), 101.

"juridical" sovereignty, even in the absence of genuine "empirical" sovereignty. Among Western scholars, Jackson's work has been especially influential for its theoretical attention to the sovereignty regime in the Third World. It examines how the transmission of sovereignty to the Third World resulted in "a reversal of classical positive sovereignty in international relations" (based on national power and capacity to act independently and exercised through a balance of power system) and produced a shift towards "negative" sovereignty, defined as "freedom from outside interference."

> Non-intervention and sovereignty ... are basically two sides of the same coin ... Negative sovereignty ... primarily involves decolonization: it is the distinctive liberty acquired by former colonies as a consequence of the international enfranchisement movement ... It is a formal-legal entitlement and therefore something which international society is capable of conferring.[8]

Jackson clarifies that the negative sovereignty regime was based essentially on a doctrine of "categorical self-determination."[9] He thus reiterates the nexus between sovereignty and decolonization; the latter, involving the dismantling of the entire colonial and trusteeship system, was the chief catalyst of the negative sovereignty regime in international relations. Once in place, this negative sovereignty regime became "the sole successor to colonialism," permitting no alternative institutional arrangement for the new states.[10] Hence the main game of the negative sovereignty regime would be played out in the "North–South" domain, which would exist side-by-side with the traditional East–West (the United States and the Soviet Union) positive sovereignty game (based on the traditional balance of power system).

In this chapter, I concur that a major shift in the sovereignty regime occurred after World War II, and that this shift revolved primarily around the non-interference norm. But this process is better described as the diffusion of "universal sovereignty," as Reus-Smit has suggested,[11] rather than the creation of a singular and overarching doctrine of "negative sovereignty." I argue that the diffusion of sovereignty was not an automatic by-product of decolonization. It had to be fought for, constructed, and

---

[8] Robert Jackson, *Quasi-States: Sovereignty, International Relations and the Third World* (Cambridge University Press, 1990), 27.

[9] Ibid., 75.

[10] Ibid., 198.

[11] Christian Reus-Smit, "Building the Liberal International Order: Locating American Agency," Paper prepared for the Annual Meeting of the American Political Science Association, Washington, DC, August 28–31, 2014, 12–13; Reus-Smit, *Individual Rights and the Making of the International System* (Cambridge University Press, 2013).

elaborated. Hence the agency role of the newly independent states was critical to the diffusion of universal sovereignty in global order-building.

To elaborate, non-intervention (which I use interchangeably with 'non-interference'), the defining norm of Jackson's "negative sovereignty" regime, was far more of a contested political concept than an a priori legal–formal condition. Though a Westphalian norm articulated in the eighteenth century and enshrined in the charter of the Latin American regional institutions and the UN,[12] non-interference in the Third World was not simply passively inherited from the "international enfranchisement movement" around the self-determination idea originating in the West.[13] It was actively constructed and defended through discourse and debate in the Third World. By equating non-intervention with self-determination, Jackson gave the impression of "negative" sovereignty having been "an historical and largely completed event."[14] Yet, the construction of the new sovereignty regime was substantially shaped by subsequent Third World strategies for coping with superpower rivalry, including strategies of neutrality or non-alignment advocated by some of its leaders, which were different from the original norm of self-determination that formed the basis of Jackson's idea of negative sovereignty. And these strategies were not "negative" in the sense of being geared to the achievement of decolonization. They were also aimed at empowering Third World countries and giving them a voice and role, especially by articulating certain norms of conduct, in international affairs. Hence, rather than consider them as part of a defensive and negative sovereignty game, I consider them as examples of positive contributions to the construction of the post-war global order.

This chapter also shows that the development of the non-interference norm was as much the product of a South–South contestation as that of a North–South one. The major disagreements and compromises about what constitutes non-interference and how it can be best defended took place within the Third World (this speaks to the issue of context in my pluralization of agency discussed in Chapter 1), rather than between the Third World and the North. Hence, although emphasis on sovereignty and non-intervention was commonplace throughout the postcolonial world, there were important variations in the understandings of

---

[12] On the origins of non-interference, see: Richard J. Vincent, *Nonintervention and International Order* (Princeton University Press, 1974); Stephen D. Krasner, *Sovereignty: Organized Hypocrisy* (Princeton University Press, 1999), especially 20–25.

[13] Jackson, *Quasi-States*.

[14] Thomas J. Biersteker and Cynthia Weber, eds., *State Sovereignty as a Social Construct* (Cambridge University Press, 1996), 10.

sovereignty not only between its original European formulation and the Third World, but also among the different regions of the Third World.[15]

Recent efforts to reconceptualize sovereignty as a "social construct" have made an important advance on the traditional "static" accounts of the sovereignty regime in world politics,[16] but much empirical work remains to be done in establishing how the social constructivist process led to the emergence of the key norms of sovereignty such as non-interference. In this chapter, I demonstrate how the norm of non-interference non-intervention (or non-alignment, which in my view is a close corollary of universal sovereignty) evolved through a series of contestations and compromises at a number of conferences held in Asia between 1947 and 1955. To this end, I trace the discourses about non-interference and regional organization building at these conferences, especially the Asia–Africa Conference at Bandung in 1955. My research reveals that despite the universal appeal of the *idea* of sovereignty, there was considerable disagreement among Third World actors over interpretations of the *norms* of sovereignty, especially non-interference and equality, contestations which produced an enduring legacy in Asian international relations.

These Asian and Afro-Asian conferences have received woefully inadequate attention and acknowledgement in contemporary writings about sovereignty.[17] The major works of sovereignty in the current literature,

---

[15] Although Jackson used the term "Third World" in his book's subtitle, his discussion was Africa-centric. It is arguable whether the concept of "negative sovereignty" focusing on boundary- maintenance and regime survival, salient in Africa, was equally applicable to Asia and other regions of the Third World. Leaders in Asia, especially in India and Indonesia, were more concerned about empowerment, gaining voice and status in international affairs.

[16] My "social constructivist" framework focuses on "the ways the meaning of sovereignty is negotiated out of interactions within intersubjectively identifiable communities." Biersteker and Weber, "The Social Construction of State Sovereignty," in *State Sovereignty as a Social Construct*, 11. See especially the chapter by Inayatullah for a treatment of Third World sovereignty as a social construct, although its view of what is "social" focuses on dependency relationships and ignores the role of normative interaction. Here, the key interactions I focus on are discursive, rather than practical; in my framework, the two are regarded as mutually constitutive and discourse is taken as a form of practice.

[17] There is a considerable literature on the Bandung Conference. The standard academic work is George McTurnan Kahin, *The Asian–African Conference: Bandung, Indonesia, April 1955* (Ithaca: Cornell University Press, 1956). Kahin witnessed the conference, although neither he nor the other authors cited could be allowed into the closed sessions of the all-important Political Committee meetings where all the leaders met. He did obtain a summary record of the conference's Proceedings, which this author has consulted at the Cornell University library. Among other authors present in Bandung in April 1955 are: Richard Wright, *The Color Curtain: A Report of the Bandung Conference* (Cleveland and New York: The World Publishing Company, 1956); Homer A. Jack, *Bandung: An On-the-Spot Description of the Asian–African Conference* (A Towards Freedom Pamphlet, undated); A. Appadorai, *The Bandung Conference* (New Delhi: The Indian Council of

including those tracing the "genealogy" and pathways of sovereignty, have paid almost no attention to these Third World regional debates.[18] In this chapter, I seek to review the discourses about sovereignty and its norms with the help of the original documents of these conferences, including those previously ignored or unavailable, such as their verbatim and summary records and minutes gathered together from archives in the USA, Indonesia, and India.[19] The findings of this chapter point to two areas in which the Asian regional gatherings, especially Bandung, had their major impact. The first was their role in delegitimizing great power military pacts, especially SEATO. The second was their role in shaping the contours of regionalism in Asia (and to some extent Africa through Nkrumah's leadership) for the next several decades, which con-

---

World Affairs, 1955); Guy J. Pauker, *The Bandung Conference* (Cambridge, MA; Center for International Studies, MIT, 1955). Two aspects of this literature are noteworthy: the works have been written either by area studies scholars (such as Kahin, Pauker, and Appadorai) or by journalists (such as Wright and Jansen), and all appeared in the immediate aftermath of the conference, before many sensitive documents of the conference were declassified. A later work by a distinguished journalist is George H. Jansen, *Afro-Asia and Non-Alignment* (London: Faber and Faber, 1966). More recent literature on the Bandung Conference includes J. A. C. Mackie, *Bandung 1955: Non-Alignment and Afro-Asian Solidarity* (Singapore: Editions Didier Millet, 2005); Kweku Ampia, *The Political and Moral Imperatives of the Bandung Conference of 1955: The Reactions of the US, UK and Japan* (London: Global Oriental, 2007); see also See Seng Tan and Amitav Acharya, eds., *Bandung Revisited: The Legacy of the 1955 Asian–African Conference for International Order* (Singapore: NUS Publishing, 2009); Christopher J. Lee, ed., *Making a World after Empire: The Bandung Moment and its Political Afterlives* (Athens, OH: Ohio University Press, 2010); Derek McDougall and Antonia Finnane, eds., *Bandung 1955: Little Histories* (Caulfield, Victoria: Monash University Press, 2010). But except to a limited degree, these do not discuss the larger issue of sovereignty norms.

[18] See for example: Jackson, *Quasi-States*; Biersteker and Weber, *State Sovereignty as a Social Construct*; Krasner, *Sovereignty: Organized Hypocrisy*; Philpott, *Revolutions in Sovereignty*; Jens Bartelson, *A Genealogy of Sovereignty* (Cambridge University Press, 1995); F. H. Hinsley, *Sovereignty*, 2nd edition (Cambridge University Press, 1986); Alan James, *Sovereign Statehood: The Basis of International Society* (London: Allen and Unwin, 1986); Nicholas Onuf, "Sovereignty: Outline of a Conceptual History," *Alternatives* 16, no. 4 (1991), 425–446. Even more recent perspectives on the "end" of sovereignty and challenges to the non-intervention norm do not look at the foundations of the non-interference regime through Asian and Afro-Asian conferences such as Bandung. Gene M. Lyons and Michael Mastanduno, eds., *Beyond Westphalia: State Sovereignty and International Intervention* (Baltimore and London: The Johns Hopkins University Press, 1995).

[19] This chapter is based on the author's collection of previously unavailable verbatim records and minutes of the proceedings of all the relevant conferences, including the ARC, Baguio, Colombo, Bogor, and Bandung Conferences. This has been supplemented by a lengthy personal interview with Abdulghani Roeslan, the Secretary-General of the Bandung Conference, especially to elaborate on and clarify points made in the latter's own writings: *The Bandung Connection: The Asia–Africa Conference in Bandung in 1955* (Jakarta: Gunung Agung (S) Pte/Ltd., 1981); *The Bandung Spirit* (Jakarta: Prapantja, 1964).

tinues today. Both outcomes applied and extended the notion of sovereignty; hence the processes of "localization" and "subsidiarity" are relevant in understanding them.

Constructing Non-interference

Although Asia was not the first region to develop the idea of regionalism (that distinction, as discussed in Chapter 6, belongs to Latin America and specifically to the pan-American ideal), it was in Asia that the first post-World War II gathering of non-Western leaders took place. In his opening address to the Asian–African Conference at Bandung in 1955, Indonesian President Sukarno described it as "the first intercontinental Conference of colored peoples in the history of mankind."[20] Sponsored by five countries, India, Pakistan, Ceylon, Burma, and Indonesia (collectively known as the Conference of South-East Asian Prime Ministers or Colombo Powers), the Bandung Conference took place from 18 to 24 April 1955. It was attended by twenty-nine countries: Afghanistan, Burma, Cambodia, Ceylon, China, Egypt, Ethiopia, Gold Coast, India, Indonesia, Iran, Iraq, Japan, Jordan, Laos, Lebanon, Liberia, Libya, Nepal, Pakistan, the Philippines, Saudi Arabia, Syria, Sudan, Thailand, Turkey, Democratic Republic of Vietnam, State of Vietnam, and the Kingdom of Yemen. Pre-independence Cyprus also participated and the African National Congress was an observer.

There had been gatherings against racialism before, notably the Ligue contre l'impérialisme et l'oppression coloniale (League against Imperialism and Colonial Oppression) held in Brussels in 1927, and the two Asian Relations Conferences (ARCs) in New Delhi in 1947 and 1949 (the latter was also called the Conference on Indonesia). However, as Sukarno himself argued, the Brussels meeting, attended by the likes of India's Jawaharlal Nehru, took place "thousands of miles away, amidst foreign people, in a foreign country, in a foreign continent. It was not assembled there by choice, but by necessity. Today the contrast is great. Our nations and countries are colonies no more. Now we are free, sovereign and independent. We are again masters in our own house. We do not need to go to other continents to confer."[21]

---

[20] Sukarno, "President Sukarno Opening Speech at the Bandung Conference," in *Asia-Africa Speaks from Bandung* (Jakarta: Ministry of Foreign Affairs, 1955). Also available at: www.cvce.eu/content/publication/2001/9/5/88d3f71c-c9f9-415a-b397-b27b8581a4f5/publishable_en.pdf.
[21] Sukarno, "President Sukarno Opening Speech at the Bandung Conference."

The first New Delhi Conference in 1947 was technically unofficial, hosted by a think-tank, the Indian Council of World Affairs (ICWA). Participants included Tibet, as well as yet-to-be independent governments; indeed host country India was then still under British colonial rule, and would continue to be for several months more. Both the New Delhi conferences were not exclusively gatherings of "colored peoples"; Australia, the United States and United Kingdom attended the first as observers, and Australia was included in the 1949 conference as a full participant.

Below, I compare the norms proposed and debated at the two ARC conferences in New Delhi (1947 and 1949) and the Bandung Conference (1955), and other intervening conferences. This shows that the non-interference norm was not of primary importance in 1947, but grows in significance as we move toward the Bandung Conference. In other words, it was socially constructed and expanded during and as a result of these gatherings.

Although these conferences were similar in many respects in their objectives, and shared many of the same participants, there were also important differences. Unlike the first ARC, Bandung was an official gathering of sovereign nations. More importantly, the ARCs focused mainly on colonialism and self-determination, while Bandung focused on Cold War issues such as military alliances and non-intervention. A common view of the ARC is that it avoided political issues and focused on non-political ones. The Secretary-General of the ICWA at the time of the ARC, A. Appadorai, noted that non-political topics were "the favourites" for the ARC because several participating countries, such as Burma and Indonesia, were yet to become independent. The agenda of the ARC reflects this: it covered eight issues: National Movements for Freedom, Racial Problems, Inter-Asian Migration, Transition from Colonial to National Economy, Agricultural Reconstruction and Industrial Development, Labor Problems and Social Services, Cultural Problems, and the Status of Women and Women's Movements.[22]

Yet, the ARC did reach "consensus" on a set of norms over political issues. These included an agreement not to provide any assistance for the continuance of "foreign domination" in any part of Asia and provision of assistance to national movements wherever possible. A third norm was that "people belonging to one country and living in another should identify themselves with the latter."[23] It extracted assurances from countries

[22] A. Appadorai, "The Asian Relations Conference in Perspective," *International Studies* 18, no. 3 (July–September 1979), 275–285.
[23] Ibid., 279.

such as India, China, Indonesia, Sri Lanka, and Burma that their existing or proposed constitutions would not contain any provision for discrimination on racial grounds. The norm of equality between all citizens irrespective of race and creed "should be the rule in all countries." The norm of equality was divided into four ingredients: "(1) complete legal equality of all citizens; (2) complete religious freedom; (3) no public social disqualification of any racial group; and (4) equality before law of persons of foreign origin who had settled in the country."[24]

The norms articulated at the ARC were not to escape unscathed during subsequent challenges. But one key norm, assistance for national movements wherever possible, was observed most strikingly in the case of Indonesia. What is more striking, many of these "rules" concerned the domestic jurisdiction of states, yet they were regarded as unexceptional and a "consensus" could be reached over them. Perhaps the non-official nature of the conference made this possible, along with the fact, as mentioned above, that several participants had not yet reached sovereign statehood. At a later stage, the mere discussion of racial equality of member states at a regional forum in Asia would be construed as a flagrant violation of sovereignty and the doctrine of non-interference. Self-determination and racial equality, rather than non-interference, were the key concerns at this point. The fear of interference, and thus the salience of non-interference, would grow alongside the escalation of the Cold War following the communist takeover in China. But in 1947, the participants in the ARC were not so much concerned with defining the rules of their mutual interaction as with demanding and articulating their sovereign status, which was closely tied to self-determination and racial equality. The latter, though conceived as an international norm, was deemed applicable to domestic contexts at a time when regime security had not been a concern.

This was possible because, at this stage, the focus was on achieving independence, not conduct of international relations. While ARC focused on promoting self-determination and the West's relations with colonies (North–South), Bandung focused on the relations among the new states (South–South). The ARC was about promoting the idea of sovereignty, hence agreement could be possible even over domestic norms, which was inspired by opposition to colonialism. While the ARC's goal was to win freedom, Bandung's goal was to "preserve" it "against all threats, including the threat posed by the new and sinister imperialism of world communism."[25] At Bandung, to bring about an "agreement on general

---

[24] Ibid., 280.
[25] Romulo, *The Meaning of Bandung*, 16.

principles" was "the basic aim."[26] Abdulghani Roeslan, the Secretary-General of the Bandung Conference, listed among the objectives of the conference the following: "to continue the struggle toward a full materi-alization of national independence" and "to determine ... the standards and procedures of present-day international relations."[27] In a subse-quent commemorative speech, he expanded on the second objective as "the formulation and establishment of certain norms for the conduct of present-day international relations and the instruments for the prac-tical application of these norms."[28] According to the official report of the Arab League Delegation to the conference, participants regarded the Declaration on World Peace as the "most important resolution" adopted at Bandung, because it "upheld the principles regulating their relations with each other and the world at large."[29]

The new emphasis on defining rules of conduct in intra-regional rela-tions reflected prevailing circumstances. The Bandung Conference was held under different circumstances than the ARC. Three factors were note-worthy. First, the communist revolution in China made non-interference more moot. Second, following the Korean War, the United States was now interested in a Pacific regional alliance, in marked contrast to its pre-1950s attitude when it had refused to support regional groupings in Asia out of deference to Asian nationalists who were likely to have viewed such efforts as unwarranted domination by outside powers. Third, Cold War ideological polarization was becoming sharper in Asia.

As such, non-interference emerged as the key norm of Asian region-alist efforts. Faced with an escalating crisis in Indo-China, the prime ministers of the five countries, India, Pakistan, Burma, Indonesia, and Ceylon, organized themselves into a group that became known as the Colombo Powers, holding their first meeting in Ceylon's capital in April 1954. In proposing the terms of a settlement in Indo-China, the drafting committee of the Colombo Conference, prodded by India and Burma, suggested "a solemn agreement of non-intervention" by the United States, the Soviet Union, the United Kingdom, and China "to refrain from giving aid to the combatants or intervening in Indo-China with troops or war material" as a specific clause in a draft joint communiqué to be issued by the Colombo Powers.[30] Pakistan,

---

[26] *The Report of the Arab League on the Bandung Conference* (Cairo: League of Arab States, 1955), 23. Henceforth cited as The Arab League Report.

[27] Abdulghani, *The Bandung Spirit*, 72.

[28] Ibid., 103.

[29] The Arab League Report, 151.

[30] *Southeast Asian Prime Ministers' Conference: Minutes of Meetings and Documents of the Conference*, Colombo, April 1954. Hereafter cited as *The Colombo Conference Minutes*.

while not being "opposed to the principle of non-intervention," objected to the inclusion of the language (presumably because that would have delegitimized US assistance to South Vietnam at a time when Pakistan had decided to join a collective defense pact with the USA). In the end, softer language was found which urged the outside powers, China, the United States, the Soviet Union, and the United Kingdom, to agree on "steps necessary to prevent the recurrence or resumption of hostilities" so that "the success of ... direct negotiations [as opposed to the prospects for a ceasefire] will be greatly helped."[31]

It was at this Colombo meeting that the idea of an Asia–Africa Conference was proposed by Indonesia under the sponsorship of the Colombo Powers. The final preparations for the conference were made in a second meeting of the Colombo Powers held in Bogor, Indonesia in December 1954. The Bogor Conference listed as one of the key objectives of Bandung the consideration of the "problems affecting national sovereignty and racialism and colonialism." It also listed the goal of the Asia–Africa Conference as being "to explore and advance" the "mutual and common interests" of Asian and African nations and "establish and further friendliness and neighbourly relations." Non-interference was upheld in three key decisions; it explained the conference's decision that acceptance of one country as a participant would not imply change in its view of any other country. And it recognized the "principle that the form of government and the way of life of any one country should in no way be subject to interference by any other."[32] Nehru opposed invitations to representatives of independence movements in dependent countries because "that would mean an interference in internal affairs, while the Colombo countries had advocated the principle of non-interference."[33]

Sovereignty was the key focus at Bandung. The nations at the conference were "united behind one simple idea – the idea of national independence."[34] The Bandung agenda was much broader and more political than that of the ARC; as in ARC, it included self-determination, including Palestine and racialism, but Bandung also focused on human rights, and world peace and world cooperation, which were not discussed as such in Delhi in 1947. But most importantly, the key issue at Bandung was non-interference: "The word and the idea of intervention was

[31] Ibid.
[32] "Joint Communiqué by the Prime Ministers of Burma, Ceylon, India, Indonesia and Pakistan," in *Conference of the Prime Ministers of the Five Colombo Countries, Bogor December 1954, Minutes of Meetings and Documents of the Conference.* Hereafter cited as *The Bogor Conference Minutes.*
[33] Ibid., First Session, 6.
[34] Abdulghani, *The Bandung Spirit*, 18.

everywhere, especially in Southeast Asia," recalled Abdulghani.[35] Both the United States and the Soviet Union were intervening. It is in the context of non-intervention that the legitimacy of "pacts" became an issue. Nehru had articulated a doctrine of non-involvement or non-alignment. For him, the key objective of Bandung was to expand the "area of peace" and to save the world from the nuclear arms race. Non-interference was also an important objective, but this is better ensured through mutual agreements such as the India–China *Panchaseel*. Non-interference was a key aspect of this. It is little known that while Nehru opposed multilateral defense agreements, he was not opposed to bilateral defense ties between states, including Third World countries and outside powers. Against this backdrop, the key purpose of Bandung was no longer to articulate the demands of self-determination, but to determine the norms of conduct in international relations. Thus, the Arab delegates would be disappointed about the relative inattention to the question of Palestine, the key unresolved issue of self-determination discussed at the conference.

Bandung showed that the key debates about sovereignty were often about what constitutes threats to it. Bandung was the scene of two major controversies over this. The first was caused by Ceylonese Prime Minister John Kotelawala's attack on communism as a second and newer form of colonialism. Referring to "those satellite states under Communist Domination in Central and Eastern Europe," he asked "if we are in opposition to colonialism, should it not be our duty to openly declare opposition to Soviet colonialism as much as to Western imperialism?"[36] Attacks on communism as a new form of colonialism were not confined to Ceylon, but were also carried out by Iraq and Turkey and, with a more moderate tone, the Philippines. Chinese Prime Minister Chou En-lai strongly objected to the mention of communism as a new "form" of colonialism. Much has been made of this episode, but what is missed is the legalistic position taken by Nehru in upholding the sovereignty of the East European states. "There is a distinct and great difference in criticizing the very basis of independent nations that are represented in the United Nations and with whom we have diplomatic relations ... and our talking about Algeria, Morocco or Tunisia," because the latter were "represented in the UN by the colonial powers," while the East European countries were "represented directly at the UN by their own representatives."[37]

It is interesting to note that Kotelawala's anger against communist colonialism was partly induced by his failure to elicit a pledge from Chou

---

[35] Ibid., 63.
[36] Proceedings of the Bandung Conference Political Committee, April 23, 1955.
[37] Speech to the Closed Session of the Bandung Conference, Proceedings of the Bandung Conference Political Committee, April 22, 1955.

En-lai to stop Cominform propaganda and external assistance to communists at home. Chou's conciliatory stance might be explained as a ploy to secure Asian support to fend off American pressure. This was undoubtedly true. But his success came at a price: he had to offer assurances of Chinese non-interference. The latter did not stop, but there was no questioning of its delegitimation.

The second point of contention at Bandung as it struggled in its objective of deciding the norms of international relations was the question of military alliances. Pakistan's Mohammed Ali asserted that Pakistan remained "an independent sovereign state" and as such had a right to do whatever was needed for its own security. Nehru took the opposite tack: the very act of choice undermined Pakistan's sovereign status, if not in a legal sense, in a substantive sense. Pakistan's legal right to enter into regional pacts undermined its moral claim to sovereignty. Incidentally, Nehru defended himself against the charge of starryeyed idealism by insisting that he was "taking a realistic view" of the pacts.[38] At the same time, he derided Turkey's "so-called realistic appreciation of the world situation."[39] It is important to bear in mind that Nehru was not against any kind of defense cooperation. In 1945, he had envisaged a "close union of the countries bordering on the Indian Ocean for defence and trade purposes."[40] Nehru supported bilateral agreements among Asian powers, similar to that India had signed with China incorporating the Five Principles.[41] But to Nehru, the Manila Treaty differed from the North Atlantic Treaty Organization (NATO), of which Turkey was a member: the Manila Treaty brought about "quite a new conception," because unlike NATO, "members of this organization are not only responsible for their own defense but also for that of areas they may designate outside of it if they so agree, this would mean creating a new form of spheres of influence." Nehru contrasted it with the Geneva Agreement on Indo-China, which he endorsed "because of its clause that no outside interference will be allowed in Indo-China."[42]

The debates over communist colonialism and regional pacts, though technically distinct, were in reality closely linked. Advocates of the regional pacts contended that these were necessary against the threat of communist interference. As Romulo pointed out, the communists were

---

[38] Speech by Nehru, Proceedings of the Bandung Conference Political Committee, April 23, 1955.

[39] Ibid.

[40] Cited in Nehru's Interview with B. Shiva Rao, reproduced in B. Shiva Rao, *India's Freedom Movement: Some Notable Figures* (New Delhi: Orient Longman, 1972), 296–299.

[41] Francis Low, *Struggle for Asia* (London: Frederick Muller, 1955), 214–215.

[42] *The Bogor Conference Minutes*, 2nd Session, 6.

routinely violating their own professed doctrine of non-interference. For the pro-pact group, the key challenge to sovereignty of the new states was subversion and infiltration. (Although Pakistan was an exception to this, it was less worried about subversion; the key goal was to secure US support against India. But without support from Romulo and Kotelawala, who were genuinely concerned about communism, Pakistan could not have got its way.) SEATO was the first pact to cover these threats; hence its relevance as a security framework. Defenders of SEATO such as Romulo argued that the pact could not violate the doctrine, since it required the consent of the party concerned before its mutual assistance provisions could be activated. Nehru, on the other hand, believed that the proliferation of regional pacts would reduce the "area of peace" and encourage great power interference and intervention in the internal affairs of the new states. For him, the non-interference norm was closely linked to the non-involvement of states in superpower rivalry through membership in regional pacts.

The Bandung Conferences resolved the contestation on the first question by declaring that "colonialism in all its manifestations is an evil which should be brought to an end." The shift from "colonialism in all its forms" to "colonialism in all its manifestations" satisfied China which interpreted it to mean not the existence of two forms of colonialism (Western and communist), but "colonialism in its political, military, economic, cultural and social manifestations."[43]

A key aspect of the Bandung Conference was the debate over principles. Prior to the conference, India and China had signed the Five Principles of Peaceful Co-existence, namely (1) mutual respect for each other's territorial integrity and sovereignty; (2) mutual non-aggression; (3) mutual non-interference in each other's internal affairs; (4) equality and mutual benefit; and (5) peaceful co-existence. At Bandung, Burma recommended these principles. But disagreement ensued over "peaceful co-existence" which was opposed by the anti-communist camp. Pakistan offered seven principles, of which three – respect for sovereignty, non-interference, and non-aggression – were to be found in the Five Principles, but added four more: right to self-determination, equality of all nations, the peaceful settlement of international disputes, and most importantly, "the right of self-defence exercised singly or collectively." Nehru objected to the last, claiming that it "covered" Pakistan's membership in Cold War pacts. In the end, the Bandung Declaration offered ten principles. Two aspects of the final list may be noted. First, "peaceful co-existence"

---

[43] Final Communiqué of the Asian–African Conference, Proceedings of the Bandung Conference Political Committee, April 24, 1955.

failed to appear in the list, replaced by "to live together in peace with one another."[44] Second, collective defense was allowed, but a sub-clause to this principle urged the "abstention from the use of arrangements of collective defence to serve the particular interests of any of the big powers."

In examining the importance of Bandung in extending universal sovereignty, one must take into account the argument that the norm had already been enshrined in the UN Charter and that the regional meetings were simply repeating well-known platitudes. But this view is misleading for two reasons. First, the countries attending the Bandung Conference felt that while the UN was important, the norms of sovereignty could not be sufficiently defended by it. This was true not just of advocates of pacts like Romulo who felt the UN did not have teeth, but also of the champions from the neutralist camp. Thus, a group of the latter wanted the conference to pass a resolution to acknowledge that the UN had done enough to address the issue of West Irian, although this was dropped. Moreover, many participants at the Asian meetings were not members of the UN and their membership, a key demand of Asian conferences as will be seen later, was by no means assured. Thus, while non-interference was a "universal" norm enshrined in the UN Charter, it does not follow that the diffusion and development of this norm occurred mainly through expansion of UN membership and did not require the advocacy and support of regional conferences. This supports the "social construction" perspective.

Assessments of Bandung tend to agree that it was more successful in "establishing the new status of Asian and African nations in international politics and their claim to a place in the counsels of the nations" than in handling "concrete problems of contemporary international relations."[45] Kahin concluded that "the Conference's major achievements were not ... to be found in its formal resolutions. More important was its educational function – the attainment by the representatives ... of a much fuller and more realistic understanding of one another's point of view."[46] A more specific and substantive claim was that it helped to diffuse world tensions, especially in view of Chou's offer of direct talks with the United States over Formosa (Taiwan).

These assessments, made in the immediate aftermath of Bandung, could not have foreseen its two long-term effects. Romulo claimed that the pro-West camp came out victorious after Bandung. He wrote a year

[44] Romulo, *The Meaning of Bandung*, 7.
[45] William Henderson, "The Development of Regionalism in Southeast Asia," *International Organization* 9, no. 4 (November 1955), 467.
[46] Kahin, *The Asian–African Conference*, 35.

later: "It is no exaggeration that the anti-communist states put both communism and neutralism on the defensive, scoring a signal diplomatic triumph for the free world."[47] But subsequent events show that the triumph of the free world did not translate into vitality and longevity for the military alliance, SEATO.

Yet, Bandung did have a normative impact on the legitimacy of great power–led alliances. Guy Pauker described the "injunction" against the "use of arrangements of collective defence to serve the particularistic interests of any of the big powers" as the "most significant aspect" of the conference.[48] The injunction, which reflected the lack of consensus among the Colombo Powers both at Bandung and earlier, served to delegitimize SEATO. It can be argued that SEATO's problems had to do with lack of teeth, rather than legitimacy. As an alliance, SEATO was quite different from NATO; it had a permanent military command, the US commitment was not automatic, but subject to its "constitutional processes," and the nature of response was not action, but consultations. Even in the case of overt aggression, the power could act only at the invitation and with the consent of the government concerned. Unlike the NATO formula of "attack on one, attack on all," SEATO adopted the Monroe Doctrine formula, applied to the Organization of American States (OAS), under which the parties merely recognize that an armed attack in the treaty area "would endanger its own peace and safety." But these limitations were not worrisome to parties. "The possibility of the United States not acting at all because of the limitations imposed by these two formulae was not a source of serious apprehension in the United Kingdom, New Zealand or Australia."[49] US Secretary of State John Dulles himself had assured that the provision regarding constitutional processes "gives all the freedom of action and power to act that is contained in NATO."[50] Furthermore, the absence of a NATO-like structure was not considered too debilitating "so long as the use of a mobile, striking force in the area rather than massive land forces is contemplated."[51]

The non-participation of the Colombo Powers of India, Burma, and Indonesia (especially the former) also affected British support for a collective defense system for Southeast Asia. Although Britain had other reasons, deference to the Colombo Powers was a key factor in its lukewarm attitude towards SEATO. Anthony Eden in his memoirs wrote

---

[47] Romulo, *The Meaning of Bandung*, 22.
[48] Pauker, *The Bandung Conference*, 18.
[49] Ralph Braibanti, "The Southeast Asia Collective Defense Treaty," *Pacific Affairs* 30, no. 4 (December 1957), 328.
[50] Ibid., 329.
[51] Ibid., 338.

that, prior to the Geneva Conference in 1954, he had communicated to Dulles his wish that they "should avoid taking any action which might lead the Governments represented at Colombo to come out publicly against our security proposals."[52] A Joint Study Group Report notes that the British members of the group believed that "strong efforts to secure the participation of the Colombo Powers in the collective security arrangement or at least their acquiescence in its formation should be made prior to the negotiation of the treaty."[53] The absence of Anthony Eden, the British Foreign Minister, from the SEATO Conference in Baguio, the Philippines, in September 1954, was officially explained as due to the situation caused by the French rejection of the European Defence Community, but there remained feelings that "Sir Anthony was not keen to attend owing to the [negative] attitude of India and Ceylon" toward the treaty.[54] During his meeting in London with Dulles, Eden had proclaimed that "without their understanding and support, no permanent South-east Asia defence organization could be fully effective."[55] A former Secretary-General of SEATO listed among the reasons for its collapse its failure "to gather new members," and noted the "ironical" fact that "it was Thailand and the Philippines whose security SEATO was principally conceived to ensure, who asked ... for its gradual phasing out ..." Echoing Nehru, he argued: "When membership is disparate and composed of great and small nations, the latter having to rely heavily on the former, the organization is bound to be at the mercy of the whip and whim of the larger nations."[56] Also significant is the fact that the Association of Southeast Asia, a clear precursor to ASEAN formed by Thailand, the Philippines, and Malaysia in 1961, noted in its founding declaration that the organization was "in no way connected with any outside power bloc and was directed against no other country."[57]

Also some of the Bandung language found its way into ASEAN. At the signing of the founding Bangkok Declaration of ASEAN, Indonesia sought to incorporate the Bandung language against pacts that serve the

---

[52] Anthony Eden, *Full Circle: The Memoirs of Sir Anthony Eden* (London: Cassell and Company, 1960), 99.

[53] "Report of the Joint US–UK Study Group on Southeast Asia," July 17, 1954, in Allen H. Kitchens and Neal H. Petersen, eds., *Foreign Relations of the United States* [hereafter cited as *FRUS*], *1952–1954, The Geneva Conference*, vol. XVI (Washington, DC: US Government Printing Office, 1981), 1415.

[54] Low, *Struggle for Asia*, 217.

[55] Ibid., 213.

[56] Konthi Suphamongkon, "From SEATO to ASEAN," undated paper (Singapore: Institute of Southeast Asian Studies), 32–35.

[57] Michael Leifer, *ASEAN and the Security of South-East Asia* (London: Routledge, 1989), 28.

particularistic interests of any great power.[58] As ASEAN's Zone of Peace, Freedom, and Neutrality (ZOPFAN) Declaration of November 27, 1997 states: "Believing in the continuing validity of the 'Declaration on the Promotion of World Peace and Cooperation' of the Bandung Conference of 1955, which among others, enunciates the principles by which states may co-exist peacefully." The Treaty of Amity and Cooperation of 1975 also acknowledges that ASEAN's goals were "consistent with" the "Ten Principles adopted by the Asian–African Conference in Bandung."

Sovereignty and Regionalism in Asia

It is a common misconception that the Asian regional conferences were aimed at the creation of a permanent regional organization. Some Western and Asian circles had expected Bandung to lead to a regional organization. In a telegram to the Canadian High Commissioner in Delhi, dated April 12, 1955, the Canadian Secretary of State for External Affairs noted:

There is the possibility that a permanent organization will develop from the Asian–African Conference, and to a certain extent duplicate the work of the United Nations and its specialized agencies. We trust that any continuing organs set up at Bandung will not displace the Colombo Plan in its special field, nor tend to supplant the United Nations.[59]

But this proved to be a false expectation. The idea of a permanent Asian regional organization never acquired much support. Immediately prior to and after the holding of the non-official ARC, two schemes were considered: the first called for "a permanent Institution meeting once in three years in an Asian country," the purpose of which would be to facilitate "exchange of ideas and cultivation of personal contacts between Asian thinkers and public workers." This would be "a non-official Conference consisting of delegations from non-official organisations in Asian countries devoted to the objective study of international affairs and not having any political party affiliations and not being engaged in any kind of propaganda." The other scheme was to set up a "new central organization" whose objective would be: "(a) To promote the study and understanding of Asian problems and relations in their Asian and world aspects; (b) to promote good-neighbourly relations between Asian

---

[58] Arnfin Jorgensen-Dahl, *Regional Organization and Order in Southeast Asia* (Basingstoke: Macmillan, 1982).

[59] Secretary of State for External Affairs to High Commissioner in India, Telegram 224, Ottawa, April 12, 1955, "ASIAN–AFRICAN CONFERENCE," DEA/12173-40, Volume #21-779, Chapter VII, Far East, Part 7, Bandung Conference of Non-Aligned Nations.

countries and peoples; and (c) to promote the freedom, peace, and well being of Asia and Asian peoples." This body would function by collecting and disseminating information, conducting study and research, holding periodic conferences, and fostering cultural and social contacts between Asian countries. The body would be governed by an Asian Council consisting of two representatives from each constituent national unit. The Asian Council was to meet twice a year and its resolutions were to be determined by voting, rather than consensus.[60]

The institution which emerged from these resembled the second scheme, i.e. for a "new central organization" that was set up in New Delhi in the name of the Asian Relations Organization (ARO). Modeled after the Institute of Pacific Relations in the USA, the ARO, however, remained moribund from the very outset. A reading of the ICWA Files shows that the Delhi secretariat was unable to elicit responses to its requests for information from national units despite repeated attempts. The ARO folded its operation quietly "sometime in the middle of 1955," significantly after the return of Nehru from Bandung, when Nehru, its president, instructed A. Appadorai, the Secretary-General, that "I think it is better to wind up the Organization because in the present political climate nothing much can be done ... almost from the start of the organization there has been conflict among member-states and in such a situation I don't think any useful work can be done."[61]

The Conference on Indonesia convened in January 1949 in New Delhi by Nehru to discuss the Dutch police action against Indonesia also raised the possibility of a permanent Asian regional organization. Carlos Romulo proposed a "small permanent secretariat in New Delhi, maybe, or Manila, to serve as a clearing house of information essential to concerted action by our various Governments, and a method of consultation on matters of common interests." He also spoke of how "many members look beyond it [the conference] to the formation of a permanent organization, a regional association *strictly within the framework of the United Nations*" (emphasis added).[62] By the time of the Baguio Conference convened by Romulo to discuss Asian cooperation, it had become even clearer that the desire for a regional organization would be subjected to the imperative of state sovereignty. At the Baguio Conference Romulo insisted that "Every state here represented retains unimpaired the right

---

[60] "Draft Scheme for a Permanent Conference Organisation," undated document found in the files on the Asian Relations Conference, Indian Council on World Affairs, New Delhi, Personal reading, January 28, 2003. Hereafter cited as ICWA Files.

[61] Appadorai, "The Asian Relations Conference in Perspective," 283.

[62] *The Conference on Indonesia, January 20–23, 1949* (Delhi: Ministry of Information and Broadcasting, 1949), 27, 40.

to meet and solve those problems by national action according to the peculiar conditions prevailing within its territory. Any proposal for common action, therefore, must be regarded not as a substitute for national action but rather as supplementary to it."[63]

By the time of Bandung, the idea of a regional organization had been out of Nehru's mind. At Bandung, there was no talk of a permanent organization. Only the Economic Committee considered a regular body. As per the Final Report of the Economic Committee, there was a discussion on the organizational aspects. The proposals varied from having a permanent organization with a permanent secretariat to one for having only informal discussions without any secretariat. Most were against the setting up of a permanent economic organization with a permanent secretariat. Burma's working paper on Mutual Aid and Economic Cooperation proposed a permanent economic secretariat and Indonesia's working paper on the Need for Economic Cooperation suggested some form of organization/secretariat.

Among those who had favored a permanent economic secretariat were Iran, Sudan, and Syria. Lebanon, Liberia, Sri Lanka, and Turkey opposed. Burma during the discussion withdrew its proposal as it felt that it was premature to establish a secretariat owing to shortage of funds and other reasons. Most (Burma, China, India, Iraq, Sri Lanka) supported a consultative committee without a permanent secretariat. Cambodia suggested periodical meetings of representatives of states on the model of the British Commonwealth prime ministers' meetings. India supported a consultative committee without a permanent secretariat and the Thai proposal was that each country might appoint within its own secretariat a liaison officer, to whom correspondence might be addressed by the various liaison officers.[64]

While still at Bandung, Nehru was asked by Chou about maintaining a "liaison office" for the next sitting of the conference, due to be held in Egypt two years later. In a note to Krishna Menon, Nehru revealed that the Joint Secretariat for Bandung could play such a role. But Burma's U Nu reacted strongly against this idea: "there should be no kind of organization or liaison office," and Nehru concurred with this view.[65]

What about process? Referring to the process developed through the series of Asian and Asian–African conferences, it can be observed that

---

[63] *Verbatim Records of the Opening Plenary Session, Final Act and Proceedings of the Baguio Conference of 1950* (Secretariat of the Baguio Conference of 1950), 13.

[64] Ibid.

[65] "Note to V. K. Krishna Menon," Bandung, April 23, 1955, in *Selected Writings of Jawaharlal Nehru*, second series, vol. XXVIII (New Delhi: Jawaharlal Nehru Memorial Fund, 2001), 124.

all debates about process were resolved in favor of the following principles: that regional meetings should be in the nature of "informal talks
without commitments"; that "there should be no question of majority or
minority votes, but that the consensus of opinion should form the basis
of conference decision"; and the "draft communiqués should simply
give the consensus of opinion on each subject rather than individual
resolutions."[66] At the ARC, contentious issues such as those related to
the Cold War were avoided because they were likely to "divide the conference."[67] It is ironic but important that Nehru, the keenest proponent
of an Asian organization, was also insistent on soft rules for the conduct
of deliberations at Asian summits. He preferred the Commonwealth
model to the formalism of the UN. The Commonwealth was an association of free states, discussions were held in a "friendly spirit," and
there was no attempt by states to impose their will on one another. It
was marked by "mutual equality and respect amongst its members" and
"when differences arise, they are accepted with tolerance and mutual
respect."[68] The preference for soft rules would have been hard to reconcile with the formal procedures that would have been needed for a
regional organization.

At the first Colombo Powers meeting, Nehru asked that they
"follow the precedent set by the Conferences of Commonwealth Prime
Ministers"; these being meetings where discussion of disputes between
members were usually avoided.[69] The next major discussion of rules of
procedure took place at the Bogor summit of the Colombo Powers. In
deciding the procedure for Bandung, the Bogor summit decided that
"any view expressed at the conference by one or more participating
country would not be binding on or be regarded as accepted by any
other, unless the latter so desired."[70] Another decision taken at Bogor
also affirmed the salience of sovereignty: "acceptance of the invitation by
any one country would in no way involve or imply any change in the status of that country or its relationship with other countries."[71] The norm
of non-interference was reinforced: "the principle that the form of government and the way of life of any country should in no way be subject to
interference by another." Inclusiveness – that "all kinds of countries will

---

[66] George H. Jansen, *Afro-Asia and Non-Alignment* (London: Faber and Faber, 1966),
148–149, 193. See also Pauker, *The Bandung Conference*, 6.

[67] Appadorai, "The Asian Relations Conference in Perspective," 279.

[68] Indian ambassador to the United States, G. L. Mehta, cited in Low, *Struggle for Asia*, 203.

[69] *The Colombo Conference Minutes.*

[70] *The Bogor Conference Minutes.*

[71] Ibid.

sit with various systems of government and differing social systems" – was "a new concept ... in the field of multilateralism."[72]

In so far as process was concerned, Bandung maintained a striking continuity with ARC, despite being an official gathering. At Bandung, the Political Committee decided on the procedure from the very outset. Nehru recommended that the rules of procedure should be "as flexible as possible."[73] In the end, Indonesian Prime Minister Ali Sastroamidjojo decided that "there will be no specific rules of procedure": that could be left to the chairman of the conference who could conduct meetings "in accordance with the generally accepted conventions of Conferences." And "there should be no 'voting'"; decisions were to be reached by consensus. Referring to this rule, Abdulghani explained it as a "deep-rooted and unquestioned practice," but not just of Indonesians or even Asians, but also of African societies.[74] "The object is to reach an acceptable consensus of opinion, and one which not only hurts the feeling or the position of no one, but which actually tends to reinforce the community feeling."[75] But he acknowledged that reaching consensus at international meetings was going to be difficult, because "every person present has, in fact, a power of veto."[76] "The rules of procedure – even though of an informal and temporary character – had much influence and a very great role in the running of the Conference ... In those brief and to the point rules of procedure, basic and important lines of policy were implied." These rules "including the principle of deliberation and consensus, were one of the keys to the success of the A-A Conference."[77]

There is a striking resemblance between the rules of procedure that prevailed through the Asian conferences and that of ASEAN. The "ASEAN Way" is known for informality, preference for consensus over majority voting, avoidance of legalistic procedures, preference for non-binding resolutions, and a tendency to avoid contentious bilateral issues in multilateral discussions. While the ASEAN Way is today known as a distinctively Southeast Asian trait, the roots of this "process-driven" approach to regionalism cannot be understood in isolation from the Asian conferences held between 1947 and 1955.[78]

---

[72] Ibid.
[73] Ibid.
[74] Abdulghani, *The Bandung Spirit*, 29.
[75] Ibid.
[76] Ibid.
[77] Abdulghani, *The Bandung Connection*, 76–77.
[78] For a critical discussion of the "ASEAN Way," see: Amitav Acharya, *Constructing a Security Community in Southeast Asia: ASEAN and the Problem of Regional Order* (London: Routledge, 2001).

The process through which the Asian norm against collective defense was developed not only provided a durable foundation for Asian multilateralism, it also helped broaden and strengthen the non-intervention norm in the global context. To be sure, there was prior development of this norm in global and regional contexts, such as in Latin America and at the founding of the UN. But Asia's was a distinctive and significant contribution.

In the drafting of the UN Charter, non-intervention had a less prominent place than other core norms of sovereignty, such as territorial integrity and the doctrine of sovereign equality of states, partly out of concern among the key players of the 1945 San Francisco Conference (where the non-Western representation was small and mostly from Latin America) that too much emphasis on non-intervention would prejudice the authority of the Security Council to carry out its enforcement functions under Chapter VII.[79] It was through Bandung and the NAM that the norm was considerably strengthened as a rule of sovereignty in the Third World. The traditional meaning of non-intervention and the scope of challenge that could undermine it (which now included membership in superpower military alliances) were broadened. The classical European exception to non-intervention (intervention justified in the name of maintaining the balance of power) had no place in the Third World sovereignty regime.

Constructing Sovereignty in Latin America, Africa, and the Middle East

Asia was not the only region to have provincialized Westphalia. Latin American countries, the first to obtain independence from colonial rule, have been "international rule innovators." Among their normative innovations is the doctrine of *uti possidetis juris*, or honoring inherited boundaries, and the principle of non-intervention.[80] The former was developed as a response to imperial collapse (especially of the Spanish empire) and the consequent inability of European great powers to maintain regional order. Later, under the banner of pan-Americanism, Latin American states developed a regional norm of "absolute nonintervention in the

---

[79] See *Documents of the United Nations Conference on International Organization, Commission I, General Provisions*, vol. VI (New York: United Nations Information Organizations, 1945).

[80] Jorge I. Dominguez, "International Cooperation in Latin America: The Design of Regional Institutions by Slow Accretion," in *Crafting Cooperation: The Design and Effects of Regional Institutions in Comparative Perspective*, ed. Amitav Acharya and Alastair Iain Johnston (Cambridge University Press, 2007), 126–127.

hemispheric community," both as an abstract principle and as a means to challenge US hegemony in the region (embodied in the "Monroe Doctrine") and its perceived hypocrisy in violating the norm of non-intervention.[81] One such rule, the Calvo Doctrine (after Argentinian jurist Carlos Calvo) rejected the right of intervention claimed by foreign powers (European and US), in order to protect their citizens resident in Latin America. Another rule, the Drago Doctrine, named after Argentinian Foreign Minister Luis Drago, challenged the US and European position that they had a right to intervene to force states to honor their sovereign debts. Over US opposition, Latin American congresses recognized revolutionary governments as de jure. Both the Calvo and Drago doctrines constituted subsidiary norms of state sovereignty in Latin America's regional order. The Latin American advocacy led the United States to abandon the Monroe Doctrine in 1933 and accept non-intervention as a basic principle in its relations with the region.

But the Latin American construction of non-intervention reflected the political aspirations of settler societies whose legal and intellectual underpinnings had considerable association with Western political traditions and legal ideas. It was part of a regional bargaining exercise in which America's southern neighbors persuaded it to accept non-intervention in exchange for their acceptance of US security protection. This would "multilateralize" the Monroe Doctrine, the original goal of which was to deter European recolonization of South America. The Asian construction of non-intervention was distinctive in the sense of being geared to a bipolar international structure. It did not allow for collective defense pacts with either superpower. And the Asian construction of non-intervention at multilateral gatherings like Bandung predated Africa's sovereignty and non-intervention regime by a decade and influenced it, not the least because several African states participated in the meetings in Asia.[82]

In the Middle East, normative agency featured a contestation between Westphalian sovereignty and what Michael Barnett calls the "norms of

---

[81] Thomas Leonard, "The New Pan Americanism in USS–Central American Relations, 1933–1954," and David Barton Castle, "Leo Stanton Rowe and the Meaning of Pan-Americanism," in *Beyond the Ideal: Pan Americanism in International Affairs*, ed. David Sheinin (Westport, CT: Praeger, 2000).

[82] On the normative link between Bandung and African regionalist concepts, see: Colin Legum, *Bandung, Cairo and Accra* (London: The Africa Bureau, 1958). The Conference of Independent African States (CIAS), convened by Kwame Nkrumah in 1958, explicitly invoked Bandung principles, including its rejection of Cold War pacts. Kwame Nkrumah, *I Speak of Freedom* (Westport, CT: Greenwood Press, 1961), 151–152, 219; Bala Mohammed, *Africa and Nonalignment* (Kano, Nigeria: Triumph Publishing Co., 1978), 21, 54–55, 184.

Arabism," which includes the "quest for independence, the cause of Palestine, and the search for [Arab] unity" and non-alignment.[83] The initial pan-Arab norms, especially those associated with Egypt's Nasser, resisted the Baghdad Pact sponsored by the United States. This pact was signed in February 1955 on the same pretext of fighting communism as had been the case with SEATO. Prior to its signing, Nasser had been judged by the US State Department to be "friendly to the West, especially to the United States." But the State Department also pointed out that Nasser had become more "reserved" toward the West since the signing of the Baghdad Pact, which he "believes will damage Egypt's position of leadership among the Arab states."[84] Nehru himself had warned before the Bandung Conference that the Baghdad Pact would make an otherwise friendly Egyptian government wary of US intentions and radicalize the Middle East, while undermining indigenous efforts at regional cooperation.[85] Among other things, Nasser viewed the Baghdad Pact as severely undermining the scheme for an indigenous Arab Collective Security System, which had been mooted by Egypt. The Bandung Conference's "spirited rhetoric of anticolonialism, independence, and rejection of alliances with the West had a major influence on Nasser."[86] Within months of the Bandung Conference, Nasser would sign an arms deal with Czechoslovakia and nationalize the Suez Canal, thereby setting the path for a major confrontation with the United States and the West in 1956. Nasser viewed the Baghdad Pact as an instrument of US and British hegemony which subverted regional aspirations and arrangements for peace and security. In rejecting the pact, he sought to strengthen nationalism, self-determination, non-intervention, and regional autonomy. Hence he simultaneously localized the global sovereignty norm and infused it with a locally developed norm against the Baghdad Pact. At the same time, the Nasserite ideal of creating a single Arab nation out of existing postcolonial states gradually faded. But this only illustrates the working of the other subsidiary norms of the region, and their supporting/strengthening

---

[83] Michael Barnett, *Dialogues in Arab Politics* (New York: Columbia University Press, 1998), 56, 106; Mark Lynch, *State Interests and Public Spheres: The International Politics of Jordan's Identity* (New York: Columbia University Press, 1999), 34; Raymond A. Hinnebusch, *The International Politics of the Middle East* (Manchester University Press, 2003), 64.

[84] British Embassy, Washington, to Foreign Office, London, US Department of State Intelligence Report No. 6830.3, "Developments relating to the Bandung Conference," March 18, 1955, D2231/283, FO 371/116982. The UK National Archives.

[85] Jawaharlal Nehru, "India and World Affairs," in *Selected Works of Jawaharlal Nehru*, vol. XXVIII (New Delhi: Jawaharlal Nehru Memorial Fund, 2000), 310.

[86] Barnett, *Dialogues in Arab Politics*, 299; Eli Podeh, *The Quest for Hegemony in the Arab World: The Struggle over the Baghdad Pact* (New York: E. J. Brill, 1995).

effect on the existing universal norms of national sovereignty.[87] Moreover, the cause of Palestine and the quest for regional autonomy, cooperation, and non-alignment continued to define the normative order of the Arab Middle East long after Nasser.

African scholars have pointed to a range of interrelated African norms, including non-interference, African solutions to African problems,[88] self-determination, and territorial integrity (which Young terms as the "norm of inter-state boundary harmony in Africa").[89] Ghana's Kwame Nkrumah, leader of the first sub-Saharan African country to gain independence, led the formulation of the general norms of an African regional order which would stress non-intervention by outside powers in African affairs[90] and the abstention of Africans in superpower-led collective defense pacts. As in the Middle East, these African norms supported the common global norms of territorial sovereignty, racial equality, liberation from colonial rule, and regional cooperation. Nkrumah had been prevented by the British (Ghana was still under British dominion status) from attending the Bandung Conference, despite his keen desire to do so. Yet he too was deeply influenced by the conference. In April 1958, Nkrumah hosted the first Conference of Independent African States. Like the Bandung meeting, the African conference was geared not only to discussing ways to secure independence from colonial rule, but also to developing norms of foreign policy conduct aimed at addressing "the central problem of how to secure peace." The Bandung principles of "abstention from the use of arrangements of collective defence to serve the particular interests of any of the great powers" were among those agreed to at the African conference.[91] As Nkrumah saw it, the conference was the first time that "Free Africans were actually meeting together to examine and consider African affairs." Moreover, the normative result of the conference was "a signal departure from established custom, a jar to the arrogant assumption of non-African nations that Africa affairs

---

[87] Michael Barnett, "Nationalism, Sovereignty, and Regional Order in Arab Politics," *International Organization* 49, no. 3 (1995), 479–510.

[88] William J. Foltz, "The Organisation of African Unity and the Resolution of Africa's Conflicts," in *Conflict Resolution in Africa*, ed. Francis M. Deng and I. William Zartman (Washington, DC: The Brookings Institution, 1991), 352.

[89] Crawford Young, "Self Determination, Territorial Integrity, and the African State System," in *Conflict Resolution in Africa*, ed. Deng and Zartman, 326, 328.

[90] In common with Nasser, Nkrumah distinguished non-intervention by outside (non-African) powers in African affairs (hence "African solutions to African problems") from involvement by African states and institutions in the internal affairs of African states. Hence, their respective brands of pan-Arabism and pan-Africanism permitted their own intervention in the domestic affairs of other countries in the region. Nasser conceived of a single Arab nation, and Nkrumah advocated an African intervention force.

[91] John Woronoff, *Organizing African Unity* (Metuchen, NJ: Scarecrow Press, 1970), 39.

were solely the concern of states outside our continent."[92] This marked
the beginning of the African subsidiary norms of regional self-reliance
in regional security and economic development. Even after Nkrumah's
eclipse, the African normative order would continue to reject superpower
intervention, espouse regional autonomy, and develop regional institutions geared to achieving African cooperation if not outright political
unity.[93]

Normative agency may involve transregional extensions of locally
developed rules. The Asian norm against intervention clearly had a
demonstrable effect on other Third World regions. The Non-Aligned
Movement (NAM), which attracted considerable membership in Latin
America, Africa, and the Middle East, was a direct offshoot of the
Bandung Conference.[94] A meeting of foreign ministers in 1961 limited
membership in the NAM to states that were not members of "a multilateral alliance concluded in the context of Great Power conflicts."[95] This
remained a core principle of NAM.

Finally, localized norms may travel from one region to another through
learning and emulation, and thereby retain a certain basic meaning across
regions. The process of diffusion can also cause new variations in their
understanding and application. African states resisting Western colonialism were moved to channel their normative resistance not only against
the apartheid regime in South Africa, but also to other regions, including
the Arab struggle against Israel over Palestine.[96] However, the process of
interregional diffusion can cause important variations. The norm of honoring postcolonial boundaries, originally developed in Latin America,
was adopted in Africa and to some extent in Asia, although more so in
the former than the latter. (In Asia, several crucial violations occurred,
especially Indonesia–Malaysia, India–Pakistan, and Vietnam with respect
to its idea of Indochina as a single entity.) Yet that norm's application in
Latin America was much more legalized than in the other regions. Thus,
to say that norm subsidiarity is a general feature of Third World regions
does not mean that these norms would have exactly the same meaning
in different regions. The Latin American doctrine of non-intervention

[92] Kwame Nkrumah, *Africa Must Unite* (New York: Praeger, 1963), 136.
[93] Robert H. Jackson and Carl G. Roseberg, "Why Africa's Weak States Persist: The
Empirical and the Juridical in Statehood," *World Politics* 35, no. 1 (1982), 259–282;
Jeffrey Herbst, "Crafting Regional Cooperation in Africa," in *Crafting Cooperation:
Regional International Institutions in International Politics*, ed. Amitav Acharya and Alastair
Iain Johnston (Cambridge University Press, 2007), 129–144.
[94] Jansen, *Afro-Asia and Non-Alignment*; A. W. Singham and Shirley Hune, *Non-Alignment
in an Age of Alignments* (London: Zed Books, 1986).
[95] Ayoob, *The Third World Security Predicament*, 104.
[96] Young, "Self Determination, Territorial Integrity, and the African State System," 325.

was a more *absolute* doctrine than in European practice, where intervention could still be justified for the sake of maintaining balance of power. Asians too zealously adopted non-intervention, but introduced another significant local variation: abstention from superpower-led military pacts. Hence while all Third World regions developed norms linked to non-intervention, this took different forms.

Around the same time that the decolonized states in Asia embraced a particularly restrictive interpretation of sovereignty and non-intervention, their former colonial masters in Europe began to move away from Westphalian sovereignty toward a greater degree of solidarism and supra-nationalism. Hence, a gap opened up in the practices around sovereignty between the former colonial powers (the original site of sovereignty) and the recently decolonized states. This faultline continued to shape not just the pattern of North–South relations in the post-war period, especially with the rise of the Non-Aligned Movement, which served to diffuse the norm of non-intervention and abstention from superpower-led collective military alliances in the Global South just as Asian regional institutions helped to institutionalize the norm at the regional level.[97] It also laid a normative foundation that has profoundly shaped post-war regional institution-building in Asia.

Conclusion

This chapter leads to three general points. First, it demonstrates the normative agency of non-Western actors in the construction of the principles of sovereignty in global order. Chapter 1 mentions that part of this agency lies in contesting dominant understandings of prevailing global norms. This chapter shows two areas in which the contestations at Bandung had their major impact. The first was in delegitimizing great power military pacts, especially SEATO, as a threat to sovereignty. The second was their role in shaping the design and effect of regional institutions in Asia. As such, this chapter shows that the view of the global sovereignty regime as a mere extension of Westphalian principles obscures a good part of the sovereignty game in the Global South. While there was basic agreement on some of the essential attributes of sovereignty, such as equality and non-interference, what constitutes equality and interference was a matter

---

[97] Jansen, *Afro-Asia and Non-Alignment*; Singham and Hune, *Non-Alignment in an Age of Alignments*. Before the first summit of NAM in Belgrade in 1961, the Preparatory Meeting of Foreign Ministers held in Cairo in June 1961 issued criteria that restricted invitations to states which were not members of "a multilateral alliance concluded in the context of Great Power conflicts." Ayoob, *The Third World Security Predicament*, 104. It is noteworthy that Africa also did not develop collective defense with great powers.

of debate. By focusing on how sovereignty was transferred from the West to the Rest through decolonization, scholars have neglected how sovereignty was actively constructed by Third World agents.

A second general point from this chapter is that the specific interpretations of sovereignty in different parts of the world created different types of regional applications of the norm, hence accentuating regional diversity in the global order. For example, while Asia rejected multilateral alliances with the United States as a threat to sovereignty, Latin America did not. Africa for its part focused on creating a boundary regime before taking up economic integration (as Western Europe and to some extent Asia did). Each region was responding to its specific context and needs, thereby creating diversity in interpretations and applications of the idea and norms of sovereignty.

4   Transforming Westphalia

The previous chapter examined the agency of non-Western countries in the global diffusion of sovereignty, which resulted in the extension of its meaning and norms in the post-World War II period. This chapter will look at the other side of the coin: their agency in the limitations of sovereignty in the post-Cold War period, especially with the help of the norms of humanitarian intervention and, later, the Responsibility to Protect (R2P). Ramesh Thakur and Thomas Weiss argue that the responsibility to protect is "the most dramatic normative development of our time."[1] The R2P poses a special challenge to these theoretical debates about agency in norm diffusion. Because of its close association with human rights and humanitarian intervention debates that long preceded it, the R2P is often associated with Western political theory and agency. While some of the proponents of the norm vigorously deny that R2P reflects the traditional North–South faultline,[2] that perception endures in the developing world. The Canadian hand behind the creation of the commission that articulated the R2P norm, the International Commission on Intervention and State Sovereignty (ICISS), and the explicit linking by its then Foreign Minister Lloyd Axworthy of the R2P with other instruments of human security such as the International Criminal Court and the Ottawa Land Mines Treaty, has led to the identification of the R2P with a distinctive Western "freedom from fear" agenda, at the expense of broader elements of human security (including but not limited to "freedom from want"). A key argument of this chapter is to demonstrate the role of non-Western actors in contesting initial ideas about intervention and helping their eventual propagation through localization, subsidiarity, and circulation processes.

---

[1] Ramesh Thakur and Thomas G. Weiss, "R2P: From Idea to Norm – and Action?" *Global Responsibility to Protect* 1, no. 1 (2009), 23. It should be noted that Thakur was a member and Weiss was research director of the International Commission on Intervention and State Sovereignty (ICISS); hence they write from a strongly sympathetic perspective.

[2] Ibid., 35.

Humanitarian Intervention

The doctrine and practice of intervention is one of the fundamental issues of sovereignty and security in world politics.[3] The classical meaning of intervention is coercive interference by an outside power or powers in the domestic politics of another state. McFarlane specifies the military nature of the interference by defining intervention as "coercive military intrusion into an internal political conflict."[4] A somewhat similar definition is provided by Vertzberger who defines intervention as a "coercive, state organized and controlled, convention breaking, goal oriented activity in another sovereign state that is intended to affect either domestic political activity in the target state, or its political structure (preservation or change), or particular foreign policies of the target state by usurping its decision-making capabilities through the use of extensive military force."[5]

While intervention has been a persistent feature of international relations,[6] it is not an unchanging phenomenon. The logic of intervention (Table 4.1), including its rationale and principles, went through rapid and dramatic changes in the immediate aftermath of the Cold War. During the Cold War, the logic of intervention was mainly geopolitical, even when couched in the language of peace and humanitarianism. It was rooted in the bipolar structure of the world which encouraged geopolitical competition and made superpowers prone to intervention for

[3] For important studies of the concept of intervention, see: James N. Rosenau, "Intervention as a Scientific Concept," *Journal of Conflict Resolution* 134 (1969), 149–171; James N. Rosenau, "The Concept of Intervention," *Journal of International Affairs* 22, no. 2 (1968), 165–176; Richard Little, "Revisiting Intervention: A Survey of Recent Developments," *Review of International Studies* 13, no. 1 (1987), 49–60; Hedley Bull, ed., *Intervention in World Politics* (Oxford: Clarendon Press, 1986); R. J. Vincent, *Nonintervention and International Order* (Princeton University Press, 1974); Oran R. Young, "Intervention and International Systems," *Journal of International Affairs* 22, no. 2 (1968), 177–187.

[4] Neil McFarlane, *Intervention and Regional Security*, Adelphi Paper no. 196 (London: IISS, 1985).

[5] Yaacov Y. I. Vertzberger, "The Calculus of Foreign Military Intervention Decisions," Paper Prepared for the Annual Convention of the International Studies Association, London, March 28–April 1, 1989.

[6] "[W]hile particularly frequent during the Cold War, foreign military interventions are neither a new phenomenon, nor are they tied necessarily to any particular international system structure ... there does not appear to be any reason to believe that the future will be fundamentally different from the past. Five crucial factors conducive to foreign military intervention – opportunities, incentives, capabilities, weak prohibitions, and limited alternative strategies – are likely to persist, and potentially even be exacerbated, in the years ahead." Bruce W. Jentleson, Ariel E. Levite, and Larry Berman, "Foreign Military Intervention in Perspective," in *Foreign Military Intervention: The Dynamics of Protracted Conflict*, ed. Ariel E. Levite, Bruce W. Jentleson, and Larry Berman (New York: Columbia University Press, 1992), 319–320.

Table 4.1. *The changing logic of intervention*

Cold War intervention	Humanitarian intervention
National interest	Collective good
Geopolitical mind-sets	Humanitarian impulse
Access to raw materials	Without regard to material gain
Bloc ideology	Universal values (e.g. human rights)
Reputation and credibility as security guarantors	Legitimacy and image as part of international community
Bilateral or likeminded (coalition of the willing/coerced)	Multilateral/inclusive

resisting territorial advances by the rival bloc and/or for ideological reasons, which often required internal regime change.[7] The most important shift in the purposes of intervention in the post-Cold War era was the increasing demand for collective humanitarian intervention.[8] In 1991, then Secretary-General of the United Nations, Javier Perez de Cuellar, claimed, "we are clearly witnessing what is probably an irresistible shift in public attitudes towards the belief that the defense of the oppressed in the name of morality should prevail over frontiers and legal documents."[9] As one commentary in November 1992 put it: "In just a few years the idea has been established that countries which fail to care decently for their citizens dilute their claim to sovereignty and forfeit invulnerability to outside political-military intervention."[10] The US-led UN intervention in Somalia in 1992, which was deemed to be the key example of the changing purpose of intervention, prompted a Carnegie Endowment study to argue: "Perhaps the most frequently invoked purpose for collective military intervention in internal conflicts of all kinds will be to ensure the delivery of humanitarian assistance to civilian populations under siege."[11]

---

[7] Phil Williams, "Intervention in the Developing World: A Northern Perspective," in *Conflict and Consensus in South–North Security*, ed. C. Thomas (Cambridge University Press, 1989), 144–158.

[8] Cited in Richard N. Gardner, "International Law and the Use of Force," in *Three Views on the Issue of Humanitarian Intervention* (Washington, DC: United States Institute of Peace, 1992), 21.

[9] Ibid., 21.

[10] "Thanksgiving 1992," *The Washington Post*, November 26, 1992, www.washingtonpost .com/archive/opinions/1992/11/26/thanksgiving-1992/2be9f308-ff36-4f67-987a-a381ee67240f/?utm_term=.0b4727e10cf2.

[11] Morton H. Halperin and David J. Scheffer (with Patricia L. Small), *Self-Determination in the New World Order* (Washington, DC: Carnegie Endowment for International Peace, 1992), 107.

To a greater degree than the traditional notion of intervention, the meaning of humanitarian intervention is contested. Some, such as Sean Murphy, see humanitarian intervention as *"the threat or use of force* by a state, group of states, or international organization primarily for the purpose of protecting the nationals of the target state from widespread deprivations of internationally recognized human rights."[12] Others, such as Fernando Téson, allow for non-military forms of humanitarian intervention. Thus, humanitarian intervention is "proportionate transboundary help, *including forcible help,* provided by governments to individuals in another state who are being denied basic human rights and who themselves would be rationally willing to revolt against their oppressive government."[13] These differences notwithstanding, it is clear that while the traditional conception of intervention disregarded sovereignty if and when the national interests of the intervener were threatened, humanitarian intervention sanctions intervention even in the absence of clear violation of the national interests of the intervening party/ies.

Humanitarian intervention became one of the most important issues of contention in global order-building in the post-Cold War era, thanks partly to the differing responses of the international community to the crises of the 1990s, such as northern Iraq, Somalia, Africa's Great Lakes region, and the former Yugoslavia. Since these debates are well known, a brief summary here suffices.

The first had to do with the problem of separating national interest from the humanitarian impulse. "It will sometimes prove impossible," argued Halperin and Schefferin highlighting what had become obvious to both the proponents and critics of the new interventionist framework, "to separate the humanitarian from the political objectives of a collective

---

[12] Sean D. Murphy, *Humanitarian Intervention: The United Nations in an Evolving World Order* (Philadelphia: University of Pennsylvania Press, 1996), 11–12 (emphasis added).

[13] Fernando Téson, *Humanitarian Intervention: An Inquiry into Law and Morality,* 2nd edition (New York: Transnational, 1997), 208 (emphasis added). On other explications of humanitarian intervention during the early post-Cold War period, see Thomas G. Weiss and Kurt M. Campbell, "Military Humanitarianism," *Survival* 33, no. 5 (1991), 451–465; David J. Scheffer, R. N. Gardner, and G. B. Helman, eds., *Three Views on the Issue of Humanitarian Intervention* (Washington, DC: United States Institute of Peace, 1992), 21; Kelly Kate Pease and David P. Forsythe, "Human Rights, Humanitarian Intervention and World Politics," *Human Rights Quarterly* 15, no. 2 (1993), 307–308; Gene M. Lyons and Michael Mastanduno, eds., *Beyond Westphalia: State Sovereignty and International Intervention* (Baltimore and London: The Johns Hopkins University Press, 1995); Martha Finnemore, "Constructing Norms of Humanitarian Intervention," in *The Culture of National Security: Norms and Identity in World Politics,* ed. Peter J. Katzenstein (Ithaca: Cornell University Press, 1996), 153–185; Nicholas J. Wheeler, *Saving Strangers: Humanitarian Intervention in International Society* (New York: Oxford University Press, 2000); Martha Finnemore, *The Purpose of Intervention* (Ithaca: Cornell University Press, 2004).

military intervention."[14] Even in Somalia, where intervention was carried out to stop large-scale starvation, the principle of humanitarianism was not deemed to have been an absolute value and the principle of national interest was not totally insignificant in the calculus of intervention. During the Cold War Somalia was a strategic prize. The military base in Berbera was an integral part of US strategic planning for the Persian Gulf. While the value of these bases in Somalia had declined (not completely, however), other geopolitical factors remained. Five Western oil companies, Conoco, Chevron, Amoco, Phillips, and Agip, had concessions to search for oil covering more than half of Somalia's national territory. The chief of Conoco oil company in Somalia, Osman Hassan Ali, pointed to the "strategic value" of Somalia as a clear factor in US intervention, including oil, the threat of Islamic fundamentalism, and the future utility of military bases.[15]

Another point of controversy about humanitarian intervention had to do with the selectivity of the intervention. In Somalia, the UN Security Council's initial reluctance to intervene prompted the then UN Secretary-General Boutros Boutros-Ghali to accuse the West of hypocrisy when it came to dealing with Africa's crises as opposed to those in the Balkans. As one observer put it, "a naked double-standard was being applied by members more concerned with 'the rich man's war' in the former Yugoslavia."[16] Yet another point of controversy about humanitarian intervention was skepticism over the claims of its advocates about "principle displacing prudence."[17] The alleged humanitarian purpose behind such intervention was subject to the criteria of "doability." The so-called Powell Doctrine, named after the US Chairman of the Joint Chiefs of Staff, General Colin Powell, had stipulated that "America will intervene only if it can win decisively and with minimal losses through the introduction of overwhelming force."[18] Humanitarian intervention required a "clear, quickly attainable goal" to satisfy domestic public opinion.[19] Indeed, the "doability" criteria had been responsible for the George H. W. Bush administration's refusal to intervene in the Balkans, with its difficult terrain and well-armed and motivated opponents, in contrast to its intervention in

---

[14] Halperin and Scheffer (with Small), *Self-Determination in the New World Order*, 109.
[15] Geoffrey York, "Why US Really Cares about Saving Somalia," *The Globe and Mail*, January 27, 1993, A11.
[16] Jeffery Clark, "Debacle in Somalia," *Foreign Affairs* 72, no. 1 (1992–93), 116
[17] William Safire, "When to Use Force," *New York Times*, January 7, 1993, A13.
[18] Charles Krauthammer, "Drawing the Line at the Genocide," *Washington Post*, December 11, 1992, www.washingtonpost.com/archive/opinions/1992/12/11/drawing-the-line-at-genocide/09159898-b9f1-434b-b5d7-c0511943d4ce/?utm_term=.5d106920eb11.
[19] "It's Our Fight Now," *Newsweek*, December 14, 1992, 35.

1991 in northern Iraq, which has an easy terrain. As *The Economist* magazine would see it: "Armed intervention, even for simple humanitarian purposes, will always be carried out selectively, because in some places it will stand no chance of success."[20]

To sum up, while the logic of the new interventionist framework in the post-Cold War era was ostensibly different from that associated with the old, the purported shift from intervention on geopolitical grounds to intervention for humanitarian purposes not only remained incomplete, but was also mired in contradictions and dilemmas. These dilemmas would be succinctly described by the then UN Secretary-General Kofi Annan in 1999:

Nothing in the UN Charter precludes a recognition that there are rights beyond borders. What the Charter does say is that "armed force shall not be used, save in the common interest." But what is that common interest? Who shall define it? Who shall defend it? Under whose authority? And with what means of intervention?[21]

Origins of R2P

The international community's quest for answers to the questions posed by Annan would lead to the establishment of the International Commission on Intervention and State Sovereignty (ICISS), under a Canadian initiative in September 2000.[22] The commission released its report in December 2001, entitled *The Responsibility to Protect: Report of the International Commission on Intervention and State Sovereignty*.[23] The origin of the R2P is commonly associated with this document. In an interview in 2012, Gareth Evans, the co-chair of the ICISS, stated:

The "Responsibility to Protect" (R2P) was an idea born in 2001. The intention was to recast the language and substance of the debate: to change prevailing

---

[20] "World Cop," *The Economist*, December 19, 1992, 10.

[21] Kofi Annan, "Two Concepts of Sovereignty," *The Economist*, September 16, 1999.

[22] There is a growing literature on R2P. Recent contributions include, especially, Ramesh Thakur and William Maley, *Theorising the Responsibility to Protect* (Cambridge University Press, 2015); Alex Bellamy and Tim Dunne, *The Oxford Handbook of the Responsibility to Protect* (Oxford University Press, 2016); Charles T. Hunt, "Emerging Powers and the Responsibility to Protect: Non-Linear Norm Dynamics in Complex International Society," *Cambridge Review of International Affairs* 29, no. 2 (2016), 761–781.

[23] *The Responsibility to Protect: Report of the International Commission on Intervention and State Sovereignty* (Ottawa: International Development Research Centre, December 2001). Hereafter, cited as *The ICISS Report*.

mind sets, so the reaction to these catastrophic human rights violations taking place behind sovereign state walls would be that they are everyone's business.[24]

Yet, to mark 2001 as its point of origin would be to belie the complex genesis and agency behind the idea, as Evans himself would acknowledge. To some extent, the end of the Cold War, the liberal moment in international relations, and the global spread of human rights and democracy may be seen as elements of the changing normative structure of world politics that had rendered the emergence of R2P likely or even inevitable. The backdrop to the ICISS was the controversies surrounding the crises of the 1990s, including northern Iraq, Somalia, and Bosnia and the failure to intervene in Rwanda, as well as subsequent interventions in Kosovo (not authorized by the UN Security Council and undertaken by NATO) and East Timor (authorized by the Council, but undertaken by a "coalition of the willing"). The mandate of the ICISS was "to wrestle with the whole range of questions – legal, moral, operational and political – rolled up in this debate, to consult with the widest possible range of opinion around the world, and to bring back a report that would help the Secretary-General and everyone else find some new common ground."[25]

In reality, the commission's most important contribution may have been in pulling together several prior threads of the norm into a coherent whole. Indeed, it is not difficult to establish that the R2P idea had its origins in a wide variety of sources and contexts. The ICISS drew explicitly upon the Just War tradition, which holds that "sometimes, states can have moral justification for resorting to armed force."[26] The ICISS Report's six-fold criteria for intervention, namely right authority, just cause, right intention, last resort, proportional means, and reasonable prospects, directly mirror the *jus ad bellum* principles of the Just War Theory, which include just cause, right intention, proper authority, last resort, probability of success, and proportionality.[27] The Just War tradition has its roots in the Greco-Roman tradition, Christian ethics, and Western philosophy. The leading sources of this doctrine include Aristotle, Cicero, St. Augustine, St. Thomas Aquinas, Grotius, Suarez, Vattel, and Vitoria. The principles of Just War thinking had found their way into modern international law governing armed conflict, including the Hague and

---

[24] Gareth Evans, "Gareth Evans on 'Responsibility to Protect' after Libya," Interview with Alan Philps, *The World Today* 68, no. 8/9 (October 2012), www.chathamhouse.org/publications/twt/archive/view/186279.

[25] *The ICISS Report*, vii.

[26] "War," *Stanford Encyclopedia of Philosophy*, http://plato.stanford.edu/entries/war/.

[27] Ibid. See also Amitav Acharya, "Redefining the Dilemmas of Humanitarian Intervention," *Australian Journal of International Affairs* 56, no. 3 (2002), 373–381.

Geneva Conventions.[28] This makes it only natural that the R2P would be seen as a Western concept, no matter how strenuously its proponents would try to deny this claim.

But the R2P norm has a much wider genesis. Weiss identifies two "prior conceptual efforts" that "had broken new ground between state sovereignty and human rights and paved the way for *The Responsibility to Protect*."[29] The first was the work on internally displaced persons by Francis M. Deng at the Brookings Institution. The second was the views of Kofi Annan on sovereignty.

Before Deng became a senior fellow and founding director of the Africa Project at Brookings, he had earlier worked as a Human Rights Officer in the United Nations Secretariat (1967–1971). His other positions included being the Ambassador of the Sudan to Canada, Denmark, Finland, Norway, Sweden, and the United States. He was Sudan's Minister of State for Foreign Affairs during 1976–1980. Later, he would serve as the Representative of the United Nations Secretary-General on Internally Displaced Persons from 1994 to 2004.

Deng's work on internally displaced persons at the Brookings Institution led to the 1996 edited volume entitled *Sovereignty and Responsibility: Conflict Management in Africa*.[30] Both the title and the subtitle of this book are of significance, because they not only underscore the African context of the redefinition of sovereignty, but also give birth to the term that named the R2P norm. Roberta Cohen, who worked with Deng on internally displaced persons (IDPs),[31] suggests that the idea of

---

[28] "War," *Stanford Encyclopedia of Philosophy*. The best articulation of the Just War tradition is Michael Walzer, *Just and Unjust Wars: A Moral Argument with Historical Illustrations* (New York: Basic Books, 1977).

[29] Thomas G. Weiss, "The Responsibility to Protect (R2P) and Modern Diplomacy," in *The Oxford Handbook of Modern Diplomacy*, ed. Andrew F. Cooper, Jorge Heine, and Ramesh Thakur (Oxford University Press, 2013), 763–778.

[30] Francis M. Deng, Sadikiel Kimaro, Terrence Lyons, Donald Rothchild, and I. William Zartman, *Sovereignty as Responsibility: Conflict Management in Africa* (Washington, DC: Brookings Institution, 1996). See also: Francis M. Deng and I. William Zartman, eds., *Conflict Resolution in Africa* (Washington, DC: Brookings Institution, 1991); Francis M. Deng and Terrence Lyons, eds., *African Reckoning: A Quest for Good Governance* (Washington, DC: Brookings Institution, 1998); and Francis M. Deng, "Reconciling Sovereignty with Responsibility: A Basis for International Humanitarian Action," in *Africa in World Politics: Post-Cold War Challenges*, ed. John W. Harbeson and Donald Rothchild (Boulder, CO: Westview Press, 1995), 295–310.

[31] Roberta Cohen, "From Sovereign Responsibility to R2P," in *The Routledge Handbook of the Responsibility to Protect*, ed. W. Andy Knight and Frazer Egerton (Abingdon: Routledge, 2012). In a telephone conversation on November 15, 2013, Deng himself told this author of the collaborative origins of "responsible sovereignty," sharing credit with other members of the Brookings Project on Sovereignty as Responsibility.

responsible sovereignty had much to do with the issue of IDPs, especially in Africa.[32]

The word "responsible" in "responsible sovereignty" implied not only the responsibility of the state to its citizens. It also meant Africa's responsibility for addressing African problems. Thus,

> sovereignty as responsibility meant that the state had to take care of its citizens and – if it needed support – call on the sub-regional, regional or continental organizations, or ultimately the international community. But if it did not do that, and its people were suffering and dying, the world would not watch and do nothing. They would find a way of getting involved.[33]

For Deng, seeking African solutions to the continent's problems was both a moral and practical necessity because of changing geopolitical circumstances. As he put it:

> During the Cold War, as we all know, we used to look at regional and even internal conflicts as proxy wars of the superpowers. And they were to be managed – sometimes resolved, sometimes aggravated – by the superpowers. With the end of the Cold War the superpowers withdrew, and we had to begin to see the conflicts in their proper context – as regional or internal. This was a positive development; they were no longer distorted as proxy wars. But by the same token we had to reapportion responsibility; we could no longer depend on the superpowers as their interests were no longer involved. We had to find internal solutions, whether domestic or sub-regional or continent-wide.[34]

Deng was not the sole inventor of the concept of responsible sovereignty, and there is some uncertainty as to how the exact phrase originated.[35] But he became the real face of the idea.[36] He was a "norm entrepreneur" par excellence. In selling the idea around the world, he would underplay the intervention part. Instead of saying "Protect human rights, or else," he would say, "I am here to help you, if you want to avoid outside intervention; protect the rights of your people, or don't abuse them." As he would put it, "the only threat to governments posed by the

---

[32] Roberta Cohen and Francis M. Deng, *Masses in Flight: The Global Crisis of Internal Displacement* (Washington, DC: Brookings Institution Press, 2012); Roberta Cohen and Francis M. Deng, eds., *The Forsaken People: Case Studies of the Internally Displaced* (Washington, DC: Brookings Institution Press, 2010).

[33] Francis M. Deng, "Idealism and Realism Negotiating Sovereignty in Divided Nations," Presented at the 2010 Dag Hammarskjöld Lecture at the Dag Hammarskjöld Foundation, Uppsala, Sweden, 2010, 13.

[34] Ibid.

[35] In a telephone conversation on November 15, 2013, Deng told this author that "responsible sovereignty" was the product of his collaboration with others at Brookings.

[36] One of his close associates (who declined to be named) told me that Deng was a "wonderful spokesperson," a "terrific salesman" for the idea.

idea of sovereignty as responsibility was when they failed to discharge their responsibilities."[37]

The term "responsible sovereignty" is without question the source of the "responsibility to protect norm." This was recognized by the ICISS's initiator, Canadian External Affairs Minister Lloyd Axworthy, and after a noticeable delay, the ICISS co-chair, Gareth Evans.[38] Hence Deng and his collaborators affirmed the view that "those governments that do not fulfill their responsibilities to their people forfeit their sovereignty. In effect, the authors redefine sovereignty as the responsibility to protect the people in a given territory."[39]

But Deng was not the only African behind the R2P idea. The second precursor to the R2P doctrine, as hinted above, was Kofi Annan. As noted, Annan's predecessor, and the first UN Secretary-General from Africa, Boutros Boutros-Ghali had "argued forcefully for humanitarian intervention in Somalia, Liberia, and Burundi, [and had] castigated western powers for focusing disproportionate attention on 'rich men's wars' in the Balkans while neglecting Africa's more numerous conflicts, and advocated the use of regional security arrangements to lighten the UN's heavy peacekeeping burden."[40] As Annan put it in his aforementioned 1999 article:

State sovereignty, in its most basic sense, is being redefined … States are now widely understood to be instruments at the service of their peoples, and not vice versa … When we read the Charter today, we are more than ever conscious that its aim is to protect individual human beings, not to protect those who abuse them.[41]

The fact that Deng and Annan were both from Africa should not be regarded as a coincidence, as most writings on R2P seem to do. The African context is also important because there are no comparable instances of intellectuals and policymakers from the Balkans, the other major theater of major conflict and genocide, offering similar visions and

[37] Francis Deng, "JISB Interview: The Responsibility to Protect," *Journal of Intervention and Statebuilding* 4, no. 1 (2010), 83.

[38] Lloyd Axworthy, *Navigating a New World: Canada's Global Future* (Toronto: Alfred A. Knopf, 2003), 414. Gareth Evans has made clear this historical link in *The Responsibility to Protect: Halting Mass Atrocity Crimes Once and for All* (Washington, DC: Brookings Institution, 2008).

[39] Amitai Etzioni, "Sovereignty as Responsibility," *Orbis* 50, no. 1 (Winter 2006), accessed December 23, 2012, www.gwu.edu/~ccps/etzioni/documents/A347a-SoverigntyasResponsibility-orbis.pdf.

[40] Adekeye Adebajo and Chris Landsberg, "The Heirs of Nkrumah: Africa's New Interventionists," *Pugwash Occasional Papers* 2, no. 1 (January 2001), accessed July 5, 2011, www.pugwash.org/reports/rc/como_africa.htm.

[41] Annan, "Two Concepts of Sovereignty."

ideas or getting involved in debates that fed into the R2P doctrine. But the African context and norm entrepreneurship would be clearer when the ICISS was set up. Sensitive to the prevailing divisions among Western and developing countries ("industrialized countries more enthusiastic in principle, developing countries more wary about providing a rationale for outside interventions"[42]) over the issue of humanitarian intervention, Canada as the Commission's sponsor deliberately sought to balance the representation in the commission. This suggests that the prospects for resistance and rejection by the developing countries were an important factor behind the commission's composition. Gareth Evans from Australia and Mohamed Sahnoun from Algeria were appointed as co-chairs, while four of its ten other members were from the developing world. These were Cyril Ramaphosa (South Africa), Fidel Ramos (Philippines), Eduardo Stein (Guatemala), and Ramesh Thakur (India) from the South. The other members of the commission were Vladimir Lukin (Russia), Giséle Côté-Harper (Canada), Lee Hamilton (USA), Michael Ignatieff (Canada), Klaus Naumann (Germany), and Cornelio Sommaruga (Switzerland).

The co-chair of the commission, Sahnoun, was an Algerian diplomat who had served, amongst other posts, as Advisor to the President of Algeria, Deputy Secretary-General of the Organization of African Unity (OAU), Deputy Secretary-General of the League of Arab States in charge of the Arab–Africa dialogue, Special Envoy of the UN Secretary-General on the Ethiopian/Eritrean conflict, Joint Representative of the UN and the OAU in the Great Lakes Region and Central Africa, and Special Representative of the UN to Somalia. Sahnoun maintained that his experience with both the AU and the UN was crucial to his advocacy of R2P.[43] Later, in a statement that clearly evokes the role of an "insider proponent" in the theory of "constitutive localization" (Chapter 2),

---

[42] Ramesh Thakur and Thomas G. Weiss, "R2P: From Idea to Norm – and Action?" *Global Responsibility to Protect* 1, no. 1 (2009), 35.

[43] Speaking of his own background, Sahnoun observes: "I started my career with the African Union and immediately I found myself involved in conflict resolutions. In the 1960s and 1970s, many African countries became independent states. Quickly they found themselves confronted with border problems. The [frontiers] had been traced by the colonial powers, and these did not take into account socio-cultural factors, ethnicity, and so on. It became urgent to find solutions and to convince the different countries to avoid conflict and eventually to respect the borders as they had been established by the colonial powers. Gradually, we arrived at agreements where the African countries accepted the borders such as they were, but also respecting minorities. Then came internal conflicts. Here we had to implement mediation and try to find a solution. It started with Biafra, and then it went on from there. I gained experience that proved itself to be very useful later, and therefore the successive Secretary-Generals of the United Nations called on me so that I could take care of these problems." "A distinguished peacemaker

he described the African context and contribution to the making of the R2P in the following words:

For Africans, the vow to which our leaders subscribed in 2005 was not new. Five years earlier they had already adopted the norm of non-indifference to mass atrocities in the African Union's Constitutive Act. The idea itself of "sovereignty as responsibility" was developed by the Sudanese scholar and diplomat, Francis Deng. And, unlike other regions, our legal systems have long acknowledged that in addition to individuals, groups and leaders having rights, they also have reciprocal duties. So the responsibility to protect is in many ways an African contribution to human rights.[44]

By all accounts, Sahnoun turned out to be a very influential member of the commission. Someone intimately involved with the working of the commission says that: "Sahnoun was really the main voice [of the Global South], and a very wise one." While the commission made every effort to transcend the North–South divide, "the views of the global South ... were integrated into the commission." Here, Sahnoun played the key role. "When Sahnoun spoke and said 'this will not wash,' that was the end of the story ... His voice always put on the brakes, but he also is a partisan of rights (having himself been tortured by the French)."[45]

The African context of the R2P norm becomes even more apparent when one takes into consideration the changing role of the OAU and the position of several key African leaders in calling for the redefinition of sovereignty as tragic events unfolded in the continent in the 1990s. These included more than a dozen civil wars of which the economic and human security impact was extremely high, and which the international community including the UN had failed to address. As two noted African specialists, Adekeye Adebajo and Chris Landsberg, put it, even though Somalia had been a major turning point in the emergence of the idea of humanitarian intervention:

After the *débâcle* in Somalia in October 1993 with the killing of 18 American soldiers, UN peacekeepers were forced to withdraw from the Horn of Africa. Since then, the UN Security Council has shown great reluctance to sanction interventions in Africa, turning down requests for missions to Burundi, Congo-Brazzaville and Liberia. The Security Council shamefully failed to act in the

---

in the United Nations – Ambassador Mohamed Sahnoun," *divainternational.ch*, accessed December 23, 2012, http://divainternational.ch/spip.php?article24.

[44] Mohamed Sahnoun, "Uphold Continent's Contribution to Human Rights," July 21, 2009, accessed May 3, 2013, http://allafrica.com/stories/200907210549.html?viewall=1.

[45] Personal correspondence with the author, December 21, 2012.

clear case of genocide against 800,000 people in Rwanda between April and June 1994.[46]

Partly as a response to this perceived neglect and double-standard (Boutros-Ghali's point), and inaction by the international community, in 1993, the OAU established a Mechanism for Conflict Prevention, Management, and Resolution which stressed the prevention of conflicts rather than peacekeeping, and sought to develop military and political instruments like the sixteen-member OAU Central Organ and its Conflict Management Center to improve the OAU's military effectiveness and provide better political analysis of conflict situations. The OAU was involved in a number of small-scale interventions, such as a Military Observer Team (MOT) to Rwanda in April 1991, a 67-strong Observer Mission in Burundi (OMIB) deployed between February and October 1994, and an Observer Mission to the Comoros Islands (OMIC) in August 1997.[47] Then there were also Nigerian-led ECOMOG interventions in civil wars in Liberia (August 1990–July 1997 and August–October 2003), Sierra Leone (February 1998–October 1999), Guinea Bissau (June 1998–April 1999), and Côte d'Ivoire (September 2002–February 2004).[48] While some of these interventions were spurred by mixed motives including the strategic and political interests of the African leaders directly affected by these conflicts, they were also inspired by "humanitarian considerations of saving lives and rescuing citizens."[49]

Even before the ICISS was set up, key African leaders in South Africa and Nigeria had openly called for a redefinition of sovereignty. Although they were neither the first nor the only ones, they were certainly among the earliest advocates of such intervention in the developing world. What was especially striking was that traditionally the dominant political ethos in Africa had been to preserve sovereignty and reject intervention,

[46] Adebajo and Landsberg, "The Heirs of Nkrumah." The authors trace the origins of the interventionist impulse to Ghana's nationalist leader Kwame Nkrumah, who had called for the establishment of an African High Command, a collective intervention force. But Nkrumah's force was meant to be used to advance African liberation from colonial rule and protection from foreign intervention, rather than for humanitarian purposes of the kind (genocide, crimes against humanity) that the contemporary African leaders and the R2P proponents are concerned with, where the perpetrators could be African leaders themselves.

[47] Adebajo and Landsberg, "The Heirs of Nkrumah."

[48] William Agyapong, "Military Intervention in Intrastate Conflicts in West Africa: Economic Community of West African States Monitoring Group as a Case Study," A Thesis Presented to the Faculty of the US Army Command and General Staff College in partial fulfillment of the requirements for the degree Master of Military Art and Science, Fort Leavenworth, Kansas, 2005, accessed December 24, 2012, www.dtic.mil/cgi-bin/GetTRDoc?AD=ADA436459.

[49] Adebajo and Landsberg, "The Heirs of Nkrumah."

although much of it was directed against outside power intervention. At an OAU meeting in Kampala in 1991, Nigerian President Olusegun Obasanjo exhorted: "An urgent aspect of security need is a re-definition of the concept of security and sovereignty ... we must ask why does sovereignty seem to confer absolute immunity on any government who [sic] commits genocide and monumental crimes ..."[50] In a similar vein, Uganda's Yoweri Museveni noted at the same meeting: "Sovereignty became a sacred cow and many crimes have been committed in its name ... If the European countries can surrender some of their sovereignty for greater development, African states can similarly surrender some of their sovereignty for greater security, both at the intra and interstate levels."[51] At the OAU summit in Ouagadougou in 1998, South African President Nelson Mandela told his fellow leaders: "Africa has a right and a duty to intervene to root out tyranny ... we must all accept that we cannot abuse the concept of national sovereignty to deny the rest of the continent the right and duty to intervene when behind those sovereign boundaries, people are being slaughtered to protect tyranny."[52] The same year, the OAU Secretary-General, Salim Ahmed Salim of Tanzania, argued that: "We should talk about the need for accountability of governments and of their national and international responsibilities. In the process, we shall be redefining sovereignty."[53] As Adebajo and Landsberg put it, "These views are revolutionary in the non-interventionist and sovereignty-obsessed context of African diplomacy in the first three decades of independence."[54]

While discussing agency, one might wonder whether the emergence of the R2P had anything to do with US leadership or advocacy. During the George W. Bush administration, some of its senior officials like Richard Haass, who was the Director of Policy Planning at the State Department during its first term, and Douglas Feith, the Under-Secretary of Defense for Policy, justified the invasion of Iraq by citing the diminishing importance of state sovereignty in the face of human suffering.[55] But this

---

[50] Ibid.

[51] Ibid.

[52] Ibid.

[53] Ibid. See also: Matthew Omolesky, "Firing into a Continent," *The American Spectator*, May 2, 2011, accessed December 24, 2012, https://spectator.org/37692_firing-continent/.

[54] Adebajo and Landsberg, "The Heirs of Nkrumah."

[55] Bellamy calls Haass "a key advocate of the American conception of sovereignty as responsibility," while not justifying the US invasion of Iraq under the pretext of R2P. Alex J. Bellamy, *Responsibility to Protect: The Global Effort to End Mass Atrocities* (Cambridge, UK: Polity Press, 2009), 24. In a speech to the International Institute for Strategic Studies on September 13, 2002, Haass traced the "departure from the traditional notion of near-absolute sovereignty" in three stages. First, Rwanda triggered and Kosovo upheld

cannot be seriously viewed as a contribution to the R2P, but rather as a self-serving and unconvincing argument which might have impeded the promotion of the norm.[56] The R2P was a convenient pretext for the invasion of Iraq, after the earlier justifications, such as WMDs and Iraq's link with terrorism, had failed to convince the international community. A more persuasive link between US policy and R2P has been made by Roberta Cohen, who has traced the genesis of the norm to the human rights promotion efforts of the Carter administration.[57] Cohen's argument is understandable, since she was part of the Carter administration's human rights team and was closely connected with human rights advocacy groups. And the link between human rights and R2P is an obvious

---

the belief that "sovereignty should only provide immunity from intervention if the government upholds basic, minimum standards of domestic conduct and human rights." 9/11 was the second stage; it was not a whole new development, but merely "accelerated new thinking that had already begun about the limits of sovereignty," and "expanded the circumstances in which most countries condoned external intervention in the affairs of a state" by adding terrorism to the list of triggers. The impending action against Iraq, Haass argued, would constitute "a third adjustment" to this evolving thinking about sovereignty, whereby classical notions of deterrence and containment had little effect in countering groups like al-Qaeda or Saddam Hussein. Saddam, argued Haass, was "someone who has repeatedly violated his international obligations and who is doing everything in his power to develop and conceal weapons of mass destruction." In view of his "history of violence against his neighbors and his own people ... and his aggressive pursuit of nuclear and other weapons," and in the "new international environment where terrorism and WMD are intersecting," "a strong case can be made for preventive military action." Richard N. Haass, "Reflections a Year after September 11," Remarks to International Institute for Strategic Studies' 2002 Annual Conference, September 13, 2002, accessed February 17, 2006, www.cfr.org/publication/5098/reflections_a_ year_after_september_11.html. In a speech in 2005, Feith asserted that: "Sovereignty means not just a country's right to command respect for its independence, but also the duty to take responsibility for what occurs on one's territory, and, in particular, to do what it takes to prevent one's territory from being used as a base for attacks against others." Douglas J. Feith, Under-Secretary of Defense for Policy, "Speech to the Council on Foreign Relations," US Department of Defense: Office of the Assistant Secretary of Defense, February 17, 2005, accessed February 17, 2006, www.defenselink. mil/transcripts/2005/tr20050217-2127.html. While Haass' statement was made at a time when the administration was already giving serious thought to invading Iraq, Feith's was clearly a post-facto rationalization of the invasion of Iraq.

[56] Weiss puts it aptly: "as the 'weapons of mass destruction' (WMDs) justification for the war fell apart and claims of close links between Saddam's regime and al-Qaeda also proved spurious, the coalition of the willing – with Washington and London as the main belligerents – began to apply *ex post facto* humanitarian language and even R2P as the main justification for their actions in Iraq. Richard Haass, the former director of the policy planning unit in the US State Department and president of the Council on Foreign Relations, spoke of sovereignty as responsibility and argued that when states fail to discharge their responsibility to fight terrorism: "America will act – ideally with partners, but alone if necessary – to hold them accountable ... Human protection was an all-too-transparent rationalization." Weiss, "The Responsibility to Protect (R2P) and Modern Diplomacy," 770.

[57] Cohen, "From Sovereign Responsibility to R2P," 7–21.

and important one. But it seems to be a stretch to link R2P retroactively with the Carter administration.[58] But the R2P had little to do with US leadership and norm entrepreneurship.

The ICISS's primary goal was to establish clear rules, procedures, and criteria of humanitarian intervention, especially those related to the decision to intervene, its timing, and its modalities. The report thus aims to make humanitarian intervention not only legitimate, but also more efficient. Last but not least, the report seeks to address the root causes of conflict and advance long-term peace.

Although not short of concrete policy proposals, the report's most significant contribution was in the conceptual domain. *The Responsibility to Protect* redefined humanitarian intervention as a responsibility (first, of the state concerned, and failing that, of the international community), and not a right (of outsiders, however they may represent the international community at large). In the aftermath of the 1991 Gulf War, for example, French Foreign Minister Roland Dumas had asserted that the international community had a "right to intervene" to alleviate human suffering caused by repression, civil disorder, inter-state conflict, or natural disasters.[59] *The Responsibility to Protect* found the phrase "right to intervene" unhelpful, because it stressed "the claims, rights and prerogatives of the potentially intervening states" over "the urgent needs of the potential beneficiaries of action,"[60] and because it failed to capture the broader tasks of prevention and follow-up peacebuilding that must accompany intervention. Under the new framework, the decision to intervene would be made from the point of view of those needing support and not those providing it. And protection would carry a broader meaning than intervention; implying not just an obligation to react, but also equally important and parallel obligations to prevent and rebuild.

Another key feature of the report was its firm insistence that humanitarian intervention was to be "an exceptional and extraordinary" measure. Two kinds of events were specified as triggers for intervention: large-scale loss of life and ethnic cleansing. Going by these criteria, natural disasters, democratic breakdowns, or conflicts that do not produce "serious and

---

[58] It is worth noting that Cohen began her association with Brookings in 1994, and continued in various capacities (Africa Fellow and Visiting Fellow (1994–2001), Co-Director of the Brookings–LSE Project on Internal Displacement (1996–2001), Senior Fellow (2001–2007), and Non-Resident Senior Fellow (2007–2016)). She worked with Deng on IDPs and continued to stress the responsible sovereignty idea. See her profile at: www.brookings.edu/experts/roberta-cohen/ (accessed October 29, 2016).

[59] Cited in Thomas G. Weiss and Kurt Campbell, "Military Humanitarianism," *Survival* 33, no. 5 (September–October 1991), 452.

[60] *The ICISS Report*, 16.

irreparable harm" to human beings would not justify the violation of sovereignty by the international community.

The report did not argue against the salience of state sovereignty as the basic organizing principle of international relations. (It helped, however, to greatly inform the reader on the debate over sovereignty, thanks to an excellent overview of the concept and challenges to it that appears in the research essays that accompany the report in a CD-ROM.) Instead, it found that the presumed tension between state sovereignty and humanitarian intervention was often exaggerated. Sovereignty "does still matter."[61] However, sovereignty was to be taken not as a right, but as a responsibility. The "primary responsibility for the protection of its people lies with the state itself." But if states were to be found unwilling or incapable of living up to that responsibility, or were willingly causing grave harm to their own people, the responsibility to protect shifted to the international community. Since the primary responsibility of "protecting" people lay with their governments, their unwillingness and/or inability to offer such protection could be construed as a legitimate trigger for international intervention.

No other policy document had gone further in specifying the criteria for humanitarian intervention. The report set down six specific and important conditions: right authority, just cause, right intention, last resort, proportional means, and reasonable prospects. The first two of these stipulations were notable not so much because of what they include as grounds for intervention as for what they purposely exclude. In defining "just cause" the report excluded intervention to restore democracy or to stop human rights abuses that do not entail large-scale killing and ethnic cleansing, and intervention by states to protect their nationals in foreign territory. "Right intention" was similarly limited to alleviation of acute human suffering rather than alteration of boundaries or even supporting claims of self-determination. Outright overthrow of oppressive regimes would not be justified, while destroying their ability to cause harm to their own people would. This was an important distinction. As with just cause, this criterion, along with the stipulation of multilateralism as a key indicator of right intention, would make humanitarian intervention less ideological and hence controversial. For example, humanitarian intervention thus defined could be usefully separated from the West's ideologically charged democratic "enlargement" campaign. Going by the right intention criterion, a unilateral US military intervention in Iraq would be unjustified, even if the Bush administration advanced a moral purpose

---

[61] Ibid., 7.

("axis of evil") behind this move. Countries such as China would have less justification in opposing humanitarian intervention as a US ploy to advance its ideological interests.

The report did not set any figures as to what constitutes "large-scale" casualties. It would be unfair to cite this as a failing of the report, but it does mean that the "one cold blooded question ... how many dead and dying are enough to require intervention?"[62] remained unresolved. While the just cause and right intention criteria would reduce the controversy about humanitarian intervention by sharply distinguishing it from political motives, drawing such distinctions in real life was not going to be easy. What about democratic breakdowns accompanied by a large-scale loss of life? In such complex situations, intervention might be justified, but the report's efforts to separate the humanitarian rationale from political ones would be compromised. The report acknowledged the possibility of "mixed motives"[63] behind intervention decisions. Demands for self-determination could still be grounds for intervention if suppression of such demand by a government led to large-scale loss of life and ethnic cleansing. In such a situation, however, could the intervening members of the international community limit themselves to saving lives without getting implicated in the political aspirations of the victims?

The "last resort" principle was described as a point marked by the failure of negotiations to achieve compromise due to intransigence of one or both parties accompanied by the prospects for imminent violence. "Proportional means" implied a minimalism in terms of the scale, intensity, and duration of military action, all of which must be commensurate with the provocation. This entailed ensuring a minimal impact on the target country's political system and strict observance of international humanitarian law. "Reasonable prospects" here was defined in terms not of the defeat of a state, but of a tangible chance of success in stopping or avoiding the atrocities and suffering that acted as a trigger for the intervention. This criterion was a reminder of the so-called "doability" principle, a corollary of the "Powell Doctrine" of the early 1990s, which contributed to the US decision to avoid intervention in Bosnia. Actions that stand no chance of offering protection or which could aggravate an existing crisis were to be avoided.

One key issue remained unresolved here: how was one to assess the chances of success or failure of humanitarian intervention or its potential to be counter-productive? Without a clear sense of this, "Armed

---

[62] "It's Our Fight Now," *Newsweek*, December 14, 1992, 35.
[63] *The ICISS Report*, 36.

intervention, even for simple humanitarian purposes, would always be carried out selectively, because in some places it will stand no chance of success."[64]

The "right authority" criterion, key to the legitimacy of humanitarian intervention, was deemed to be important enough to deserve treatment in a separate chapter. The UN was designated as the most appropriate authority, the chief "applicator of legitimacy" in humanitarian interventions. While acknowledging its limitations and imperfections, the report left "absolutely no doubt" that the Security Council remained the best place for authorizing humanitarian intervention. The task of the report was not to seek alternatives to the Council, but to make that mechanism work better. The report mandates Council approval in all cases of intervention while urging it to act promptly on such requests. The document made a plea for a "code of conduct" for the Permanent Five to govern the use of the veto in intervention decisions, calling on the P-5 not to resort to the veto where their vital national interests are not involved (e.g. China in relation to the renewal of the UN force in Macedonia), and to resort to "constructive abstention."

This was a crucial issue. The prospects of a global consensus on humanitarian intervention would be critically dependent on the kind of reform to the Security Council veto that the report itself advocated. It might have been helpful for the report to have spelled out the principles and modalities that could be included in the proposed "code of conduct." But its decision not to do so reflected a pragmatic realization that there existed no imminent prospects of gaining the consent of the P-5 in reforming the Charter to prevent the capricious use of the veto. What would happen if the Security Council failed to act? The report recommended going to the General Assembly under the "Uniting for Peace" procedures. (The extreme rarity of resort to this procedure raised questions about how practical this suggestion would be in the event of strong opposition from one or more members of the P-5.) Action by regional or sub-regional organizations found less favor. Regional bodies might have a better understanding of the conflict and a greater stake in their neighborhoods returning to peace (although this has not always been true). But their interest in, and capacity for, intervention would be limited. Sovereignty concerns, and fear of being subjected to similar intervention in the future once a precedent had been set, would be a major inhibiting factor. Most regional organizations – NATO being the clear exception – lacked the resources to undertake collective military action even under

---

[64] "World Cop," *The Economist*, December 19, 1992, 10.

the most urgent provocation. The problems encountered by the OAU in Chad and ASEAN's failure to intervene in East Timor offer good examples of such resource constraints.

Intervention by a regional organization in a non-member state was a far more controversial enterprise, as demonstrated in NATO's intervention in Kosovo. The report acknowledged the problematic nature of this intervention. But its language carried enough ambiguity to lend justification to the questionable US view that the intervention was justified in view of the possibility of a spill-over of the Kosovo conflict to neighboring NATO member states. In general, the report took an ambiguous stand on the role of ad hoc coalitions – the so-called "coalitions of the willing" – in undertaking humanitarian intervention. It endorsed intervention by ad hoc coalitions with the approval of the Security Council: duly authorized by the Council, "a multinational coalition of allies can offer a more credible and efficient military force when robust action was needed and warranted."[65] But even here, the speed and efficiency of an intervention would not guarantee its legitimacy. And what of interventions by ad hoc coalitions undertaken without Security Council authorization? *The Responsibility to Protect* argued that a coalition-of-the-willing approach would be better than inaction by the Security Council, especially in the face of acute humanitarian crises. It acknowledged that such interventions "do not ... find wide favour"[66] in the international community. The parties to the Kosovo intervention were willing to "acknowledge its highly exceptional character"[67] and would have preferred Security Council authorization. If so, then the tepid discussion of the commission against such interventions, reflecting perhaps sharp divisions within the panel over this issue, was one of the main failings of the report. Even those who strongly believe in the cause of humanitarian intervention, including this author, find the "coalition of the willing" approach undesirable and controversial because of its questionable basis in international law, and because such interventions are usually dominated by powerful states. By not insisting on severe qualifications on such approaches, the report undermined the commission's seemingly genuine desire to separate humanitarian intervention from the ideological and geopolitical interests of the great powers. Could the international community be reasonably assured that P-5 members would not manipulate the process of Security Council authorization so as to make a coalition-of-the-willing approach dominated by

---

[65] Ibid., 52.
[66] Ibid., 54.
[67] Ibid.

one or more among them more likely, especially where the latter might serve their geopolitical interests?

The final part of *The Responsibility to Protect* devoted itself to operational principles that would enhance the efficiency of humanitarian intervention and reduce the chances of mistakes and mishaps that might be politically costly. Here, the focus was on the importance of clear objectives, the need for an unambiguous mandate, and the availability of adequate resources. An important aspect of the report's recommendation was that the intervening authorities should not be guided by force protection as their principal objective, and that they should accept limitations on the use of force and proportionality of retaliation against threats. Unity of command, interoperability among multinational forces, and good communications among them were stressed as being key to the success of humanitarian intervention.

Responses to R2P: Localization and Circulation

The R2P attracted a decidedly mixed response from the developing world. Some remained unconvinced that the implementation of the recommendations of the report would change the basic reality that the developing countries would still have precious little say over the Security Council decisions to intervene. Those engaging in humanitarian intervention are most likely to be advanced countries, and those who are its target are most likely to be developing countries. R2P-based humanitarian intervention will remain the prerogative of the strong against the weak; it can never be attempted against powerful states. The report recognized this reality but dismisses it: "the reality that interventions may not be able to be mounted in every case where there is justification for doing so, is no reason for them not to be mounted in the first place."[68] However, without adequate Security Council reform, it might be difficult to separate the responsibility to protect from great power self-interest.

The report of the commission was sidelined by the September 11 attacks on the United States and the consequent preoccupation of the international community over the US-led global war on terror, which severely damaged multilateralism. The war on terror reinstated strategic intervention ahead of the humanitarian variety, notwithstanding the United States's belated and self-serving justification offered by the Bush administration that its invasion of Iraq was a humanitarian action (as it became clearer that evidence could not be found to support the

---

[68] *The ICISS Report*, 37.

Table 4.2. *Selected initial responses to R2P*

CHINA: "[T]he concept of the 'responsibility to protect' should be understood and applied correctly. At present, there are still various understandings and interpretations about this concept by many member states. Therefore the Security Council should refrain from invoking the concept of 'the responsibility to protect.' Still less should the concept be abused ... [T]he responsibility to protect civilians lies primarily with the Governments of the countries concerned. While the international community and other external parties can provide support and assistance and urge the parties concerned seriously to implement the provisions of humanitarian law and to avoid harming civilians, they should not infringe upon the sovereignty and territorial integrity of the countries concerned, nor should they enforce intervention by circumventing the Governments of such countries."

INDONESIA: "We need a consensus on the responsibility to protect people from genocide, ethnic cleansing and crimes against humanity. To this end, force should be used only when all other means have failed."

MALAYSIA: "Actions must be in accordance with the respect for the sovereignty and territorial integrity of states as well as observing the principle of non-interference."

BOTSWANA: "We embrace the concept of 'responsibility to protect.'"

GHANA: "We hold the view that in the event of the failure by both governments and armed groups to abide by their commitments under international humanitarian law, conventions and agreements, it behooves the United Nations to intervene and protect innocent populations against such crimes as genocide, ethnic cleansing and other gross human rights violations."

NIGERIA: "[The t]ime has come for the international community to reexamine when it is its responsibility to protect, without prejudice to the sovereignty of Member States. Genocide, ethnic cleansing and crimes committed against unarmed civilians in situations of conflict are grim reminders that the time is right for the international community to determine when to exercise its responsibility to protect."

ZIMBABWE: "The vision that we must present for a future United Nations should not be one filled with vague concepts that provide an opportunity for those states that seek to interfere in the internal affairs of other states. Concepts such as 'humanitarian intervention' and the 'responsibility to protect' need careful scrutiny in order to test the motives of their proponents."[1]

ARGENTINA: "[T]he responsibility to protect civilians in conflict is a central principle of humanity that must be depoliticized and transformed into joint action of Security Council members and international organzsations."

MEXICO: "We all know that the debate about the responsibility to protect is interlinked with the fundamental principles of international law. Despite the consensus reached in 2005, we cannot deny that mistrust prevails on this matter. While some States see in this new principle the mere continuance of interventionist practices aimed at destabilizing political regimes, others promote its application in a selective manner, limiting its scope to cases significant for their political interests."

VENEZUELA: "Today we claim from the peoples, in this case the people of Venezuela, a new international economic order, but it is also eminently a new international political order, let's not allow a handful of countries try to reinterpret with impunity the principles of the International Law to give way to doctrines like 'Preemptive War,' how do they threaten us with preemptive war!, and the now so called 'Responsibility to Protect,' but we have to ask ourselves who is going to protect us, how are they going to protect us."[2]

(cont.)

Table 4.2. (*cont.*)

---

[1]President R. G. Mugabe, World Summit General Assembly, 60th Session, September 14–16, 2005.
[2]President Hugo Chavez Frías, World Summit General Assembly, 60th Session, September 14–16, 2005.
Sources: New York: International Coalition for the Responsibility to Protect, Institute for Global Policy: "Government Statements on the Responsibility to Protect Asia-Pacific Region, 2005–2007," accessed April 19, 2015, http://responsibilitytoprotect.org/R2P%20 Government%20statements%20Asia%20Pacific%202005-2007.pdf; "Government Statements on the Responsibility to Protect Africa Region 2005–2008," accessed April 19, 2015, http://www.responsibilitytoprotect.org/files/Govt%20Statements%20 2005-2007--Africa%20pdf.pdf; "Government Statements on the Responsibility to Protect Latin-America Region 2005–2007," accessed April 19, 2015, http://www .responsibilitytoprotect.org/files/R2P%20Government%20statements%20Latin%20 America%202005-2007.pdf.

war's original rationale, the Iraqi possession of WMDs). More important, American decision-making leading to the attack on Iraq violated almost every criterion of humanitarian intervention laid down by the R2P (which mirror the traditional principles of the "just war" doctrine), including: "right authority," "just cause," "right intention," "last resort," "proportional means," and "reasonable prospects." But the principle of R2P received a new boost in the 2004 Report of the Secretary-General's High-Level Panel on Threats, Challenges and Change. The panelists

endorsed the emerging norm that there is a collective international responsibility to protect, exercisable by the Security Council authorizing military intervention as a last resort, in the event of genocide and other large-scale killing, ethnic cleansing or serious violations of international humanitarian law which sovereign Governments have proved powerless or unwilling to prevent.

The criteria specified by the report to justify humanitarian intervention correspond closely to the criteria found in the R2P report.[69]

A further and more significant lease of life for the norm came at the UN General Assembly Summit in September 2005. At the summit, leaders agreed to the following text:

Each individual State has the responsibility to protect its populations from genocide, war crimes, ethnic cleansing and crimes against humanity. This responsibility entails the prevention of such crimes, including their incitement, through appropriate and necessary means. We accept that responsibility and will act in accordance with it. The international community should, as appropriate,

---

[69] *A More Secure World: Our Shared Responsibility*, Report of the Secretary-General's High-Level Panel on Threats, Challenges and Change (New York: United Nations, 2004), 66, 106.

encourage and help States to exercise this responsibility and support the United Nations in establishing an early warning capability.[70]

Despite this endorsement, the R2P has faced major hurdles in becoming the standard bearer of a new norm of humanitarian intervention that would significantly reduce the salience of non-intervention. The developing countries in particular remained wary of its recommendations, while on the other extreme, some advocates of humanitarian intervention argue unhappily that it keeps the threshold of intervention too high to cover situations like Burma.[71] As Ramesh Thakur, a member of the ICISS and one of the most influential voices on R2P, notes, "The crisis over 'humanitarian intervention' arose because too many developing countries concluded that, intoxicated by its triumph in the cold war [sic], a newly aggressive West was trying to ram its values, priorities and agenda down their throats."[72] At a UN debate over the R2P, Egypt on behalf of the Non-Aligned Movement noted that "mixed feelings and thoughts on implementing R2P still persist. There are concerns about the possible abuse of R2P by expanding its application to situations that fall beyond the four areas defined in the 2005 World Summit Document, misusing it to legitimize unilateral coercive measures or intervention in the internal affairs of States."[73] According to another assessment:

Some fear that R2P will be misused as reasoning for neo-colonialist "Western" interventions. Many in the global south have thus solidified this position, often through the Group of 77 or the Non-Aligned Movement, against what they feel is intended to strengthen the influence and power of Northern governments to the detriment of the South. Although justifications for intervention in Iraq based on humanitarian grounds in 2003 were quickly discredited by most governments, there is still a sense that R2P could be used in the future for these types of politically-motivated interventions.[74]

[70] 2005 World Summit Outcome (UN General Assembly, September 15, 2005), www.responsibilitytoprotect.org/index.php/component/content/article/35-r2pcs-topics/398-general-assembly-r2p-excerpt-from-outcome-document.
[71] Ramesh Thakur, "Developing Countries and the Intervention–Sovereignty Debate," in The United Nations and Global Security, ed. Richard M. Price and Mark W. Zacher (New York: Palgrave Macmillan, 2004), 193–208; Thakur, "Iraq and the Responsibility to Protect," Behind the Headlines 62, no. 1 (2004), 1.
[72] Ramesh Thakur, The Responsibility to Protect: Norms, Laws and the Use of Force in International Politics (London: Routledge, 2011), 159.
[73] H. E. Ambassador Maged A. Abdelaziz, The Permanent Representative on behalf of the Non-Aligned Movement, "Statement," www.responsibilitytoprotect.org/NAM_Egypt_ENG.pdf.
[74] "The Americas," International Coalition for the R2P, accessed April 19, 2015, www.responsibilitytoprotect.org/index.php/pages/1287.

Some initial responses to R2P were couched in the same terms as earlier misgivings about the idea of humanitarian intervention, which had been put forth in words such as the comments of Malaysia's Foreign Minister Syed Hamid Albar: "We have to be wary all the time of new concepts and new philosophies that will compromise sovereignty in the name of humanitarian intervention, in the name of globalisation which is another form of trying to interfere in the domestic affairs of another country."[75]

At the regional level, the R2P has elicited different attitudes and responses in different regions.[76] As Edward Luck, an advisor to then UN Secretary-General Ban Ki Moon on R2P, recognizes, regions are not consistent in their attitude toward R2P, because "no two situations are identical."[77] It is perhaps in Africa that the R2P norm has found the greatest resonance. Following on from its shift to a more pro-intervention stance in the 1990s, the Constitutive Act of the African Union (successor to OAU), adopted at Lome, Togo in July 2000 and entered into force on May 26, 2001, recognizes "the right of the Union to intervene in a Member State pursuant to a decision of the Assembly in respect of grave circumstances, namely: war crimes, genocide and crimes against humanity."[78] This Act has been lauded as "the first international treaty to recognize the right to intervene for a humanitarian purpose (humanitarian intervention)."[79] It should be noted, however, that it does not specify whether "the definition of intervention is to be restricted to the use of force or it is to be viewed broadly as including mediation, peacekeeping missions, sanctions and any other non-forcible measures."[80] Moreover, the R2P clearly failed in the case of the Sudan. The then US Secretary of State Condoleezza Rice admitted, "one of the real regrets I've had

---

[75] "Malaysia Opposes UN Probe of East Timor Atrocities," *Agence France Presse*, October 7, 1999.

[76] Carla Barqueiro, Kate Seaman, and Katherine Teresa Towey, "Regional Organizations and Responsibility to Protect: Normative Reframing or Normative Change?" *Politics and Governance* 4, no. 3 (2016), 37–49.

[77] Edward Luck, "Statement to the Informal Interactive Dialogue on the Role of Regional and Sub-regional Arrangements in Implementing the Responsibility to Protect," *International Coalition for the R2P*, July 12, 2011, http://responsibilitytoprotect.org/Ed%20Luck%20General%20Assembly%20Debate%20Statement.pdf.

[78] "The Constitutive Act of the African Union," Lome, Togo, July 11, 2000, www.achpr.org/instruments/au-constitutive-act/.

[79] Evarist Baimu and Kathryn Sturman, "Amendment to the African Union's Right to Intervene: A Shift from Human Security to Regime Security?" *African Security Review* 12, no. 2 (2003), 37–45.

[80] Ibid. See also C. Packer and D. Rukare, "The New African Union and its Constitutive Act," *American Journal of International Law* 96, no. 2 (2002), 372.

is that we haven't been able to do something about Sudan."[81] But such outside inaction may have triggered the AU to undertake intervention, albeit with mixed results. The AU's mission in Somalia has been praised for its effectiveness in ensuring a modicum of order and stability in a highly fragile situation.[82]

In the subsequent Libyan intervention in 2011, Africa seemed wary and subject to conflicting sentiments. While all three African members of the Security Council (Gabon, Nigeria, and South Africa) voted to support Resolution 1973 that authorized NATO intervention, ten weeks later an AU communiqué spoke of "the importance of respect of the letter and spirit of resolution 1973," which was aimed at NATO's pursuit of regime change in Libya. "Clearly the AU was suspicious of France and Britain's motivations for foreign intervention in Libya, and perceived the enterprise as a project in regime change disguised as humanitarian intervention."[83]

Generally though, Africa has been much more receptive to the R2P norm than Asia. Unlike Africa, there were few insider proponents of the norm in Asia. Notable exceptions might be Anwar Ibrahim, the former Deputy Prime Minister of Malaysia, who proposed the idea of "Constructive Intervention," or Surin Pitsuwan, the former Thai Foreign Minister, who reframed Anwar's idea into the notion of "Flexible Engagement." But none of these progressive ideas about diluting sovereignty came close to advocating military intervention or even hard peacekeeping of the kind advocated by African leaders and policymakers.[84]

The differences between Africa and Asia over R2P are especially striking and deserve some explanation because the two regions, which jointly participated at the 1955 Asia–Africa Conference in Bandung, Indonesia, started with a similar normative predisposition toward state sovereignty. Like Asia, Africa used to be a bastion of the non-intervention norm.[85] The localization–subsidiarity framework is relevant in explaining the changing African attitudes toward sovereignty and the difference compared with Asia. Consistent with the localization framework, a key factor in explaining this difference is the greater availability of "insider proponents" for

[81] "Meet the Press," transcript for December 21, 2008, www.msnbc.msn.com/id/28337897/ns/meet_the_press/t/meet-press-transcript-dec/.
[82] Jeffrey Gettleman, "African Union Force Makes Strides Inside Somalia," *New York Times*, November 24, 2011.
[83] Thomas Alberts, "The African Union and Libya – On the Horns of a Dilemma," *All Africa*, November 2, 2011, http://allafrica.com/stories/201111030819.html.
[84] Acharya, *Whose Ideas Matter?*, 126–128.
[85] Robert H. Jackson and Carl G. Rosberg, "Why Africa's Weak States Persist: The Empirical and the Juridical in Statehood," *World Politics* 35, no. 1 (1982), 1–24.

Africa such as Mbeki, Obasanjo, and Salim, in addition to global players of African background such as Deng, Annan, and Sahnoun. Another
condition of norm localization is also at play here: regional ideology or
"cognitive prior" such as a pan-nationalist ideology countering nationalist sentiments. In Africa, a stronger prior sense of pan-Africanism was
an important factor. Asia's cognitive prior, by contrast, had remained
unchanged. Compared with other parts of the developing world, Asia
remains a tightly sovereignty-bound region.[86] To sum up, Africa's relative acceptance of the R2P can be explained by the favorable conditions of norm localization and subsidiarity found there, especially as the
norm resonated with prior ideas such as Nkrumah's notion of an African
High Command, the advocacy by African leaders of intervention to cope
with multiple intra-state conflicts with inter-state implications which the
outside world cared little about, and lack of comparable pan-Asian cognitive priors and insider advocacy in Asia.

The case of East Timor in 1999 dramatically illustrated the lack of
willingness among Asian countries to undertake intervention to protect
the lives of a people endangered by the actions of their own government. Here, the reluctance of Indonesia's neighbors to intervene, despite
clear evidence of large-scale atrocities, was partly due to an unwillingness
to interfere in Indonesia's domestic affairs and partly due to a lack of
capacity to intervene. There is some evidence of a greater willingness to
accept this norm in Southeast Asia, but the extent of this is a matter of
debate. Although Asian regional bodies, such as ASEAN and the ASEAN
Regional Forum, have not yet developed a collective role or instrument
to undertake intervention comparable to those in Africa, some analysts
have discerned that the "processes of norm localization are producing
an accommodation" between R2P and the principle of non-interference
in Southeast Asia.[87] The tentative moves by ASEAN toward a regional

---

[86] This is also the case when one compares Asia with Latin America. In Latin America, military takeover of a civilian government could trigger its suspension from the OAS, which
then is mandated to seek the restoration of civilian rule. In Asia, no regional organization
espouses such intrusive measures.

[87] Alex Bellamy and Catherine Drummond, "The Responsibility to Protect in Southeast
Asia: between Non-interference and Sovereignty as Responsibility," *The Pacific Review*
24, no. 2 (2011), 179–200. See also Alex Bellamy and Mark Beeson, "The Responsibility
to Protect in Southeast Asia: Can ASEAN Reconcile Humanitarianism and Sovereignty,"
Asian Security 6, no. 3 (2010), 262–279; Alex Bellamy and Paul Williams, "The
New Politics of Protection? Côte d'Ivoire, Libya and the Responsibility to Protect,"
International Affairs 87, no. 4 (2011), 825–850. This view has been challenged by others,
such as Capie, who argues that the norm has not been localized primarily because it has
been pushed more by outsider proponents than local ones, and that "many states [in
Southeast Asia] still see the broader R2P norm as a potential threat to sovereignty and
regime security, and as such have not internalized many of its key aspects." David Capie,

human rights mechanism could be a catalyst for such a shift, thereby leading to a dilution of state sovereignty.[88]

In the Middle East, the debate over the R2P norm entered a new stage with the Libyan crisis. One striking development was the otherwise pro-sovereignty Arab League's authorization of the Libyan intervention. At its meeting in Cairo on March 12, 2011, the League affirmed "the necessity to respect international humanitarian law" and called "for an end to the crimes against the Libyan people." It also called for the international community "to ensure the safety and security of Libyan citizens." Additionally it asked the UN Security Council to help deal with the Libyan situation including the "measures to impose immediately a no-fly zone on Libyan military aviation."[89] The subsequent UNSC Resolution 1973 adopted on March 17, 2011 approved a no-fly zone over Libya and called for "all necessary measures" to protect civilians. It was hailed as "the first instance where the norm has been backed by a UNSC Chapter VII resolution and used as grounds for intervention in an ongoing crisis." As such, Libya was supposed to have "had the impact of revitalizing this emerging norm and putting it back on the map."[90] This certainly delighted the norm's proponents. According to Bellamy, "The Responsibility to Protect (RtoP) played an important role in shaping the world's response to actual and threatened atrocities in Libya … Where it was once a term of art employed by a handful of like-minded countries, activists, and scholars, but regarded with suspicion by much of the rest of the world, RtoP has become a commonly accepted frame of reference for preventing and responding to mass atrocities."[91]

A more cautious if generally positive view, while calling Libya "a triumph for R2P," because it showed that "It is possible for the international

---

"The Responsibility to Protect Norm in Southeast Asia: Framing, Resistance and the Localization Myth," *Pacific Review* 25, no. 1 (2012), 76. See also: Pierre P. Lizée, "Asia and the Responsibility to Protect: What Now?" *PacNet*, no. 56, September 27, 2011, http://csis.org/files/publication/pac1156.pdf.

[88] Sriprapha Petcharamesree, "ASEAN Human Rights Regime and Mainstreaming the Responsibility to Protect: Challenges and Prospects," *Global Responsibility to Protect* 8, nos. 2–3 (2016), 133–157.

[89] "Timeline: Arab League," *BBC News*, November 15, 2011, http://news.bbc.co.uk/2/hi/middle_east/country_profiles/1550977.stm; "Arab League, Egypt back rebels in Libyan endgame," *Reuters*, August 22, 2011, www.reuters.com/article/2011/08/22/us-arabs-libya-idustre77l37q20110822; Sami Aboudi, "Arab League tells Syria to End Bloodshed Soon," *Reuters*, August 27, 2011, http://www.reuters.com/article/2011/08/28/us-syria-arableague-idUSTRE77Q17F20110828.

[90] Benedetta Berti and Gallia Lindenstrauss, "The International Action in Libya: Revitalizing the Responsibility to Protect," *Canada Free Press*, April 5, 2011, www.canadafreepress.com/index.php/article/35176.

[91] Alex Bellamy, "Libya and the Responsibility to Protect: The Exception and the Norm," *Ethics and International Affairs* 25, no. 3 (October 2011), 263–269.

community, working through the authenticated, UN-centred structures and procedures of organised multilateralism, to deploy international force to neutralise the military might of a thug and intervene between him and his victims with reduced civilian casualties and little risk of military casualties," found no convincing argument as to "whether international military action in Libya will promote consolidation or softening of the R2P norm."[92] Indeed, a weakening of the norm was evident in the Syrian crisis. The perception that British and French actions in carrying out the Libyan intervention clearly exceeded the UN mandate persuaded its initial African backers, Nigeria and South Africa, into changing their positions within the AU from support for to opposition to the intervention. It also made it more difficult that another such mandate was provided in the case of Syria. Overall, although power considerations mattered, especially Russian support for the Syrian regime and the greater military capacity of the Assad regime to resist outside intervention compared with that of the Gaddafi regime in Libya, "the Libyan crisis ... sharpened normative divisions" over the application of R2P to Syria, thereby preventing collective action in the international community.[93]

The Libyan operation produced an important backlash against the R2P, leading to an attempt to institute checks and balances against its abuse. This is consistent with the idea of norm circulation, whereby the failing of a norm triggers a feedback effect that conditions its subsequent application. A good example of this is Brazil's proposal for "responsibility while protecting" ("RWP") introduced in November 2011. The proposal, coming from a BRICS and G20 member, not only demands that the application of R2P be consistent with the principles of last resort and proportionality (which were already in the ICISS Report), but also calls for greater accountability during the operations undertaken in the name of the R2P.[94] To this end, it calls for "a monitoring and review mechanism whereby it can be ensured that states have the opportunity to debate the implementation of a UN Security Council mandate."[95]

---

[92] Ramesh Thakur, "Has R2P Worked in Libya?" *The Canberra Times*, September 19, 2011, www.canberratimes.com.au/news/opinion/editorial/general/has-r2p-worked-in-libya/2296301.aspx.

[93] Nathalie Tocci, *On Power and Norms: Libya, Syria and the Responsibility to Protect* (Washington, DC: The Transatlantic Academy, 2014), 21.

[94] Kristen Boon, "The Responsibility to Protect," *Opinio Juris* (2012), http://opiniojuris.org/2012/11/13/the-responsibility-to-protect/.

[95] Noele Crossley, "The Responsibility to Protect in 2012: R2P Fails in Syria, Brazil's 'RWP' Emerges," *Global Policy*, December 28, 2012, www.globalpolicyjournal.com/blog/28/12/2012/responsibility-protect-2012-r2p-fails-syria-brazil%E2%80%99s-%E2%80%98rwp%E2%80%99-emerges.

Although the proposal is yet to be realized, it has attracted a good deal of attention in the debate over how to move the R2P forward.[96] Gareth Evans describes the Brazilian proposal as a "way forward" for the R2P in the wake of the Libyan controversy:

The [Brazilian] proposals are for a set of criteria to be fully debated before the Security Council approves any use of military force, and for some kind of enhanced monitoring and review process that would enable such mandates to be seriously debated by all Council members during their implementation … If such criteria – all setting quite high hurdles – were visible and consistently applied, it should be a lot easier to avoid the "slippery slope" argument which has contributed to the Security Council paralysis on Syria, making some countries unwilling to even foreshadow non-military measures such as targeted sanctions or International Criminal Court investigation because of their concern that military coercion would be the inevitable next step if lesser measures failed.[97]

A final challenge to R2P is the attitude of the emerging powers of the Global South. Their attitude has not been singular or consistent, rather varying from case to case.[98] Some analysts see a general shift on the part of the BRICS towards greater acceptance, support and even ownership of the norm. As Stuenkel observes: the "'non- Western' emerging … powers' views on the norm in question are far more nuanced" than commonly portrayed. "The BRICS are in fundamental agreement about the principle that undergirds R2P … [but] the BRICS at times diverge from Western countries not about the existence of the norm, but about when and how to apply it."[99] Their support has not been unconditional,

---

[96] Oliver Stuenkel, "Brazil and Responsibility to Protect: A Case of Agency and Norm Entrepreneurship in the Global South," *International Relations* 30, no. 3 (2016), 375–390.

[97] "Gareth Evans on 'Responsibility to Protect' after Libya," Interview with Gareth Evans by Alan Philps for *The World Today*, Chatham House. New York: Global Centre for the Responsibility to Protect, October 1, 2012, available at www.globalr2p.org/media/files/gareth-evans-on-responsibility-to-protect-after-libya.pdf.

[98] Oliver Stuenkel, "The BRICS and the Future of R2P," *Global Responsibility to Protect* 6, no. 1 (2014), 3–28; Tim Dunne and Sarah Teitt, "Contested Intervention: China, India, and the Responsibility to Protect," *Global Governance: A Review of Multilateralism and International Organizations* 21, no. 3 (2015), 371–391; Courtney J. Fung, "China and the Responsibility to Protect: From Opposition to Advocacy," United States Institute of Peace, June 8, 2016, www.usip.org/publications/2016/06/08/china-and-the-responsibility-protect-opposition-advocacy; Dan Krause, "It is Changing After All: India's Stance on 'Responsibility to Protect,'" *Observer Research Foundation*, April 2016, www.orfonline.org/wp-content/uploads/2016/04/ORF_OccasionalPaper_90.pdf; Stamatis Laskaris and Joakim Kreutz, "Rising Powers and the Responsibility to Protect: Will the Norm Survive in the Age of BRICS?" *Global Affairs* 1, no. 2 (2015), 149–158; Karen Smith, "South Africa and the Responsibility to Protect: From Champion to Sceptic," *International Relations* 30, no. 3 (2016), 391–405.

[99] Stuenkel, "The BRICS and the Future of R2P."

but comes with demands for greater fairness and checks and balances against its abuse.

Some final observations about the state of R2P in the emerging global order may be made. Overall, the response of different regions to the R2P has not been uniform. There are major differences between Asia and Africa, with the former adopting a more critical stance. The support of the Arab League for the Syrian intervention suggests another variation, hinting at the possibility of context-dependent support. This speaks to the diversity of normative approaches to sovereignty and security in world politics. More generally, the attitude of non-Western countries to R2P has been neither one of unquestionable opposition, nor one of passive acceptance. Rather, it is better described as one of active construction of the norm through the different forms of agency identified in Chapter 2, including localization, subsidiarity processes, and circulation. Moreover, recent and ongoing crises, especially in Libya and Syria, show the agency of both the Western and the emerging powers. As Tocci puts it,

Western and BRICS countries alike played crucial roles in determining the overall international responses to both crises. In doing so, all major international actors involved contributed to the ongoing global normative conversation about when and how to respond to mass atrocities, with likely long-term implications for the responsibility to protect.[100]

Moreover, these crises and those beforehand reveal a resistance and feedback effect, prompting new ideas and mechanisms to govern the application of the norm, including checks and balances – both formal and informal – with significant implications for legitimating norm-governing behavior in world politics.

[100] Tocci, *On Power and Norms: Libya, Syria and the Responsibility to Protect*, 2, 51–75.

5   Redefining Security

The exercise of agency in world politics, as noted in Chapter 1, involves challenging accepted understandings of key ideas as well as offering alternative ideas. In this process, the social and political context in which alternative ideas and approaches emerge assumes great importance. During the Cold War, the dominant idea of security was national security.[1] It reflected the primary security concerns and predicament of Western countries, especially the United States, and equated "security with the absence of a military threat or with the protection of the nation [state] from external overthrow or attack."[2] But many security studies scholars – especially from the non-Western world – found the national security concept too restrictive, and advocated a redefinition and broadening of the concept, taking into account the context of the non-Western world.[3] Analyzing this debate, this chapter examines how the concept of

---

[1] There is a vast literature on the evolution of the concept of security and of security studies. A small sampling from diverse perspectives might include: Barry Buzan and Lene Hansen, *The Evolution of International Security Studies* (Cambridge University Press, 2009); Buzan's earlier seminal work on security *People, States and Fear: An Agenda for International Security Studies in the Post-Cold War Era* (New York: Harvester Wheatsheaf, 1991); Ken Booth, *Theory of World Security* (Cambridge University Press, 2007); Shahrbanou Tadjbakhsh and Anuradha M. Chenoy, *Human Security: Concepts and Implications* (New York: Routledge, 2007); Christina Rowley and Jutta Weldes, "The Evolution of International Security Studies and the Everyday: Suggestions from the Buffyverse," *Security Dialogue* 43, no. 6 (2012), 513–530; Roland Dannreuther, *International Security: The Contemporary Agenda*, 2nd edition (Cambridge, UK: Polity Press, 2013); Barry Buzan and Ole Waever, "Security Studies: Past, Present, and Future," in *Contemporary Security Studies*, ed. Alan Collins, 4th edition (Oxford University Press 2016).

[2] Helga Haftendorn, "The Security Puzzle: Theory-Building and Discipline-Building in International Security," *International Studies Quarterly* 35, no. 1 (March 1991), 3–18.

[3] Among the key writings questioning the relevance of national security in the Third World during the Cold War are: Mohammed Ayoob, "Security in the Third World: The Worm about to Turn," *International Affairs* 60, no. 1 (1984), 41–51; Soedjatmoko, "Patterns of Armed Conflict in the Third World," *Alternatives* 10, no. 4 (1985), 477–493; Mohammed Ayoob, ed., *Regional Security in the Third World* (London: Croom Helm, 1986); Edward Azar and Chung-in Moon, "Third World National Security: Towards a New Conceptual Framework," *International Interactions* 11, no. 2 (1984), 103–135; Edward Azar and Chung-in Moon, eds., *National Security in the Third World* (Aldershot: Edward Elgar, 1988);

national security came to be challenged from the vantage-point of the
Third World (it is worth noting that on the debates over security the term
Third World has been extensively used, compared with "Global South"
or "non-Western") and led to the emergence of an alternative understanding of security – human security – in the post-Cold War era. While
the concept of "national security" was being broadened in Western literature and redefined in the West, this neglected the distinctive security
predicament of Third World countries, and remained mainly focused on
the security of the state, rather than security of the people. The distinctive non-Western contribution to the evolution of security thinking is the
idea of human security (which itself was an offshoot of the concept of
"human development" that emerged in the 1990s).

During the Cold War, superpower diplomacy carefully distinguished
the "central strategic balance" (involving superpower nuclear deterrence
and their European alliances) from regional conflict and regional security (conflict and conflict-management issues arising primarily in the
Third World). In the academic literature, what was considered "mainstream" focused on "the centrality of the East–West divide to the rest
of global politics."[4] Attention to problems of regional instability in the
Third World was given only to the extent that they had the potential to
affect the superpower relationship.

In the latter stages of the Cold War, the dominant concept of security,
with its main referent point being "national security," came under challenge. Critics found the national security paradigm too restrictive, and
advocated a redefinition and broadening of security studies. As a result,
a debate would emerge and continue over which phenomena should
be included within the purview of the new security studies agenda and
which should not. While the advocates of a broader notion of security call
for the inclusion, among other things, of economic, ecological, demographic (refugees and illegal migration), narcotic, and gender issues,[5]

Yezid Sayigh, *Confronting the 1990s: Security in the Developing Countries*, Adelphi Papers no.
251 (London: International Institute for Strategic Studies, 1990); Mohammed Ayoob,
"The Security Problematic of the Third World," *World Politics* 43, no. 2 (January 1991),
257–283. See also: Brian L. Job, ed., *The (In)Security Dilemma: The National Security of
Third World States* (Boulder, CO: Lynne Rienner, 1992). Caroline Thomas provides a succinct overview of the place of Third World issues in international security studies in "New
Directions in Thinking about Security in the Third World," in *New Thinking about Strategy
and International Security*, ed. Ken Booth (London: HarperCollins, 1991), 267–289.
[4] Hugh Macdonald, "Strategic Studies," *Millennium: Journal of International Studies* 16,
no. 2 (1987), 333–336.
[5] The following are some examples of such work criticizing the traditional concept of
national security and offering a broader notion encompassing diverse issue areas:
Richard Ullman, "Redefining Security," *International Security* 8, no. 1 (Summer 1983),
129–153; Michael Renner, *National Security: The Economic and Environmental Dimensions*,

others warn against too much broadening, citing the danger of security becoming a catch-all concept, and urging the retention of the original state-centric and war-centric focus of security studies.[6]

Worldwatch Paper no. 89 (Washington, DC: The Worldwatch Institute, 1989); Arthur H. Westing, "An Expanded Concept of International Security," in Arthur H. Westing, ed., *Global Resources and International Conflict* (New York: Oxford University Press, 1986), 183–200; Jessica Tuchman Mathews, "Redefining Security," *Foreign Affairs*, 68, no. 2 (1989), 162–177; Gro Harlem Brundtland, "The Environment, Security and Development," with Appendix, *SIPRI Yearbook 1993* (Oxford University Press, 1993), 15–36; Norman Meyers, "Environmental Security," *Foreign Policy*, no. 74 (1989), 23–41; Thomas F. Homer-Dixon, *Environmental Change and Human Conflict*, Working Paper (Cambridge, MA: American Academy of the Arts and Sciences, 1990); Dennis Pirages, "Environmental Security and Social Evolution," *International Studies Notes* 16, no. 1 (Winter 1991), 8–12; Neville Brown, "Climate, Ecology and International Security," *Survival* 31, no. 6 (November/December 1989), 484–499; *Environmental Security: A Report Contributing to the Concept of Comprehensive International Security* (Oslo: International Peace Research Institute, 1989); *Our Common Future: Report of the World Commission on Environment and Development* (Oxford University Press, 1987); Hans W. Maull, "Energy and Resources: The Strategic Dimensions," *Survival* 31, no. 6 (November/ December 1989), 500–518; Edward N. Krapels, *Oil and Security: Problems and Prospects of Importing Countries*, Adelphi Papers no. 136 (London: International Institute for Strategic Studies, 1977); F. A. M. Alting von Geusau and J. Pelkmans, eds., *National Economic Security: Perceptions, Threats and Policies* (Tilburg, the Netherlands: John F. Kennedy Institute, 1982), 47–61; Raimo Vayrynen, "Towards a Comprehensive Definition of Security: Pitfalls and Promises," Paper prepared for the 31st Annual Convention of the International Studies Association, Washington, DC, April 10–14, 1990; Klaus Knorr and Frank Trager, *Economic Issues and National Security* (Lawrence: University Press of Kansas, 1977); Stephen D. Krasner, "National Security and Economics," in *National Security Affairs*, ed. B. Thomas Trout and James E. Harf (New Brunswick: Transaction Books, 1982), 313–328; Giacomo Luciani, "The Economic Content of Security," *Journal of Public Policy* 8, no. 2 (April–June 1989), 151–173; Al Gedicks, "The New Resource Wars," *Raw Materials Reports* 1, no. 2 (1982), 8–13; Joseph J. Romm, *Defining National Security: The Non-Military Aspects* (New York: Council on Foreign Relations Press, 1993), 51–80; J. Ann Tickner, "Redefining Security: A Feminist Perspective," Paper Presented to the Annual Meeting of the Northwestern Political Science and Northeast International Studies Association, November 1989; Brad Roberts, "Human Rights and International Security," *The Washington Quarterly* 13, no. 2 (Spring 1990), 65–75.
[6] For important contributions to the debate over the merits and pitfalls of broadening the concept of security, see: Buzan, *People, States and Fear*; R. B. J. Walker, *The Concept of Security and International Relations Theory*, Working paper no. 3, First Annual Conference on Discourse, Peace, Security and International Society, Ballyvaughn, Ireland, August 9–16, 1987; Stephen M. Walt, "The Renaissance of Security Studies," *International Studies Quarterly* 35, no. 2 (1991), 211–239; Edward A. Kolodziej, "Renaissance in Security Studies: Caveat Lector," *International Studies Quarterly* 36, no. 4 (December 1992), 421–438; Sean M. Lynn-Jones, "International Security Studies," *International Studies Notes* 16, no. 3 (Fall/Winter 1992), 53–63; Daniel Deudney, "The Case Against Linking Environmental Degradation and National Security," *Millennium: Journal of International Studies* 19, no. 3 (1990), 461–476; Stuart Croft and Terry Terriff, "Forum: 'What is Security and Security Studies?' Revisited," *Arms Control* 13, no. 3 (December 1992), 463–544; Joseph S. Nye, "The Contribution of Strategic Studies: Future Challenges," in *The Changing Strategic Landscape*, Part I, Adelphi Paper no. 235 (London: The International Institute for Strategic Studies, 1989), 20–34; Haftendorn, "The Security Puzzle"; Simon Dalby, "Security, Modernity and Ecology: The Dilemmas of Post-Cold War Security Discourse," *Alternatives: Global, Local, Political* 17, no. 1 (1992), 95–134.

Yet, the initial debate over redefining national security in the West was itself limited. Just like the traditional concept, it paid little attention to conflicts in the non-Western world.[7] This "exclusion" was evident in both policy and academic arenas. In a survey of the field published in 1988, Nye and Lynn-Jones acknowledged "ethnocentric biases" (attributable to the development of the field primarily in the United States) which had led security studies scholars to concentrate on issues relating to "superpower rivalry, nuclear arms control, and American policy debates" while neglecting "many equally significant issues" including "regional security issues (apart from Western Europe), domestic politics, and economic security."[8] Yet it was in the Third World that most instances of international violence could be found.[9]

It was in this context that a body of writings on the "Third World security predicament" (to use Ayoob's term) in the 1980s and 1990s made a significant contribution to the further evolution of security studies.[10]

---

[7] "Mainstream" work on security studies focused on "the Cold War and the centrality of the East–West divide to the rest of global politics." Hugh Macdonald, "Strategic Studies," *Millennium: Journal of International Studies* 16, no. 2 (1987), 333–336.

[8] Joseph S. Nye, Jr. and Sean M. Lynn-Jones, "International Security Studies: A Report of a Conference on the State of the Field," *International Security* 12, no. 4 (Spring 1988), 27.

[9] Between 1945 and 1986, there were some 127 "significant wars." Out of these, only 2 occurred in Europe, while Latin America accounted for 26, Africa 31, the Middle East 24, and Asia 44. According to this estimate, the Third World was the scene of more than 98 percent of all international conflicts. Evan Luard, *War in International Society* (London: I. B. Tauris, 1986), Appendix 5.

[10] The major contributions to the literature on Third World security at this point include: Mohammed Ayoob, "Security in the Third World: The Worm about to Turn," *International Affairs* 60, no. 1 (1984), 41–51; Mohammed Ayoob, "Regional Security and the Third World," in *Regional Security in the Third World*, ed. Mohammed Ayoob (London: Croom Helm, 1986), 3–23; Bahgat Korany, "Strategic Studies and the Third World: A Critical Appraisal," *International Social Science Journal* 38, no. 4 (1986), 547–562; Udo Steinbach, "Sources of Third World Conflict," in *Third World Conflict and International Security*, Adelphi Papers no. 166 (London: International Institute for Strategic Studies, 1981), 21–28; Soedjatmoko, "Patterns of Armed Conflict in the Third World"; Edward Azar and Chung-in Moon, "Third World National Security: Towards a New Conceptual Framework," *International Interactions* 11, no. 2 (1984), 103–135; Barry Buzan, "The Concept of National Security for Developing Countries with Special Reference to Southeast Asia," Paper presented to the Workshop on Leadership and Security in Southeast Asia, Institute of Southeast Asian Studies, Singapore, December 10–12, 1987; Barry Buzan, "People, States and Fear: The National Security Problem in the Third World," in *National Security in the Third World*, ed. Edward Azar and Chung-in Moon (Aldershot: Edward Elgar, 1988), 14–43; Caroline Thomas, *In Search of Security: The Third World in International Relations* (Brighton: Wheatsheaf Books, 1987), 1; Yezid Sayigh, *Confronting the 1990s: Security in the Developing Countries*, Adelphi Papers no. 251 (London: International Institute for Strategic Studies, 1990); Mohammed Ayoob, "The Security Predicament of the Third World State," in *The (In)Security Dilemma: The National Security of Third World States*, ed. Brian L. Job (Boulder, CO: Lynne Rienner, 1992); Mohammed Ayoob, "The Security Problematic of the Third World," *World Politics* 43, no. 2 (January 1991), 257–283; Steven R. David, "Explaining Third World

A key objective of this literature was to stress the lack of fit between the concept of national security and the security situation in the Third World. The Third World experience challenged the idea of national security in three key areas, which may be briefly discussed. The first was the centrality of domestic politics in security. An early and crucial aspect of the understanding of the "Third World" category was the recognition of the "weakness" of its constituent units not only as *powers*, but, more importantly, as *states*. This weakness was partly due to the lack of fit between a state's postcolonial territorial structure and its ethnic and societal dimensions. The construction of the Westphalian nation-state was seldom a success in the Third World. As Steinbach pointed out, "The concept of 'nation', introduced by colonial powers or by small elites who saw in it the prerequisite for the fulfillment of their own political aspirations, materialized in a way which went against territorial, ethnic, religious, geographical or culturo-historical traditions."[11] Mohammed Ayoob drew attention to the fact that most Third World states lack "unconditional legitimacy," including a "capacity to ensure the habitual identification of their inhabitants with the post-colonial structures that have emerged within colonially dictated boundaries."[12]

Moreover, in the Third World, internal threats frequently spilled across national boundaries to fuel inter-state discord. Ethnic minorities fighting the dominant elite rarely honored state boundaries, often seeking sanctuary in neighboring states where the regime and population might be more sympathetic to their cause. Weak states were prone to suffer from foreign intervention. Neighboring states often meddled in their inter-ethnic relations. Outside powers take advantage of their domestic strife to advance their economic and ideological interests.

Several studies established that the vast majority of conflicts in the Third World were intra-state in nature (anti-regime insurrections, civil wars, tribal conflicts, etc.). A study by Istvan Kende found that of the 120 wars during the 1945–1976 period, 102 were internal wars (including anti-regime wars and tribal conflicts), while another study by Kidron and Segal covering the 1973–1986 period found a mix of 66 internal

---

Alignment," *World Politics* 43, no. 2 (January 1991), 232–256. Caroline Thomas provides a succinct overview of the place of Third World issues in international security studies in her "New Directions in Thinking about Security in the Third World," in *New Thinking about Strategy and International Security*, ed. Ken Booth (London: HarperCollins, 1991), 267–289; and Mohammed Ayoob, *The Third World Security Predicament: State Making, Regional Conflict, and the International System* (Boulder, CO: Lynne Rienner, 1995).

[11] Steinbach, "Sources of Third World Conflict," 21.
[12] Ayoob, "Regional Security and the Third World," 9–10.

wars and 30 border wars.[13] Thus, whereas national security in the West was focused on external threats to the sovereign state, for Third World states, security was essentially an inward-looking concept.

Second, the concept of national security made no distinction between the security of the "state" and that of the "regime" which presides over the state. Yet such a distinction was fundamental to understanding the "insecurity dilemma" in the Third World.[14] The distinction was noted by Ayoob, who argued that "regime security," rather than national security, was a salient feature of the security predicament of the Third World because:

In the absence of a consensus on fundamental issues and in the absence of open political debate and contest, many of these states are ruled by regimes with narrow support bases – both politically and socially ... Since it is these regimes ... who define the threats to the security of their respective states, it is no wonder that they define it primarily in terms of regime security rather than the security of the society as a whole.[15]

Thus, the literature on Third World security disagreed with the concept of national security by claiming that the security predicament of post-colonial states was mainly internal, rather than external, in nature. The basic attributes of "security" in the Third World would seem to involve not just the physical protection of the core values of the state from external military threats, but also considerations such as the fragility of the nation-state and regime survival in the domestic context.[16] Most postcolonial societies exhibited a lack of consensus on the basic rules of political accommodation, power-sharing, and governance. Regime-creation and regime-maintenance were often a product of violent societal struggles, governed by no stable constitutional framework. The narrow base of Third World regimes and the various challenges to their survival affected the way in which "national security" policy was articulated and pursued. In such a milieu, the regime's instinct for self-preservation often takes precedence over the security interests of the society or the nation. National security became a fig-leaf for regime survival.

A third aspect of national security was its focus on military threats and the consequent ignoring of non-military ones. While, as noted earlier, this bias had been challenged, especially during the final decades of the Cold War, it remained influential. For example, Stephen Walt's survey

---

[13] Cited in Thomas, "New Directions in Thinking about Security in the Third World," 269.

[14] Brian L. Job, "The Insecurity Dilemma", in *The (In)Security Dilemma*, ed. Job.

[15] Ayoob, "Regional Security and the Third World," 11.

[16] Amitav Acharya, "Regionalism and Regime Security in the Third World: Comparing the Origins of the ASEAN and the GCC," in *The (In)security Dilemma*, ed. Job, 143–164.

of security studies in 1991 rejected the inclusion of such phenomena as "pollution, disease, child abuse, or economic recessions" in security studies, because, as he put it, this would "destroy its intellectual coherence." Walt also argued that "the fact that other hazards exist does not mean that the danger of war has been eliminated."[17] On the more specific case of ecological issues, some argued that conflict and violence in the international system had little to do with ecological degradation.[18]

But even before it became fashionable to accept a wider definition of security, threats such as resource scarcity, environmental degradation, overpopulation, and underdevelopment could be much more intimately linked to the security predicament of the Third World than that of the developed countries. Summarizing this predicament, Caroline Thomas noted that "security in the context of the Third World does not simply refer to the military dimension, as is often assumed in the Western discussions of the concept, but to the *whole range of dimensions of a state's existence which has been taken care of in the more developed states, especially those in the West.*"[19] The link between economics and security was especially pronounced in the Third World. As Rosenbaum and Tyler argued: "The terms development and security are closely linked in the lexicon of the LDCs," not only because "a semblance of security and stability is a prerequisite for successful economic development," but also because "It is also generally understood within the Third World that economic development can contribute to national security; an economically weak nation can be exploited or defeated more easily by foreign powers and may be exposed periodically to the violent wrath of dissatisfied citizens."[20] Broadening this perspective, Vayrynen held that "Because of the fragility of social system, the marginal costs of economic vulnerability, ecological degradation and ethnic fragmentation are greater problems in developing countries than in industrialized countries (where the absolute damage may be greater, however)," and therefore, "In developing countries, the notion of national security cannot be separated from the non-military threats to security."[21]

---

[17] Stephen M. Walt, "The Renaissance of Security Studies," *International Studies Quarterly* 35, no. 2 (1991), 213.

[18] Daniel Deudney, "The Case against Linking Environmental Degradation and National Security," *Millennium: Journal of International Studies* 19, no. 3 (1990), 464–465.

[19] Thomas, *In Search of Security*, 1. Emphasis added.

[20] H. John Rosenbaum and William G. Tyler, "South–South Relations: The Economic and Political Content of Interactions among Developing Countries," *International Organization* 29, no. 1 (1975), 248.

[21] Vayrynen, "Towards a Comprehensive Definition of Security: Pitfalls and Promises," 10.

In the emerging awareness of climate change as a threat to global security, the risk of conflicts and instability linked to environmental degradation in the Third World found a central place. Of the three categories of conflict identified by Homer-Dixon as being related to environmental degradation in his influential work on the subject,[22] two – "simple scarcity conflicts" (conflict over natural resources such as rivers, water, fish, and agriculturally productive land) and "relative deprivation conflicts" (the impact of environmental degradation in limiting growth and thereby causing popular discontent and conflict) – were most acute in the Third World. Moreover, environmental degradation originating in the Third World is increasingly a potential basis for conflict *between* the North and the South, as poorer nations demand a greater share of the world's wealth and Third World environmental refugees aggravate existing "group-identity conflicts" (the problems of social assimilation of the migrant population) in host countries.

From National Security to Human Security

Thus, as security studies adapted itself to post-Cold War realities, the security predicament of Third World states provided a helpful point of departure for appreciating the limitations of the "dominant understanding" and moving it toward a broader and more inclusive notion of security. This redefinition was crucial to understanding the problems of conflict and order in the post-Cold War period. And it led to the emergence of the concept of human security.

A major challenge to the national security paradigm was the idea of comprehensive security. It had strong Asian roots, having been developed by Japan. During the Cold War, several Southeast Asian governments also formulated their own versions of comprehensive security.[23] Comprehensive security in Japan reflected a concern with economic issues, including the supply of international energy and food.[24] It also reflected Japan's vulnerability to

major threats to economic livelihood and standard of living of the Japanese people from the denial of access to markets for Japanese goods, the expropriation

---

[22] Thomas F. Homer-Dixon, "On the Threshold: Environmental Change as Causes of Acute Conflict," *International Security* 16, no. 2 (Fall 1991), 76–116.

[23] Muthiah Alagappa, "Comprehensive Security: Interpretations in ASEAN Countries," in *Asian Security Issues: Regional and Global*, ed. Robert A. Scalapino, Seizaburo Sata, Jusuf Wanandi, and Sung-Joo Han (Berkeley: University of California, Institute of East Asian Studies, 1988), 58.

[24] Yukio Satoh, *The Evolution of Japan's Security Policy*, Adelphi Paper no. 178 (London: IISS, 1982), 7.

of Japanese property and exclusion of Japanese investment projects abroad, and from a withholding of vital supplies of goods, materials and services to Japanese enterprises home and abroad.[25]

In ASEAN, comprehensive security doctrines similarly focused on economic insecurities, but added important political dimensions related to domestic stability and regime survival. Singapore developed its own doctrine of "Total Defense," in which several non-military instruments, such as psychological defense, augmented military deterrence and defensive capabilities were part of the overall national security strategy. In the case of Indonesia, "national resilience" consisted of "ideological, political, economic, socio-cultural and security-cum-defence aspects."[26]

The idea of comprehensive security represented a major attempt not only to redefine national security, but also to translate it into policy, especially in Asia. It also helped to influence or localize the European idea of "common security." The latter had emerged from the ashes of the Cold War through the institutional mechanism of the Conference on Security and Co-operation in Europe (CSCE, later the Organization for Security and Co-operation in Europe, or OSCE). Common security stipulated that security should be pursued multilaterally based on the principle of inclusiveness. Security policies should promote reassurance, rather than deterrence. In Asia, common security became localized as "cooperative security," with less emphasis on military confidence-building measures as with the OSCE and more on a broader agenda of non-military or "non-traditional" challenges and cooperation.[27] Thus:

There are three principal themes which form the core of cooperative security. The first is the acceptance and practice of inclusivity, referring both to participants – the non-like-minded as well as the like-minded – and to subject matter, thereby broadening the security discourse beyond direct and traditional military threat to encompass nonconventional security challenges such as environmental, ecological, and demographic phenomena that can exacerbate inter-state relations and even promote the application of armed force. The second is the promotion of "habits of dialogue" whereby the regional actors acknowledge the long-term benefits of undertaking regular consultations with the possibilities of establishing more formal and even official decision-making multilateral meetings on a regular schedule. The third is the premise that many – perhaps most – questions of security no longer are amenable to unilateral action but require

[25] J. W. M. Chapman, R. Drifte, and I. T. M. Gow, *Japan's Quest for Comprehensive Security: Defence, Diplomacy, Dependence* (London: Frances Pinter, 1983), 149.

[26] Alagappa, "Comprehensive Security," 62.

[27] Mohamed Jawhar Hassan and Thangam Ramnath, eds., *Conceptualizing Asia-Pacific Security* (Kuala Lumpur: Institute for Strategic and International Studies, 1996); for an overview of security concepts and approaches in Asia, see: Muthiah Alagappa, ed., *Asian Security Practice: Material and Ideational Influences* (Stanford University Press, 1998).

cooperative approaches across actors within a country as well as cross-national and intergovernmental.[28]

The ideas of comprehensive and cooperative security formed an important backdrop to the emergence of human security as a key alternative notion of security for the post-Cold War era. Emerging in the 1990s, the idea of human security rekindled the debate over what security means and how best to achieve it. It not only represents the most powerful challenge to date to the idea of national security, it also highlights the ideational and normative agency of non-Western scholars and contexts.[29]

While the prior contentions over the concept of security in both the academic and the policy world were over broadening the threat-spectrum ("security against what?"), the debate sparked by human security has mainly been over the question, "whose security?" The idea of human security was first proposed by the United Nations Development Program's (UNDP) *Human Development Report* for 1994.[30] Although the essence of human security as "security for the people" may have previous antecedents, its clearest lineage was in the idea of human development. And the main progenitor of that idea was Pakistani economist Mahbub ul Haq. There is an interesting parallel here with the R2P norm. Just as that norm had to some extent been conceived in the context of Africa and pushed by African policymakers and public intellectuals, human security was conceived in the context of Asia, especially South Asia, and proposed by South Asian policy intellectuals.

---

[28] David B. Dewitt and Amitav Acharya, "Cooperative Security and Development Assistance: The Relationship between Security and Development with Reference to Eastern Asia," Eastern Asia Policy Papers no. 16. (Toronto: Joint Centre for Asia Pacific Studies, 1996), 9–10.

[29] For examples of some of the best conceptual writings on the idea of human security from non-Western scholars, see: Shahrbanou Tadjbakhsh and Anuradha M. Chenoy, *Human Security: Concepts and Implications* (New York: Routledge, 2007); Amartya Sen, "Why Human Security?" Speech at the International Symposium on Human Security, Tokyo, July 28, 2000, www.humansecurity-chs.org/activities/outreach/Sen2000.pdf; Shahrbanou Tadjbakhsh, "Human Security in International Organizations: Blessing or Scourge?" *Human Security Journal* 4 (Summer 2007), 8–15; Amitav Acharya, *Human Security: Ethical, Normative and Educational Frameworks in Southeast Asia* (Paris; UNESCO, 2007); Amitav Acharya, "Human Security," in *The Globalisation of World Politics*,ed. John Baylis, Steve Smith and Patricia Owens, 5th edition (Oxford University Press, 2010); Amitav Acharya, Subrat Singhdeo, and M. Rajarethnam, eds., *Human Security: From Concept to Practice* (Singapore and London: World Scientific, 2011). See also: Astri Suhrke, "Human Security and Interests of States," *Security Dialogue* 30, no. 3 (1999), 265–276; Sadako Ogata and Johan Cels, "Human Security – Protecting and Empowering the People," *Global Governance* 9, no. 3 (2003), 273–282; Neil MacFarlane and Khong Yuen Foong, *Human Security and the UN: A Critical History* (Bloomington: Indiana University Press, 2006).

[30] United Nations, *Human Development Report* (New York: United Nations Development Program, 1994).

Haq, to whom belongs the credit for the idea of the Human
Development Report (HDR) and the Human Development Index
(HDI), was born in Pakistan and educated first at Lahore University,
with a second BA in economics from Cambridge University in the
UK.[31] Haq's PhD was from Yale University.[32] At Cambridge University,
he was a contemporary of Indian economists Amartya Sen and
Manmohan Singh (India's future Prime Minister). Sen, who went on
to win the Nobel Prize in Economics in 1998, would collaborate closely
with Haq in developing the HDR and HDI under the auspices of the
UNDP. Both economists shared many ideas about human development. Haq worked in Pakistan's Planning Commission in late 1957
through the late 1960s. From 1970 to 1982, he was the Director of
Policy Planning at the World Bank and the chief economist to Robert
McNamara, then the president of the World Bank. He also served as a
cabinet minister under Pakistan's General Zia ul Haq in 1982.[33] During
his work in Pakistan in the 1980s, he led the shift from a pure growth-
oriented approach to a distribution-oriented approach, a focus that was
also reflected in his advocacy of policies to promote madrasahs, women's
development, youth development, and institutions of learning. His concern with education, women, youth, and stronger institutions became
the basic building blocks of the concept of human development in the
1990s. In 1989, he joined the UNDP as a Special Advisor, and launched

[31] Haq was helped by a team of consultants, including Paul Streeten, Gustav Ranis,
Keith Griffin, Frances Stewart, Lord (Meghnad) Desai, and Sudhir Anand. Amartya
Sen and Tam Dalyell, "Obituary: Mahbub ul Haq," *The Independent*, August 3, 1998,
accessed December 24, 2012, www.independent.co.uk/arts-entertainment/obituary-
mahbub-ul-haq-1169323.html. The Indian economist Amartya Sen is also given credit
for the HDR and HDI, as a "close friend and collaborator" of Haq. Helen Clark,
"Foreward," *Human Development Report 2010* (United Nations Development Program),
accessed 25 December 2012, http://hdr.undp.org/en/reports/global/hdr2010. While Sen
calls Haq "the pioneering leader of the human development approach," he also mentions Haq "harnessing" "several voices of discontent [that] were demanding an approach
broader than standard economic measurements provided and were proposing constructive departures." Amartya Sen, "Introduction," *Human Development Report 2010*,
accessed December 25, 2012, http://hdr.undp.org/en/reports/global/hdr20.
[32] I am grateful to Ben Scafalni, a graduate student at American University, for providing
me access to his detailed research into Haq's life and his role in developing the concepts
of both human development and human security through his work under my super-
vision. See: Ben Sclafani, "Human Security in Pakistan: Domestic and International
Dimensions," Substantial Research Paper, School of International Service, American
University, Washington, DC, October 2011.
[33] M. S. Jillani and Masooda Bano, "From 'Growth' to 'Growth with a Social Conscience':
Haq as an Economic Planner in Pakistan," in *Pioneering the Human Development
Revolution: An Intellectual Biography of Mahbub Ul Haq*, ed. Khadija Haq and Richard
Ponzio (New Delhi: Oxford University Press, 2008), 18–41.

the HDR in 1990. Five years later, the 1994 HDR carried the first articulation of the concept of human security. Haq returned to Pakistan to
found the Human Development Center in Islamabad and worked on the
HDR/HDI until 1997. When he died in 1998 "more than 100 countries
were already producing human development reports."[34] The HDR's offshoot, the HDI, was conceived as a fresh way of measuring development
by combining indicators of life expectancy, educational attainment, and
income.

The core aspect of the human development idea is the rejection of the
view that growth equaled development. Instead development is viewed as
a much broader notion, where "people are moved to the center stage,"[35]
with the basic purpose of human development being to "enlarge people's
choices."[36] This broader concept, to be called human development,

is the most holistic development model that exists today. It embraces every development issue, including economic growth, social investment, people's empowerment, provision of basic needs and social safety nets, political and cultural
freedoms and all other aspects of people's lives.[37]

Thus defined, human development focuses on building human capabilities to confront and overcome poverty, illiteracy, diseases, discrimination, restrictions on political freedom, and the threat of violent conflict.
"Individual freedoms and rights matter a great deal, but people are
restricted in what they can do with that freedom if they are poor, ill,
illiterate, discriminated against, threatened by violent conflict or denied a

---

[34] "Mahbub ul Haq (Obituary)," *The Economist*, July 23, 1998.
[35] Mahbub ul Haq, *Reflections on Human Development* (New Delhi: Oxford University Press, 1995), 16.
[36] Ibid., 14.
[37] Ibid., 23. Human development was of course not the first concept to have its origins in the non-Western world and regional milieu. The best-known regional and "non-Western" critique and reconstruction of development was of course Dependency Theory, which was to a large extent a Latin American invention. While human development emerged at a time when Dependency Theory with "its pessimistic world view, and 'outdated' language of 'exploitation'" had gone out of fashion, thanks partly to the impressive growth of some developing countries, especially in East Asia, the two concepts share a concern against accepting the virtues of orthodox liberal development models (GDP growth rates and free trade) and with inequality as an obstacle to true development. Human development places less stress on "exploitation" of the South by the North as the reason for underdevelopment, and puts more blame on the South's own excesses, such as defense spending and failure to allocate adequate resources to education and health. On the relationship between and relevance of Dependency Theory and human development theory, see: "Dependency theory – Is It All Over Now?" accessed January 1, 2013, www.guardian.co.uk/global-development/poverty-matters/2012/mar/01/do-not-drop-dependency-theory.

political voice ..."[38] GDP growth alone will not satisfy the basic needs of the world's poor. True development depended "on the quality and distribution of economic growth, not only on the quantity of such growth."[39] High economic growth does not always trickle down to the people and more efficient policies should be implemented to expand the well-being of a country's citizens.

From a people-centric notion of development came a people-centric notion of security. As Haq would put it, "We need to fashion a new concept of human security that is reflected in the lives of our people, not in the weapons of our country."[40] In his words:

human development dealt with the betterment of human lives and ability for a community to thrive. Human security sought to highlight the levels of human development achieved, but to the "security" of gains made by focusing on "downside risks" of political conflict, war, economic fluctuations, natural disasters, extreme impoverishment, environmental pollution, ill health, illiteracy, and other social menaces.[41]

Although the message was intended for a global audience, South Asia formed a major context of Haq's work. "He was particularly concerned with the countries of South Asia; his own, Pakistan, and India ... He was shocked that it [South Asia] had fallen behind sub-Saharan Africa, to become the most deprived region in the world."[42] This sad state of affairs could be blamed particularly on the "guns versus butter" problem. High military expenditure came at the expense of a country's development. It was "tragically comic" that India and Pakistan were "bleeding their economies" to pay for arms.[43] In his book *Reflections on Human Development*, he pointed out that the national priorities chosen by a country or its rulers – "guns or butter, an elitist model of development or an egalitarian one, political authoritarianism or political democracy, a command economy or participatory development" – were an essential element of human development.[44]

It has been suggested that Haq's interest in a people-centric approach to security was inspired by his experience with India's partition. Sen

---

[38] United Nations Development Program, *Human Development Report 2005: International Cooperation at a Crossroads* (New York: United Nations Development Program, 2005), 18–19.

[39] Haq, *Reflections on Human Development*, 15.

[40] Cited in Kanti Bajpai, "Human Security: Concept and Measurement," 2000, Manuscript.

[41] Khadija Haq and Richard Ponzio, *Pioneering the Human Development Revolution: An Intellectual Biography of Mahbub ul Haq* (New Delhi: Oxford University Press, 2008), 114.

[42] "Mahbub ul Haq (Obituary)."

[43] Ibid.

[44] Haq, *Reflections on Human Development*, 14.

believed that "the Pakistani experience of Mahbub influenced him. His family was from Kashmir; he nearly died at the time of partition."[45] Sen further maintains that, while "we may underestimate him if we try to link him to his past," and it might be better to think of him "as a global intellectual, rather than as someone who [was] informed by local upbringing," "that locality must have also played a part."[46]

The 1994 Human Development Report defined the scope of human security to include threats in seven areas:[47]

1. Economic security: Economic security requires an assured basic income for individuals, usually from productive and remunerative work, or in the last resort, from some publicly financed safety net. In this sense, only about a quarter of the world's people may at present be economically secure.
2. Food security: This requires that all people at all times have both physical and economic access to basic food. According to the United Nations, the overall availability of food is not a problem, rather the problem often is the poor distribution of food and a lack of purchasing power.
3. Health security: Health security aims to guarantee a minimum protection from diseases and unhealthy lifestyles.
4. Environmental security: Environmental security aims to protect people from the short- and long-term ravages of nature, human-made threats in nature, and deterioration of the natural environment. In developing countries, one of the greatest environmental threats is that to water. Water scarcity is increasingly becoming a factor in ethnic strife and political tension. Water pollution also leads to the lack of safe sanitation in developing countries. In industrial countries, one of the major threats is air pollution. Global warming, believed to be caused by the emission of greenhouse gases, is another environmental security issue.
5. Personal security: This refers to the protection of people from physical violence, whether from the state or external states, from violent individuals and sub-state factors, from domestic abuse, and from predatory adults. For many people, the greatest source of anxiety is

[45] Amartya Sen, "A 20th Anniversary Human Development Discussion with Amartya Sen," http://hdr.undp.org/en/media/Amartya-Sen-interview-transcript.1.pdf.
[46] Sen, "A 20th Anniversary Human Development Discussion with Amartya Sen."
[47] United Nations, *Human Development Report 1994*, as cited in the Report of the Commission on Global Governance, *Our Global Neighbourhood* (Oxford University Press, 1995).

crime, particularly violent crime. Industrial and traffic accidents are also great risks.

6. Community security: This is aimed to protect people from the loss of traditional relationships and values and from sectarian and ethnic violence.
7. Political security: Political security is concerned with whether people live in a society that honors their basic human rights. Along with repressing individuals and groups, governments may try to exercise control over ideas and information.

One of the main criticisms of the UNDP definition, mainly from the West, was that it left the definition and scope of human security too broad. Defenders of the report, mainly from the developing world, countered that a broad definition is both necessary and desirable given the wider constituency of the UN. A major critic of the UNDP report was the Canadian government under the foreign policy leadership of Lloyd Axworthy.[48] While acknowledging the report as the source of the "specific phrase" human security, Canada critiqued it for focusing too much on threats associated with underdevelopment and ignoring "human insecurity resulting from violent conflict."[49] In the Canadian view, human security is "security of the people" and the UN Charter, the Universal Declaration of Human Rights, and the Geneva Conventions are the "core elements" of the doctrine of human security. "The concept of human security has increasingly centered on the human costs of violent conflict."[50] This understanding of human security was shared by a few other like-minded middle powers, such as Norway, which joined hands with Ottawa in establishing a Human Security Partnership. The partnership identified a nine-point agenda of human security focused on land mines, formation of an International Criminal Court, human rights, international humanitarian law, women and children in armed conflict, small arms proliferation, child soldiers, child labor, and Northern co-operation.[51]

A different understanding of human security, which gave priority to "freedom from want" (see Table 5.1), was developed by Japan and ASEAN proponents, reflecting the influence of their prior notions of

[48] On the origins of the Canadian use of human security, see Jennifer Ross, "Is Canada's Human Security Policy Really the 'Axworthy' Doctrine?" *Canadian Foreign Policy* 8, no. 2 (Winter 2001), 75–93.
[49] Department of Foreign Affairs and International Trade (DFAIT), "Human Security: Safety for People in a Changing World" (Ottawa: DFAIT, April 1999).
[50] Ibid.
[51] "Canada, Norway Change their Ways: New Approach Bases Foreign Policy on Human Issues," *The Ottawa Citizen*, May 28, 1998, A18.

Table 5.1. *Two conceptions of human security*

	Freedom from want	Freedom from fear
Original proponents	Development economists (Haq, Sen)	Western governments (Canada, Norway)
Main stimulus	Dissatisfaction over orthodox growth-oriented development models; guns versus butter concerns	End of the Cold War; rise of complex emergencies, ethnic strife, state failure, humanitarian intervention
Type of threats addressed	Non-military and non-traditional security concerns: poverty, environmental degradation, disease, etc.	Armed conflicts, violence against individuals
Main policy goal	Promoting human development, defined as "building human capabilities – the range of things that people can do, and what they can be ... The most basic capabilities for human development are leading a long and healthy life, being educated and having adequate resources for a decent standard of living ... [and] social and political participation in society." These capabilities are undermined by poverty, disease and ill-health, illiteracy, discrimination, threat of violent conflict, and denial of political and civil liberties (HDR, 2005, 18–19).	Protecting people in conflict zones. Reducing the human costs of conflict through bans on land mines and child soldiers, protecting human rights, developing peacebuilding mechanisms.
Policy frameworks	Human Development Index Commission on Human Security	Ottawa Treaty to ban land mines; International Criminal Court, International Commission on Humanitarian Intervention and State Sovereignty

comprehensive security.[52] Official statements by Japan on human security came to reveal important areas of disagreement with the Canadian formulation.[53] While acknowledging that "[t]here are two basic aspects to human security – freedom from fear and freedom from want," the Japanese Foreign Ministry criticized those who "focus solely" on the first aspect and related initiatives such as control of small arms and prosecution of war crimes. While these are important:

> In Japan's view, however, human security is a much broader concept. We believe that freedom from want is no less critical than freedom from fear. So long as its objectives are to ensure the survival and dignity of individuals as human beings, it is necessary to go beyond thinking of human security solely in terms of protecting human life in conflict situations.

I do not argue that the divergent perspectives on human security, such as those held by Japan and Canada, are symptomatic of a value-clash between Western liberalism and "Asian values." This would be misleading. After all, the Canadian approach was also geared to addressing the internal conflicts and humanitarian crises which are more commonplace in the non-Western world. Disagreements about human security are as much West–West and East–East as East–West. But they do to a certain extent reflect the distinctive security predicaments of Western and non-Western countries.

To a large extent, countries in the developing world had already embraced a broader conception of security with reference to economic underdevelopment and resource constraints. They would now embrace human security more in the sense of "freedom from want," rather than the exclusively "freedom from fear" aspect championed by Canada (and others such as Norway). This is hardly surprising, since the construction and

[52] Tatsuro Matsumae and Lincoln Chen, eds., *Common Security in Asia: The New Concept of Human Security* (Tokyo: Tokai University Press, 1995); William T. Tow, Ramesh Thakur, and In-Taek Hyun, eds., *Asia's Emerging Regional Order: Reconciling Traditional and Human Security* (Tokyo and New York: United Nations University Press, 2000); Statement by Director-General (of the Foreign Ministry of Japan) at the International Conference on Human Security in a Globalized World, Ulan Bator, May 8, 2000, www.mofa.go.jp/policy/human_secu/speech0005.html; Pranee Thiparat, ed., *The Quest for Human Security: The Next Phase of ASEAN?* (Bangkok: Institute of Security and International Studies, 2001). See also: Tadashi Yamamoto, "Human Security: What It Means and What It Entails," in *The Asia Pacific in the New Millennium: Political and Security Challenges*, ed. Mely Caballero-Anthony and Mohamed Jawhar Hassan (Kuala Lumpur: Institute of Strategic and International Studies, 2001), 573–582; Mei Zhaorung, "Human Security and the State," *The Asia–Australia Papers*, no. 2 (September 1999); Hans van Ginkel and Edward Newman, "In Quest for Human Security," *Japan Review of International Affairs* 14 (Spring 2000), 59–82.
[53] Statement by Director-General (of the Foreign Ministry of Japan) at the International Conference on Human Security in a Globalized World.

localization (Chapter 2) of ideas and norms often happens on the basis of prior beliefs and practices as well as the context and need of actors. We have seen that addressing economic underdevelopment (hence "freedom from want") had already been important to the developing world. The "freedom from want" also renders the concept of human security less controversial for governments in the developing world suspicious of, and uncomfortable with, the close association between human security and human rights promotion and humanitarian intervention.

In Asia, for example, the economic aspect of human security was highlighted in the aftermath of the regional economic crisis in 1997. The crisis dramatically increased the incidence of poverty, undermined the fruits of decades of development, caused widespread political instability (the most dramatic case being Indonesia), and aggravated economic competition and inter-state tensions over refugees and illegal migration. Moreover, the crisis underscored the crucial need for social safety nets for the poor, something ignored in the heady days of growth. As such, the crisis helped to persuade initially skeptical Asian policymakers of the relevance of the concept of human security to the region. (More discussion of this later in this chapter.)

But the two elements of human security have become progressively reconciled. Human security is now seen as both "freedom from fear" and "freedom from want." Four major developments have produced this convergence: (1) the growing incidence of civil wars and intra-state conflicts which now far outnumber conventional inter-state conflicts (with the former more likely to cause civilian suffering than the latter); (2) the spread of democratization (democracies constitute a majority of state actors in the international system today); (3) the advent of humanitarian intervention, or the principle that the international community is justified in intervening in the internal affairs of states accused of gross violation of human rights; and (4) the widespread poverty, unemployment, and social dislocation caused by the economic crises of the 1990s (which were felt more in the developing world) and those of 2008–2009 (which were felt in the West as well as the developing world), which have been blamed on the uneven effects of globalization. What is striking is that these developments are generally in keeping with the prior and ongoing security challenges facing the non-Western world, but are now accepted as threatening global security as a whole. Hence, the differing approaches to human security are no longer seen as mutually exclusive, but as complementary and evolving understandings of a complex and larger paradigm of human security in response to emerging challenges, responses which collectively shift the focus of security analysis from national, state, and regime security to the society and the individual.

Like the notion of national security and its broadening to include non-military threats to the state, the concept of human security has also been contested. The key issue here is whether "securitization" of "freedom from want" is meaningful or morally desirable and defensible. The theory of securitization and de-securitization was originally developed by the Copenhagen school led by Ole Waever.[54] Simply stated, securitization involves considering an issue, such as extremism, natural disasters, climate change, pandemics, drug trafficking, etc., as a *security threat*.[55] Securitization explains how non-military threats are brought into the domain of security policy with a view to raising their profile in the national agenda of governments and thereby mobilizing greater attention and resources to address them.[56] But when it comes to human security, securitization is a double-edged sword.

Among the benefits of securitization are the prospects for giving more attention to threats, mobilization of greater resources to address the threats, and the creation of new and better organizations and institutions for addressing such threats. Critics argue that securitization might lead to the militarization of certain threats and reinforce the hands of the state. After all, who does the securitizing and with what concept: national or human security?[57] In certain societies, securitization can be a threat to democracy and civil liberties by empowering the military at the expense of the civil society. States usually securitize an issue by invoking national security, rather than the security of individuals or the people. Civil society groups may securitize by invoking human security, rather than national security, but when there is a conflict between them and governments, the latter usually win, especially in developing countries with a tendency to slide toward authoritarianism. Despite these concerns, however, the idea of human security is generally seen as more people-centered and a healthy move toward a more relevant concept of security for the post-Cold War era and the twenty-first century.

[54] Ole Waever, "Securitization and Desecuritization," in *On Security*, ed. Ronnie D. Lipschutz (New York: Columbia University Press, 1998), 46–86.

[55] Securitization "is the move that takes politics beyond the established rules of the game and frames the issue either as a special kind of politics or as above politics" and it "can thus be seen as a more extreme version of politicization." Desecuritization, on the other hand, refers to the reverse process. It involves the "shifting of issues out of emergency mode and into the normal bargaining processes of the political sphere." Barry Buzan, Ole Waever, and Jaap de Wilde, *Security: A New Framework for Analysis* (Boulder, CO: Lynne Rienner, 1998).

[56] Amitav Acharya, "What is Non-Traditional Security?" Presentation prepared for the Institute of Defence and Strategic Studies, Singapore, September 12, 2006; Amitav Acharya, "Non-Traditional Security: The Concept, Theory and Research Agenda," Presented at the Institute for International Relations, Hanoi, September 14, 2006.

[57] Mely Caballero-Anthony, Ralf Emmers, and Amitav Acharya, eds., *Non-Traditional Security in Asia: Dynamics of Securitisation* (London: Ashgate, 2006); Mely Caballero-Anthony, ed., *An Introduction to Non-Traditional Security Studies* (London: Sage, 2015).

Human Security in the Post-Cold War Era

In the evolution of the idea of security, what was once regarded as the distinctive security predicament of the Third World has come to define the central security challenge of the international community as a whole. What were regarded as regional conflicts within the "periphery" came to be recognized as the "core" issues of the security studies agenda, especially that which deals with human security. In that sense, the shift from bipolarity to multipolarity to the unipolar moment has made little difference to the source of conflicts in many parts of the developing world where conflicts continue to be rooted in essentially domestic and intra-regional factors related to weak national integration, economic underdevelopment, and competition for political legitimacy and control.

We know this well because, thanks to the idea of human security, the trends in armed violence – a key indicator of human security – are better captured today than during the Cold War. The human security idea impressed upon the international community the need to pay closer international attention to internal conflicts around the world, and estimate both military and civilian casualties and the broader effects of armed violence. A major offshoot of this awareness was the *Human Security Report*, the first of which was released in 2005. That report claimed a 40 percent drop in armed conflicts (with at least twenty-five battle-related deaths, where one of the parties was a state) in the world since 1991, as well as a 98 percent decline in the average number of battle deaths per conflict per year.[58] But this optimism has to be qualified. In 2005, the UNDP Human Development Report found that while fewer conflicts might be occurring in the world, the share of those conflicts occurring in poor countries has increased.[59] Deaths directly or indirectly attributed to the conflict in the Democratic Republic of the Congo, for example, have

---

[58] Human Security Centre, *Human Security Report 2005: War and Peace in the 21st Century* (New York: Oxford University Press, 2005). The report listed several reasons for this, such as rising economic interdependence (which increases the costs of conflict); growing democratization (the underlying assumption here being that democracies tend to be better at peaceful resolution of conflicts); a growing number of international institutions that can mediate in conflicts; the impact of international norms against violence, including war crimes and genocide; the end of colonialism; and the end of the Cold War. A specific reason identified by the report is the dramatic increase in the UN's role in areas such as preventive diplomacy and peacemaking activities, post-conflict peace-building, the willingness of the UN Security Council to use military action to enforce peace agreements, the deterrent effects of war crime trials by the war crimes tribunals and the International Criminal Court (ICC), and the greater resort to reconciliation and addressing the root causes of conflict (ibid., Part V).

[59] United Nations Development Program (UNDP), *Human Development Report 2005: International Cooperation at a Crossroads* (New York: United Nations Development Program, 2005), 12.

surpassed casualties sustained by Britain in World Wars I and II combined. And the conflict in Sudan's Darfur region has displaced nearly 2 million people.[60] Campaigns of organized violence against civilians increased by 56 percent between 1989 and 2005. Although most of these kill relatively few people, these figures support the popularly held belief that civilians are increasingly being victimized in the post-Cold War era by the perpetrators of political violence.[61]

The number of armed conflicts, defined as conflict between two parties, at least one of which is a government of a state, leading to a minimum of twenty-five battle-related deaths, has risen recently. It dropped from fifty-one in 1991 (the peak year for armed conflicts in the post-Cold War era) to thirty-one in 2010, the lowest number of such conflicts in the post-Cold War era. But the year 2014 saw an upsurge, with a total of forty armed conflicts, the highest number since 1999. Moreover, 2014 also saw the highest number of battle-related deaths since 1989.[62] Conflicts claiming more than a thousand lives, defined as wars, declined from sixteen in 1988 to seven in 2013, but increased to eleven in 2014.[63]

Moreover, one of the key trends is the steady decline of conventional inter-state conflict and the growth of intra-state and internationalized conflicts (see Figure 5.1). In 2014, according to the Uppsala Conflict Data Project (UCPD), there was only one large-scale inter-state conflict (between India and Pakistan).[64] This is consistent with the security predicament and lessons from the developing world, which, as discussed at the outset, had identified domestic or intra-state conflicts as being more numerous than inter-state conflicts.

A good deal of literature on global security in the post-Cold War era revolves around the notion of failing and failed states.[65] These are states with a number of shared characteristics:

There is no failed state (broadly, a state in anarchy) without disharmonies between communities ... In most failed states, regimes prey on their own constituents ... failed states cannot control their peripheral regions, especially those

[60] Ibid.
[61] Human Security Centre, *Human Security Brief 2006* (Vancouver: Liu Institute for Global Issues, University of British Columbia, 2006).
[62] Therése Pettersson and Peter Wallensteen, "Armed Conflicts, 1946–2014," *Journal of Peace Research* 52, no. 4 (2015), 536.
[63] Ibid., 539.
[64] Ibid., 537.
[65] On failed states, see: Dan Halvorson, *States of Disorder: Understanding State Failure and Intervention in the Periphery* (New York: Routledge, 2013); Derick W. Brinkerhoff, "State Fragility and Failure as Wicked Problems: Beyond Naming and Taming," *Third World Quarterly* 35, no. 2 (2014), 333–344; Zaryab Iqbal and Harvey Starr, *State Failure in the Modern World* (Stanford University Press, 2015).

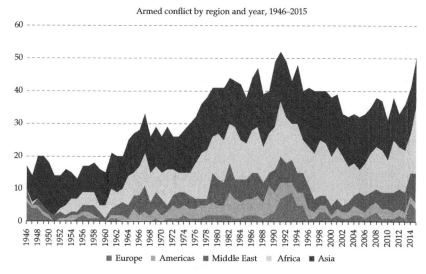

Figure 5.1 Number of armed conflicts by type, 1946–2015
Source: Uppsala Conflict Data Project (UCDP), Uppsala University.

regions occupied by out-groups ... Another indicator of state failure is the growth of criminal violence ... Failed states provide only limited quantities of other essential political goods.[66]

A report by the Congressional Research Service identifies four conditions of failing and failed states:[67]

1. peace and stability ("Failing states are often in conflict, at risk of conflict and instability, or newly emerging from conflict. Lacking physical security, other state functions are often compromised");
2. effective governance ("Countries can also be hampered by poor governance, corruption, and inadequate provisions of fundamental services");
3. territorial control and porous borders ("Weak and failing states may lack effective control of their territory ... providing space where instability can fester"); and
4. economic sustainability ("as a consequence of other security and political deficiencies, weak and failing states often lack the conditions to achieve lasting economic development").

[66] Robert I. Rotberg, *When States Fail: Causes and Consequences* (Princeton University Press, 2003), 5–6.
[67] L. S. Wyler, *Weak and Failing States: Evolving Security Threats and US Policy* (Washington, DC: Congressional Research Service, 2008), 3–4; as cited in Andrew Taylor, *State Failure* (Basingstoke: Palgrave Macmillan, 2013), 18.

Table 5.2. *Top 20 fragile states, 2016*

1	Somalia
2	South Sudan
3	Central African Republic
4	Sudan
5	Yemen
6	Syria
7	Chad
8	Congo (DR)
9	Afghanistan
10	Haiti
11	Iraq
12	Guinea
13	Nigeria
14	Pakistan
15	Burundi
16	Zimbabwe
17	Guinea Bissau
18	Eritrea
19	Niger
20	Kenya

Source: The Failed States Index (Washington, DC: The Fund for Peace, 2016), accessed October 28, 2016, http://fsi.fundforpeace .org/. The index measures a state's vulnerability to conflict or collapse using social, economic, and political indicators, and focusing on state capacity and legitimacy.

A related category is fragile states, "highlighting not only the normal pressures that all states experience, but also ... identifying when those pressures are pushing a state towards the brink of failure."[68] (See Table 5.2.) Other relevant concepts used in analyzing security threats today are "limited statehood" and "limited sovereignty." According to Risse, "areas of limited statehood are those that lack the capacity to implement and enforce central decisions and/or a monopoly on the use of force." Arguing that "it is possible to observe governance and the provision of collective goods even under conditions of limited statehood," he "highlights the Western and Eurocentric bias of contemporary social science notions of statehood and governance," which have limited applicability to such cases.[69] It is not difficult to see important echoes in the conditions that

[68] *The Failed States Index* (Washington, DC: The Fund for Peace, 2016), accessed October 28, 2016, http://fsi.fundforpeace.org/.
[69] Thomas Risse, "Governance in Areas of Limited Statehood," in *The Oxford Handbook of Governance*, ed. David Levi-Faur (Oxford University Press, 2012); see also Thomas Risse, "Governance under Limited Sovereignty," Paper presented at the Annual Convention

define the contemporary notion of failing and failed states and limited statehood, or the picture of weak states presided over by illegitimate regimes painted by the earlier literature on Third World security, as discussed at the outset of this chapter.

Many other threats to human security are found disproportionately in the developing world. One is the issue of child soldiers. According to one study, "of ongoing or recently ended conflicts, 68% (37 out of 55) have children under 18 serving as combatants" and "80% of these conflicts ... include fighters under the age of 15."[70] Another source of human insecurity is land mines and unexploded ordnance. Despite the justified optimism generated by the Ottawa Treaty on banning land mines, some 10 million stockpiled land mines remained to be destroyed by 2011.[71] Moreover, 80 percent of those killed or injured by land mines are civilians.[72] Organized crime claims more lives: in Mexico in 2011, the death toll from drug-related organized criminal violence was higher than the battle-death toll of the war in Afghanistan or Sudan or Iraq.[73]

Wars damaging the environment is another key element of human security that is also salient in the developing world. This happened with the US use of the Agent Orange defoliant during the Vietnam War and Saddam Hussein's burning of Kuwaiti oil wells in the 1990/1 Gulf War leading to massive air and land pollution. Similar links can be made between conflict and outbreak of disease. Disease accounts for most of the 3.9 million people who have died in the conflict in the Democratic Republic of Congo.[74] As the *Human Security Report* puts it, "war-exacerbated disease and malnutrition kill far more people than missiles, bombs and bullets."[75]

Next, the link between development and security remains a major issue of global human security. (See Table 5.3 for an overview of poverty, disease, refugees, and human insecurity.) Many armed conflicts have

of the American Political Science Association, Washington DC, September 1–5, 2010, accessed October 28, 2016, www.princeton.edu/~pcglobal/conferences/basics/papers/risse_paper.pdf.

[70] Peter W. Singer, *Children at War* (New York: Pantheon, 2005), citing from Human Security Centre, *Human Security Report 2005: War and Peace in the 21st Century* (Oxford University Press, 2005), 113.

[71] UN Office for Disarmament Affairs, *Landmines*, accessed November 26, 2012, www.un.org/disarmament/convarms/Landmines.

[72] United Nations Global Issues, "Demining," UN.org, accessed October 31, 2016, www.un.org/en/globalissues/demining/.

[73] Human Security Report Project, *Human Security Report 2013: The Decline in Global Violence: Evidence, Explanation, and Contestation* (Vancouver: Human Security Press, 2013).

[74] Human Security Centre, *Human Security Report 2005*, 45.

[75] Ibid.

Table 5.3. *Poverty, disease, refugees, and human insecurity*

While extreme poverty in the world has declined, with the proportion of the world's population living at or below US$1.90 day dropping from 44% in 1981 and 37% in 1990 to 12.7% in 2012 (The World Bank, "Poverty," 2015), there were 6.3 million deaths among children under the age of five in 2013 (World Health Organization (WHO) 2014).

More than 34 million people have died from HIV-related causes, with a global death rate of about 1.2 million people in 2014 alone (WHO, HIV/AIDS, Fact sheet no. 360, July 2015).

Deaths from tuberculosis fell by 47% between 1990 and 2015, but in 2014, the disease produced 9.6 million illnesses and 1.5 million deaths. Low- and middle-income countries account for more than 95% of TB deaths (WHO, "Tuberculosis," 2015).

Almost half of the world's population, some 3.2 billion people, are at risk of malaria. Sub-Saharan Africa accounts for 89% of malaria cases and 91% of malaria deaths (WHO, "Malaria," 2015). The Ebola outbreak in West Africa claimed 11,314 lives (although it could be an underestimate) in the 19 months after it was first reported in March 2014 in six countries; Liberia, Guinea, Sierra Leone, Nigeria, the United States, and Mali (BBC News "Ebola: Mapping the Outbreak," November 6, 2015).

Other recent pandemics include the 2003 SARS (Severe Acute Respiratory Syndrome) outbreak in Asia, the 2009 H1N1 "swine flu" outbreak, which killed more than 18,000 people, and the 2012 Middle-East Respiratory Syndrome (MERS-CoV) which infected 1,179 people in twenty-five countries and caused 442 deaths. The director general of WHO warns that the world is "ill prepared for severe and sustained disease" (Meera Senthilingam, "Are We Ready for the Next Global Epidemic?" February 13, 2015).

"Globally, one in every 122 humans is now either a refugee, internally displaced, or seeking asylum," reported the United Nations High Commissioner for Refugees (UNHCR) in June 2015. Forcible displacement of people reached an all-time high, rising to 59.5 million by the end of 2014 compared with 37.5 million a decade before (UNHCR, "Worldwide Displacement Hits All-time High," 2015).

Sources: The World Bank, "Poverty," accessed November 29, 2015, www.worldbank.org/en/topic/poverty/overview; World Health Organization, "Children: Reducing Mortality," Fact sheet no. 178, September 2014, accessed November 29, 2015, www.who.int/mediacentre/factsheets/fs178/en/; World Health Organization, "HIV/AIDS," Fact sheet no. 360, July 2015, accessed November 29, 2015, www.who.int/mediacentre/factsheets/fs360/en/; World Health Organization, "Tuberculosis," Fact sheet no. 104, October 2015, accessed November 29, 2015, www.who.int/mediacentre/factsheets/fs104/en/; World Health Organization, "Malaria," Fact sheet no. 94, October 2015, accessed November 29, 2015, www.who.int/mediacentre/factsheets/fs094/en/); BBC News, "Ebola: Mapping the Outbreak," BBC News, November 6, 2015, accessed November 20, 2015, www.bbc.com/news/world-africa-28755033; Meera Senthilingam, "Are We Ready for the Next Global Epidemic?" February 13, 2015, accessed November 29, 2015, www.cnn.com/2015/02/13/health/are-we-ready-for-global-outbreak/; UNHCR, "Worldwide Displacement Hits All-time High as War and Persecution Increase," News Stories, June 18, 2015, accessed December 4, 2015, www.unhcr.org/558193896.html.

indirect consequences for human life and well-being. Wars are a major source of economic disruption, disease, and ecological destruction, which in turn undermine human development and thus create a vicious cycle of conflict and underdevelopment. As the *Human Development Report, 2005* puts it: "Conflict undermines nutrition and public health, destroys education systems, devastates livelihoods and retards prospects for economic growth." It found that of the fifty-two countries that are reversing or stagnating in their attempts to reduce child mortality, thirty have experienced conflict since 1990.[76] A British White Paper on International Development notes:

Violent conflict reverses economic growth, causes hunger, destroys roads, schools and clinics, and forces people to flee across borders ... Women and girls are particularly vulnerable because they suffer sexual violence and exploitation. And violent conflict and insecurity can spill over into neighbouring countries and provide cover for terrorists or organised criminal groups.[77]

Terrorism and the war on terror have emerged as a major challenge to global human security. Although the challenge is global, as seen in recent attacks in Paris, Brussels, and other European locations, the developing world continues to bear the brunt of deaths in terrorist attacks and civil wars. International terrorist incidents increased threefold worldwide between 2002 and 2005, the number of fatalities increasing fivefold.[78] Most of the increases were associated with the war in Iraq, where the number of fatalities in attacks grew from about 1,700 in 2004 to approximately 3,400 in 2005.[79] In Iraq, a team of American and Iraqi epidemiologists estimates that the country's mortality rate has more than doubled since the US invasion: from 5.5 deaths per 1,000 people in the year before the invasion to 13.3 deaths per 1,000 people per year in the post-invasion period.[80] The *Armed Conflict Survey 2015*, conducted by the International Institute for Strategic Studies (IISS), shows that while the number of armed conflicts in the world declined from sixty-three in 2008 to forty-two in 2014, there was a marked increase in the number of fatalities during the same period, from 56,000 in 2008 to 180,000 in

---

[76] Ibid., 12.
[77] *Eliminating World Poverty: Making Governance Work for the Poor*, A White Paper on International Development Presented to Parliament by the Secretary of State for International Development by Command of Her Majesty, July 2006, www.dfid.gov.uk/pubs/files/whitepaper2006/wp2006section3.pdf, 37.
[78] Human Security Centre, *Human Security Brief 2006*.
[79] NCTC Fact Sheet and Observations Related to 2005 Terrorist Incidents, www.NCTC.Gov.
[80] David Brown, "Study Claims Iraq's 'Excess' Death Toll Has Reached 655,000," *Washington Post*, October 11, 2006, A12.

2014.[81] Significantly, Iraq (where conflicts can be linked to the lingering effects of the US-led war on terror) and Syria (where the US shied away from humanitarian intervention owing to the shadow of Iraq) make up about half of deaths, about 88,000 in 2014.[82]

The central point of this chapter is that the distinctive issues of insecurity in the Third World not only challenged the concept of national security dominant in the West, they also continue to inform the analysis of conflicts in the post-Cold War era and the twenty-first century. This has necessitated a fundamental rethinking of the concept of security. The idea of national security and its traditional referent points, such as large-scale regional conflicts and nuclear weapons, have not disappeared.[83] But the insights and lessons of the conflict and instability in the Third World have become more central and more integrated to security thinking and approach in both the Western and the non-Western worlds, thereby paving the way for the emergence of the idea of "global security."

---

[81] The International Institute for Strategic Studies, *The IISS Armed Conflict Survey 2015*, Press Statement (London: Arundel House, May 20, 2015), www.iiss.org/en/about%20us/press%20room/press%20releases/press%20releases/archive/2015-4fe9/may-6219/armed-conflict-survey-2015-press-statement-a0be, 1.

[82] Ibid., 2.

[83] Whether viewed as freedom from fear or freedom from want, the concept of human security has not replaced national security, whether in Western or in developing countries. The European migrant and refugee crisis vividly demonstrates this. The International Organization for Migration (IOM) estimated that more than 464,000 migrants crossed into Europe by sea in the first nine months of 2015, with Syrians making up 39 percent of them. Jeanne Park, "Europe's Migration Crisis," CFR Backgrounder, September 23, 2015, accessed December 4, 2015, www.cfr.org/migration/europes-migration-crisis/p32874. In 2015, 3,770 migrants died in the Mediterranean. "Migrant Crisis: Migration to Europe Explained in Graphics," BBC News, March 4, 2016, accessed June 6, 2016, www.bbc.com/news/world-europe-34131911. Yet, the response of the EU countries has been divided and mixed, with the wealthier countries like Germany showing a more welcoming attitude toward the migrants than others, such as Croatia, Poland, Hungary, and the Czech Republic, but also because the whole issue of migration and refugees, especially from Islamic countries like Syria, Iraq, and Afghanistan, has been framed as a national security issue and linked to the threat to terrorism. As Khalid Koser of the Brookings Institution notes, "We used to think of migration as a human security issue: protecting people and providing assistance. Now we clearly perceive – or misperceive – migration as a national security issue." Cited in Jeanne Park, "Europe's Migration Crisis," Council on Foreign Relations, September 23, 2015, www.cfr.org/refugees-and-the-displaced/europes-migration-crisis/p32874.

6   Regionalism and the Making of Global Order

Chapter 1 has argued that agency in building global order can be exercised at the regional level. Regionalism is often seen to be of more immediate relevance to the security and economic concerns of nations, and easier to participate in, than global institutions. While Chapter 5 looked at the issue of agency in the transition from national to human security, this chapter looks at the exercise of agency through regional security institutions and its implications for global order-building. Chapter 2 has already discussed the role of regionalisms in Asia, Latin America, Africa, and the Middle East in provincializing (localizing) the Westphalian norm of sovereignty and building new subsidiary norms of non-intervention. This chapter looks at how regionalism in a variety of forms (some EU-inspired, others not) has contributed to the expansion and redefinition of sovereignty and security. Moreover, this chapter shows how the growing recognition of the varied context and agency in regionalism, especially between the EU and other parts of the world, has produced a newer, more inclusive understanding of regionalism that is especially important for constructing global order.

Regionalism[1] has been a longstanding normative force in international relations, predating the universal organization.[2] As Martin Rochester notes, "regional (or 'limited membership') intergovernmental

---

[1] The definition of regionalism varies. A broad definition is offered by *The Oxford Handbook on Comparative Regionalism* which views it as a "primarily state-led process of building and sustaining formal regional institutions and organizations among at least three states." Tanja A. Börzel and Thomas Risse, "Introduction: Framework of the Handbook and Conceptual Clarifications," in *Oxford Handbook of Comparative Regionalism*, ed. Tanja A. Börzel and Thomas Risse (Oxford University Press, 2016), 7.

[2] Not all scholars would agree on my normative view of regionalism. But I argue that this is captured in terms of its original objectives of peaceful resolution of conflict and desire for a more decentralized world order. Regionalism embodies the prescriptive view that solutions at the regional level should receive prior consideration, regional institutions are important contributors to peace in their own areas, there should be regional solutions to regional problems, and that responses to collective action problems should be tried first at the regional level if possible, before taking them to external actors and institutions.

organizations predated universal organizations and had always exceeded the latter in number."[3] Regionalism in Latin America began with a series of congresses starting with the Congreso Anfictiónico de Panamá (Congress of Panama) organized by Simón Bolívar in 1826 in Panama. The major forms of regionalism that emerged in the nineteenth and twentieth centuries, including pan-Americanism, pan-Africanism, pan-Arabism, and pan-Asianism, were founded on shared conceptions of history and culture (sometimes imagined) and a common project for the advancement of decolonization. They were multidimensional, encompassing racial, social, economic, and political unity, rather than reflecting a purely political or strategic purpose. Although these ideologies were later taken up and pursued by formal intergovernmental regional institutions like the OAS, the Arab League, and the OAU, they are best seen as a form of inter-societal, rather than intergovernmental, regionalism. While some aspired to the creation of nation-states out of colonial structures, others, like Nkrumah of Africa, Nasser of the Arab world, Aung San of Southeast Asia, and Nehru of wider Asia, openly envisioned federations or at least supranational entities.

A common feature of these regionalist movements was their anti-imperialist and anti-hegemonial aspirations and agendas. They were not only associated with independence movements, but also rejected the collective hegemony of the great powers over the weak. The non-Western regionalist ideas and institutional forms (Japan's Co-Prosperity sphere being a major exception) were generally more progressive and emancipatory than the Concert of Europe, which is often regarded as a key precursor to European regionalism. While the Concert of Europe was essentially conservative or reactionary, regionalist ideologies in Asia, Africa, and Latin America were geared to anti-colonialism, national liberation, protecting sovereignty, and challenging the dominance of big powers (as with Latin America's resistance to the Monroe Doctrine). This also differentiated them from the more progressive European groupings, such as the Council of Europe (founded in 1949) and the European Economic Community (EEC) (founded in 1957), which aimed at taming nationalism (and sovereignty in the case of the EEC) by protecting and promoting human rights, democracy, and the rule of law as key prerequisites for peace and prosperity.

Moreover, these regionalist movements outside Europe were led not just by political elites who would later become the leaders of individual countries, but also by intellectuals, poets (such as the ardent pan-Asianist

---

[3] J. Martin Rochester, "The Rise and Fall of Regionalism as a Field of Study," *International Organization* 40, no. 4 (Autumn 1986), 785–786.

and the Nobel literature prize winner Rabindranath Tagore of India), and art-lovers (such as Okakura Tenshin of Japan who famously coined the phrase "Asia is One"). Pan-Africanism was championed by people from diverse backgrounds, including the Trinidadian lawyer and writer Henry Sylvester Williams (1869–1911) who organized the First Pan-African Conference in London in 1900, Americo-Liberian educator and politician Edward Wilmot Blyden, and the American W. E. B. Du Bois.[4]

In 1948, K. M. Panikkar, an Indian scholar-diplomat, published one of the first books on regionalism in the English language in the non-Western world.[5] In this book, Panikkar rejected the hegemonic notion of regionalism, suggested by realist thinkers such as E. H. Carr, Walter Lippmann, and Winston Churchill. To them, regional arrangements meant the geostrategic spheres of influence of existing or prospective great powers. Walter Lippmann, for example, identified four such regional systems: an Atlantic system managed by the USA and the USSR; a Russian system, a Chinese system, and eventually an Indian system. Within such hegemonic regional systems, "the preponderance of a great power was to be recognised; each small power was to accept the protection of the great power in whose region it found itself, and was to forego the right to form alliances with any extra-regional power."[6] Winston Churchill similarly envisaged a number of regional systems as part of the proposed world organization (UN), including in Europe, Asia Minor, Scandinavia, Danubia, the Balkans, and the Far East.[7]

Rejecting these, Panikkar argued that the traditional idea of regional organization, which he identified in the Armed Neutrality of Northern Powers in the Napoleonic War, the US Monroe Doctrine, the concept of Mitteleuropa advocated by Friedrich Naumann for the Danubian regions, and the exclusive economic and political blocs developed by Nazi Germany in Europe and imperial Japan in East Asia, assumed the "establishment of the paramountcy of a Great Power in a defined geographical region." Hence, "so far, regional organization has meant nothing more than a polite phraseology for *lebensraum*."[8] Against this

---

[4] An important aspect here is that many of the champions of pan-Africanism were not from Africa itself, attesting to the possibility of an outside-in or sympathetic regionalism.

[5] K. M. Panikkar, "Regionalism and World Security," in *Regionalism and Security*, ed. K. M. Panikkar et al. (New Delhi: Indian Council of World Affairs, 1948). Indian interest in regionalism is shown in A. P. Rana, "Regionalism as an Approach to International Order: A Conceptual Overview," *International Studies* 18, no. 4 (October 1979), 491–535.

[6] Hedley Bull, *The Anarchical Society* (London: Macmillan, 1977), 222–223.

[7] Winston Churchill, *The Hinge of Fate* (Boston: Houghton Mifflin, 1950), 711–712.

[8] Panikkar, "Regionalism and World Security," 1.

hegemonic concept, Pannikar advanced what might be seen as an alternative conception of regionalism:

The conditions of different regions in the world differ so much that the promotion of higher standards of living, for example, has a different meaning in relation to the people of South-east Asia to what it has in European countries. The programme of any action to give effect to this object has to be worked out in terms of particular regions. Similar is the case with conditions of social progress ... Besides, from the point of view of standards of living, social and economic progress, and the observance of human rights and fundamental freedoms, it is the regions further away from Europe and America that require urgent attention.[9]

Panikkar's statement showed that scholars and policymakers (he was both) in regions other than Europe or America were thinking of regionalism as a way of addressing the most pressing challenges that these societies faced. More importantly, he saw regionalism not as the prerogative of the great powers in extending their influence over their weaker neighbors. In this respect, it was an outright rejection of the idea of great power-managed regional orders advocated by Churchill. Instead, regionalism was seen as a means for all regions – especially the regions "further away from Europe and America" including those which would be subsequently known as the "Third World" – to address their social, economic, and political (including human rights) needs and challenges.

Panikkar's statement also underscored the sheer diversity of regions in terms of economic, social, and political conditions, with the clear implication that no single institution, formula, or approach can apply to all of them. Although he was referring to the practical problems that regionalism might address, given the diversity of regions, can any single theory or model explain the prospects and outcome of regionalism in all parts of the world? In short, Panikkar presented regionalism as more than a European formula or an American doctrine (one chapter of the book was about Europe, the rest covered the Arab League, the Inter-American System, South-East Asia, the Indian Ocean, and the Pacific), and challenged the hitherto conflation of regionalism and regional organization with regional power blocs or spheres of influence. Hegemonic regionalism, or the idea that world order should be managed by a number of regional groups each under its respective local great power/s, had also been challenged by Latin American countries, in the form of the Calvo Doctrine (1868) and the Drago Doctrine (1902), which stressed the importance of local autonomy and disapproved of intervention by great powers like the United States in Latin American affairs. Decades later,

[9] Ibid., 5–6.

India's first Prime Minister, who also was one of the most influential voices of the newly independent countries, vigorously criticized the idea of regional power blocs as the "continuation of power politics on a vaster scale" and thus detrimental to "world peace and cooperation."[10]

After World War II, these alternative ideas about regionalism from the developing world conformed closely to the subsidiarity model, with the sense that it was advocated by weaker nations who wanted some autonomy from the exclusive universal collective security system being organized by the USA. The most vocal advocacy of this form of regionalism came from the Latin American states during the debates over the drafting of the UN Charter at the San Francisco Conference in 1945. They, along with other newly independent or soon to be independent countries (especially in the Arab world), argued that an all-powerful Security Council would dominate regional institutions which also aimed at providing mechanisms for conflict control within their respective regions.[11] While the United States expressed a strong preference for universalism, delegates from twenty-one Latin American countries fervently demanded a place for regionalism within the UN Charter, contesting the US preference for universalism which sought to give the sole authority of maintaining global peace and security to the UN Security Council. Some Latin American delegations, such as Brazil, went to the extent of arguing that matters pertaining to the security of regions should be resolved exclusively by regional groups of the area, with "the intervention of the Security Council in the solution of these questions only being justified when they endanger the peace of more than one regional group."[12] Others accepted a place for regionalism in the UN system, but subject to the overall authority of the Security Council. Either way, they showed a strong passion for regionalism, drawing upon the experience in building regionalism over the previous five decades. This was brought out clearly in the statement of the delegate from Mexico, Ambassador Castillo Najera, who referred to the desire of the delegations of the American nations to showcase and preserve their "Pan-American ideal." As he put it, "the first consideration of the delegations of the American nations was to safeguard their greatest achievement, the most precious flower of cooperation for security through peaceful means."[13] The delegate from

---

[10] Jawaharlal Nehru, *The Discovery of India* (New Delhi: Oxford, 1946), 539.

[11] For the classic review of the regionalist arguments, see: Minerva Etzioni, *The Majority of One: Towards a Theory of Regional Compatibility* (Beverly Hills: Sage, 1970).

[12] Statement by the Brazilian Delegation before Commission III, May 14, 1945, Document 269, p. 5 (UNCIO, vol. XII, 1945), 768.

[13] Statement by Ambassador Castillo Najera, Delegate of Mexico, before Commission III, Security Council, June 14, 1945, Document 972 (UNCIO, vol. XI, 1945: 54), 7.

Venezuela, Parra Perez, characterized the pro-regionalist attitude of the American nations as a "question of safeguarding a whole tradition [the Inter-American system] which was dear to our continent, that of a living organism and a very active one."[14] Delegations from the newly formed Arab League submitted the League's Charter as an example of regional arrangements that should find a place in the new global security system.

Regionalist doctrines of conflict control which emerged from this "universalist–regionalist debate" made three specific claims.[15] First, geographic neighbors have a better understanding of local disputes than distant actors operating through a global body, and the former are better able to provide assistance to victims of aggression than the latter. Second, regional organizations are "stepping-stones" toward world organization; regional collaboration and coordination on major issues could be useful experience for states in the progress toward global collective security. Third, regional arrangements could diminish the scope for the involvement of the great powers, and keep conflicts from spreading beyond a limited geographic area.

The success of the regionalists in arguing their position was evident from the UN Charter that emerged from the San Francisco Conference. The UN Charter listed mediation by regional agencies as one of the techniques of international conflict control (Article 33/1, Chapter VI), while UN members were encouraged to "make every effort to achieve pacific settlement of local disputes through such regional arrangements ..." (Article 52/2, Chapter VIII), before taking the matter up with the Security Council. Senator Arthur Vandenberg, the head of the US delegation to the San Francisco Conference, recognized the special role of the Latin American countries in securing regional organizations due recognition under the UN Charter:

we have found a sound and practical formula for putting regional organizations into effective gear with the global institution which we here erect on behalf of the world's peace and security ... We do not thus subtract from global unity ... on the contrary, we weld these regional king-links into the global chain ... one of these king-links is particularly dear to the hearts of the twenty-one republics in this Western Hemisphere. It is a precious inheritance with 50 years of benign history

---

[14] Statement by Parra Perez, Delegate of Venezuela, before Commission III, Security Council, June 14, 1945, Document 972 (UNCIO, vol. XI, 1945: 56), 9.

[15] For analyses of the universalist and regionalist positions, see: Francis W. Wilcox, "Regionalism and the United Nations," *International Organization* 19, no. 3 (1965), 789–811; Ernst Haas, "Regionalism, Functionalism and Universal Organization," *World Politics* 8, no. 2 (January 1956), 238–263; Inis Claude, *Swords into Plowshares* (New York: Random House, 1964), chapter 6; Norman J. Padelford, "Regional Organizations and the United Nations," *International Organization* 8, no. 2 (1954), 203–216.

behind it ... There are other regional arrangements of great honor and validity. I exclude none of them when I speak of Pan-Americanism as a symbol. I simply point to it as being the oldest and happiest regional arrangement in the world.[16]

Although the advocates of regionalism compromised by accepting that regional arrangements should only function under the final authority of the UN Security Council, rather than independent of it, the advocacy of the non-Western delegations was crucial in giving regionalism a legal basis as a means of dispute settlement and collective security under the UN Charter, and allowed regionalism to grow more relevant as the authority of the Security Council was undermined by the Cold War stalemate between the United States and the Soviet Union.

As the Cold War unfolded, the idea of regionalism as great power spheres of influence (or what might be called "hegemonic regionalism") which had been rejected by Pannikar and Nehru resurfaced when both the superpowers in Europe established military alliances, with NATO and the Warsaw Pact becoming "symbols of the continuity and immobility of international politics in Europe."[17] But outside Europe, regional alliances fared much worse. This was evident in the case of SEATO, CENTO, and the Inter-American Security System. The decline and eventual demise of SEATO and CENTO could be attributed to three factors. First, the credibility of these groups suffered due to weak commitments on the part of the great power patrons. While in the case of NATO American response to Soviet aggression was assumed to be automatic, the Asian allies in CENTO and SEATO were disappointed by the level of assurances and security guarantees offered by the United States. A second factor was the divergent nature of security objectives between the great power partners on the one hand and their Third World clients on the other. Many of the Third World partners saw internal challenges to regime survival as the main threat to security, rather than an overt communist aggression or subversion that had been advanced by the United States as the major rationale for creating these groupings. Third, SEATO and CENTO were also criticized for inciting great power rivalry in the regional theaters since alliance with one superpower would invite response and competitive coalition-building by the other superpower. Finally, the superpower detente of the early 1970s severely undermined the credibility of the American commitment to anti-Soviet regional coalitions in the Third

[16] Statement by Senator Arthur Vandenberg, before Commission III, Security Council, June 14, 1945, Document 972 (UNCIO, vol. XI, 1945: 52), 5.
[17] Hedley Bull, "European Security Alliances in the 1980s," in *The Future of European Alliance Systems: NATO and the Warsaw Pact*, ed. Arlene Idol Broadhurst (Boulder, CO: Westview Press, 1982), 3–18, 9.

World. Detente also raised the unsavory prospect of a superpower condominium that might compromise or ignore the security interests of the Third World states in general. The disbanding of SEATO in 1975 and CENTO in 1979 put an end to more than a decade of defunct existence resulting from the disillusionment of the Third World partners on the one hand and lack of interest on the part of the great power patrons on the other. In the context of CENTO, Lenczowski has pointed out that it "either did not quite fit the new political conditions of the world, or had disappointed its Asian members by failing to give them adequate assurances and guarantees."[18] The same applies to SEATO, which had become virtually defunct by the early 1970s. Its two regional members – Thailand and the Philippines – opted for a more "homegrown" regional framework which the establishment of ASEAN in 1967 offered.

In the meantime, the subsidiarity framework of regionalism, represented in the three "original" macro-regional political groups, the OAS, the Arab League, and the OAU (created in 1963), did perform an important role in conflict control in their respective regions. Examples include: the League's mediation in the Iraq–Kuwait dispute over the former's irredentist claim to the latter; the OAU's role in disputes between Algeria and Morocco (1963), Ethiopia and Somalia (1964), and Rwanda and Burundi (1967); and the OAS's involvement in conflicts between Costa Rica and Nicaragua (1948 and again in 1955), Honduras and Nicaragua (1957), Panama and Cuba (1959), Venezuela and Dominican Republic (1960), and Haiti and Dominican Republic (1963).[19] They also confirmed that despite the assumed complementarity between universalism and regionalism as approaches to conflict management, the UN and the regional groups have been increasingly in competition with each other, and that the decline of regional groups can at least be partly explained by the success of the UN.

But a variety of factors contributed to the weakness and declining performance of these macro-regional groupings:

1. Politicization of the dispute-settlement process. Although all three
   groups provided for specific institutions and procedures for pacific

---

[18] George Lenczowski, *The Middle East in World Affairs* (Ithaca: Cornell University Press, 1980), 161.
[19] In general, Haas concluded that the effectiveness of the OAS declined sharply after the 1965 Dominican Republic crisis, coinciding with the emergence of the Soviet–Cuban alliance and the declining hegemony of the USA within the OAS. The Arab League's decline could be traced to the Camp David Accords in 1979; while for the OAU, a creditable performance during the 1966–1975 period was followed by a poor record during the 1976–1984 period. Ernst B. Haas, *Why We Still Need the United Nations* (Berkeley, CA: University of California, Institute of International Studies), 29–34.

settlement of disputes, these were undermined by personalized and politicized processes of diplomacy by leaders of member states which became commonplace.[20]

2. Lack of resources, material and human. This was evident in the case of the OAU's peacekeeping operation in Chad.
3. Unsuitability of mediation in internal conflicts, which accounted for a large percentage of conflicts in the Third World.[21]
4. Failure to limit superpower meddling and intervention in regional affairs. Although a major objective of all three groups was to ensure autonomy, defined by Zartman as a condition in which regional "actions and responses predominate over external influences,"[22] in real life Cold War divisions and superpower intervention inevitably found their way to regional mediation efforts. Superpower involvement was the result of both "pull" (the solicitation by regional actors

[20] Boutros Boutros-Ghali, "The League of Arab States and the Organization of African Unity," in *The Organization of African Unity after Ten Years: Comparative Perspectives*, ed. Yassin El-Ayouty (New York: Praeger, 1975), 50–61. See also: Henry Wiseman, "The OAU: Peacekeeping and Conflict Resolution," in *The OAU after Twenty Years*, ed. Yassin El-Ayouty and I. William Zartman (New York: Praeger, 1984), 123–153.

[21] For a study of the constraints on regional organizations in regulating internal conflict, see: Linda B. Miller, "Regional Organization and the Regulation of Internal Conflict," *World Politics* 19, no. 4 (July 1967), 582–600. For the most part, the "original" regional groups did not view intra-state conflicts as constituting the major part of their conflict-control agenda. Preoccupied as they were with the problems of colonialism, the Cold War, regional pariahs, and inter-member conflict resolution, the Arab League, the OAU, and the OAS tended to avoid getting involved in domestic conflicts of their members unless such conflicts attracted a high degree of external involvement. The OAU, for example, more or less ignored such internal conflicts as the ethnic revolt in southern Sudan, the intense factional battle in Chad, and guerrilla warfare in the Eritrean province of Ethiopia. But even in cases where regional groups sought to play a role in internal conflicts of their members, the record of success was hardly impressive. A study by Joseph Nye of the overall conflict-resolution role of the OAS, OAU, and Arab League shows the almost complete failure of the latter two groups in deciding the outcome of internal conflicts (the 1964–1965 Congo crisis and the 1967–1970 Nigerian civil war in the case of the OAU and the 1958 Lebanese crisis and the 1962–1967 Yemen civil war in the case of the Arab League). In the case of the OAU, Nye concludes that "Regional consensus and impartiality did not break down in cases of interstate conflict, but did in cases of primarily internal conflict." Nye's study also shows that the interest of the regional group with regard to these conflicts was largely related to the objective of preventing external intervention. For example, Congo became a serious concern to the OAU only after the Belgian–American parachute drop, although before that Toshombe was widely disliked within the OAU as an "externally imposed traitor." The Arab League's involvement in the Lebanon crisis of 1958 was largely inspired by the fact that the crisis had assumed the nature of an inter-state dispute since Lebanon had accused the UAR of instigating the strife. Joseph S. Nye, *Peace in Parts: Integration and Conflict in Regional Organization* (Boston: Little Brown, 1971), chapter 5.

[22] I. William Zartman, "Africa as a Subordinate State-system in International Relations," in *Regional Politics and World Order*, ed. Richard A. Falk and Saul H. Mendlovitz (San Francisco: W. H. Freeman, 1971), 386.

of superpower involvement to enhance their security and bargaining positions) and "push" (the interest of the superpowers in extending their global role) factors, but together it served to undermine regional autonomy and regionalist doctrines about conflict isolation.

5. Conflicts involving states that were excluded from the regional organization. An important predicament of the original groups was that the major security issue in their respective regions involved the role of a non-member country: Israel in the case of the Arab League, South Africa and Rhodesia in the case of the OAU, and Cuba in the case of the OAS. This led to the distortion of their originally intended roles; instead of serving as an impartial instrument of mediation and arbitration, the macro-regional groupings assumed the role of an alliance (including defense cooperation) vis-à-vis the regional pariahs which were not subject to their jurisdiction or norms.[23]

6. The revival of the UN's peace and security role. In the final stages of the Cold War, regional organizations were upstaged by the two superpowers' preference for engaging the UN for agreements on a number of regional conflicts. Regional organizations were avoided partly because the superpowers could not exercise direct control over the negotiation process through them, unlike the UN Security Council where they enjoyed a veto power. Thus, the UN's role in several regional conflicts (Afghanistan, the Iran–Iraq War, Angola, Namibia, and Cambodia, and to a lesser extent Central America) contrasts sharply with the virtual irrelevance of the OAS in the Nicaragua–El Salvador conflict, the total failure of the League to deal with the Lebanese crisis, the Iran–Iraq War, and the Iraqi invasion of Kuwait, and the OAU's lack of effectiveness in the Morocco–Polsario and Chad conflicts.

7. The emergence of sub-regional groupings, which were not only more cohesive but competed with the macro-regional groupings for the regional conflict-control role.

The decline of the OAU, OAS, and the Arab League coincided with the emergence of sub-regional organizations, such as the Association of Southeast Asian Nations (ASEAN), the Gulf Cooperation Council (GCC), the Economic Community of West Asian States (ECOWAS), Mercosur (now UNASUR), the Contadora Group, the Organization of Frontline States (OFLS), and the Southern African Development Coordination Conference (SADCC, which later became the Southern

---

[23] Wilcox, "Regionalism and the United Nations."

African Development Community: SADC).[24] Like the original regional organizations, the sub-regional groupings were instruments for conflict control within their respective regions. But while ostensibly multipurpose in objective (with the exception of Contadora, which was basically a framework for conflict management), they had a narrow, specific security agenda; for example, ASEAN with the Cambodia conflict, the GCC with the Iran–Iraq War, the Contadora with the Nicaragua–El Salvador conflict, and SADCC and OFLS with South Africa. A study of five sub-regional groupings – ASEAN, GCC, SADCC, OECS, and SPF – concluded that they had made "greater progress in implementing means for conflict avoidance/conflict resolution than either the collective defense or the larger regional security organizations that preceded them."[25] In reality, however, there were great variations among them: ASEAN in particular proved much more effective in managing the Cambodia conflict and the Contadora Group the Central American conflict, than the GCC in dealing with the Iran–Iraq War. The OFLS was an important platform against the apartheid regime in South Africa. While none could displace the role of outside actors, including the UN (this was never their goal anyway), they were useful and important complements to the overall process of regional conflict management.

Aside from hegemonic regionalism and regional conflict-control organizations like the OAS, OAU, and the Arab League, another conception of regionalism acquired prominence in the post-war period. This was rooted firmly within the liberal perspective on international relations. Its most sophisticated expression is regional integration theory.[26] While the first framework of regionalism was expressed in the form of Cold War regional alliances and the second framework through macro-regional political groups, the empirical referent objects of the third framework were micro-regional economic organizations, the original model of which was provided by the establishment of the European Coal and Steel Community (ECSC) in 1951, which later evolved into the European Economic Community and later the European Union (EU). Although commonly known as regional integration, it would be

---

[24] Although a number of other sub-regional groupings emerged at this time, they did not provide for specific or formal institutions for pacific settlement of disputes among their members. These include: the South Pacific Forum (SPF), the Organization of Eastern Caribbean States (OECS), and the Southern African Development Coordination Committee (SADCC).

[25] William T. Tow, *Subregional Security Cooperation in the Third World* (Boulder, CO: Lynne Rienner, 1990), 77, 81.

[26] Joseph S. Nye, "Neorealism and Neoliberalism," *World Politics* 40, no. 2 (January 1988), 239.

more accurate, following Wiener and Diez, to call this form of regionalism "European integration," and the academic literature that it inspired
"European integration theory."[27]

Though not strictly with a security function, this conception of regionalism promised to go "beyond the nation-state" and to enable states to
overcome the security dilemma associated with it. The sovereignty-eroding
potential of this form of regionalism (which I call *integrative* regionalism in this chapter) was captured from a neofunctionalist standpoint
by Ernst Haas, who defined integration as "a process whereby political
actors in several distinct national settings are persuaded to shift their loy-
alties, expectations, and political activities towards a new centre, whose
institutions possess or demand jurisdiction over the preexisting national
states."[28] Karl Deutsch, a transactionalist, was more explicit in recognizing the potential of integrative regionalism to overcome the sovereignty
trap and the security dilemma. He defined regional integration as

the attainment, within a territory, of a "sense of community" and of institutions
and practices strong enough and widespread enough to assure, for a "long" time,
dependable expectations of "peaceful change" among its population.[29]

Deutsch envisaged two such kinds of "security communities," an "amalgamated" variety, in which the political units transferred their claim to
sovereignty to a new center, and a "pluralistic" variety, in which war
would no longer be accepted as a legitimate means of problem solving
among nominally sovereign states.[30]

While the EEC made rapid progress, albeit with periodic setbacks,
experiments in regional integration outside Europe did not take off.
Although in the developing world several micro-regional groups sought
to emulate the EEC, none succeeded in achieving a level of integration
that would create the conditions for a security community, whether the
amalgamated or the pluralistic variety. Neither could economic regionalism based on the EEC model, involving market centralization and

---

[27] Antje Wiener and Thomas Diez, eds., *European Integration Theory* (Oxford University
Press, 2004).

[28] Ernst B. Haas, *The Uniting of Europe: Political, Economic and Social Forces, 1950–1957*, 2nd
edition (Stanford University Press, 1968), 16.

[29] Karl Deutsch et al., *Political Community in the North Atlantic Area* (Princeton University
Press, 1957), 5. For a more recent restatement and elaboration of the "security com-
munity" concept, see Emmanuel Adler and Michael Barnett, eds., *Security Communities*
(Cambridge University Press, 1998).

[30] The idea of a security community was resurrected after the Cold War, albeit modified
with a heavy infusion of constructivist concepts, such as ideas, norms, and socialization which were only implicit in the original theory. See: Adler and Barnett, *Security
Communities*; Acharya, *Constructing a Security Community in Southeast Asia*, 1st edition
(London and New York: Routledge 2001).

generation of welfare gains, produce the desired "spill-over" effect lead-ing to cooperation over security issues. In general, regional economic integration in the Third World proved to be "much more rudimentary than in Europe, more obscure in purpose and uncertain in content."[31] Micro-regional integration groups which proliferated in Africa and Latin America have "founder[ed] on the reefs of distrust, non-cooperation and parochial nationalism," thereby raising basic questions regarding the applicability of the functionalist approach to the Third World.[32]

The limits of the regional integration experience in the Third World are most seriously exemplified in Latin America, which was once thought to have the best potential for such experiments. The Central American Common Market, once regarded as the very model of the neofunction-alist approach, has suffered a long paralysis. The Latin American Free Trade Area was abolished in 1980, as members realized the futility of developing a free trade area and a common market due to different lev-els of development and conflicts over the distribution of benefits among them. In Africa, similar trends characterized integration efforts with the eclipse of the East African Community and the UDEAC. The Economic Community of West African States (ECOWAS), set up in 1975, showed some potential for integration, but it could not deliver on its initial prom-ise of developing into "an economic Union that coordinates domestic policies at the regional level."[33]

Explaining why the West European model of integration did not travel well to other parts of the world, Ernst Haas, in a comparative analysis of the Western hemisphere, the Arab region, and the European members of the Soviet Bloc, concluded that the conditions required for integra-tion in the EEC area, such as an industrial economy and liberal politics, did not obtain elsewhere. He thus concluded that "Whatever assur-ance may be warranted in our discussion of European integration is not

---

[31] Lincoln Gordon, "Economic Regionalism Reconsidered," *World Politics* 13, no. 2 (1961), 245.

[32] Charles A. Duffy and Werner J. Feld, "Whither Regional Integration Theory?" in *Comparative Regional Systems* (New York: Pergamon Press, 1980), 497. Haas acknowl-edged that the "application [of the neofunctionalist model] to the third world ... suf-ficed only to accurately predict difficulties and failures of regional integration, while in the European case some successful positive prediction has been achieved." Ernst B. Haas, "The Study of Regional Integration: Reflections on the Joys and Anguish of Pretheorising," in *Regional Politics and World Order*, ed. Richard A. Falk and Saul H. Mendlovitz (San Francisco: Institute of Contemporary Studies, 1972), 117.

[33] Julius Emeka Okolo, "Integrative and Cooperative Regionalism: The Economic Community of West African States," *International Organization* 39, no. 1 (Winter 1985), 121–153.

readily transferable to other regional contexts."[34] Haas did not imply that regional integration in other parts of the world, driven by "different functional pursuits" than that in Western Europe and "responding to a different set of converging interests," would not succeed. On the contrary, other regions will have their own functional objectives and approaches to integration, or "impulses peculiar to them." These different purposes and trajectories, Haas concluded, meant that there could be no "universal 'law of integration' deduced from the European example."[35]

Haas' prescient warning seemed to have been ignored by many scholars of regionalism, who tended to use the EC (and later the EU) as a benchmark to judge the performance of non-European regional institutions. This EU-centrism persisted even after it suffered setbacks and regional integration theories derived from it became "obsolescent."[36] The EC revived subsequently, especially with the adoption of the Single European Act that entered into force in 1992. But the relevance of its regionalist model for other parts of the world remained a matter of debate. Moreover, a good deal of the literature on the reasons for the failure of integration efforts (and theories) in the developing world have focused on negative factors, such as instability, pervasiveness of poverty, and regime paternalism. But these explanations often obscure the positive forces such as the norms of decolonization and nationalism which may have prevented regional institution-building and integration in the postcolonial world.

The Diffusion of Regionalism after the Cold War

The study of regionalism began to change in the post-Cold War era, especially with the advent of the "new regionalism" literature.[37] The major impetus for it was disillusionment with the narrow focus of existing approaches which stressed formal structures and intergovernmental interactions, to the exclusion of non-state actors and informal linkages and processes of interaction. It was also a natural response to globalization, especially the challenge posed by transnational actors and challenges

---

[34] Ernst B. Haas, "International Integration: The European and the Universal Process," *International Organization* 15, no. 3 (Summer 1961), 378.

[35] Ibid., 389.

[36] Ernst B. Haas, *The Obsolescence of Regional Integration Theory*, Research Series no. 25 (Berkeley: University of California, Institute of International Studies, 1975).

[37] The first volume of the UNU-Wider (World Institute for Development Economics Research) sponsored project was Björn Hettne, András Inotai, and Osvaldo Sunkel, *Globalism and the New Regionalism* (Basingstoke: Palgrave Macmillan, 1999). See also: Mario Telò, *European Union and New Regionalism: Regional Actors and Global Governance in a Post-Hegemonic Era* (London: Ashgate, 2007).

to the nation-state, such as migration, refugees, environmental degradation, transnational crime, and financial volatility. Existing formal regional institutions seemed ill-equipped to address such challenges at first, and even as some of them (including the EU) were adapting to such challenges, ad hoc, bottom-up, and informal networks and responses were emerging around these issue areas which the literature on regionalism needed to account for.

The other major development[38] that broadened the scope of regionalism studies was the advent of constructivism. While the new regionalism literature was inspired by a critique of formal regionalism, the constructivist approach to regionalism (which was not wholly distinct from, but overlapping with, new regionalism) was motivated by a desire to counter the rationalist and materialist assumptions of previous theories, such as neofunctionalism and neoliberal institutionalism. The so-called constructivist turn in IR theory, especially after the end of the Cold War, brought in ideational and normative elements to the study of regionalism and introduced the notion of socialization, in marked contrast to the neofunctionalist emphasis on "the instrumental motives of actors," which takes "self-interest for granted and relies on it for delineating actor perceptions."[39]

These newer theories have helped to redefine and broaden the study of regionalism and regional integration and are better able to capture the agency of non-European regionalisms in world politics. By positing that regionalism could be driven by inter-subjective forces rather than purely rationalist ones and judged in terms of normative outcomes rather than purely material ones, constructivism has not only transformed the study of European regionalism, but has also encouraged new ways of studying regionalism in the non-Western world, such as Southeast Asian, Latin American, Arab, and African regionalisms, where culture and identity could be defining issues, and whose contributions could be mainly in the normative domain while their formal regional institutions are not integrative in the neofunctionalist sense.[40] Together, new regionalism and constructivism have seriously challenged, if not yet displaced, the dominance of European models.

While not necessarily conforming to the EU model, regionalisms and regional institutions in the developing world have been increasingly

---

[38] I have not dealt with critical perspectives, but these accentuated the emphasis of new regionalism on informal sectors and provided a powerful critique of EU-type neoliberalism.

[39] Haas, "The Study of Regional Integration," 117.

[40] See, for example: Acharya, *Constructing a Security Community in Southeast Asia*; Acharya, *Whose Ideas Matter?*

challenged and conditioned by the sovereignty-eroding effects of globalization and humanitarian intervention. Since the 1990s, regionalisms
around the world have faced the pressure to become more "intrusive"
and less sovereignty-bound, in the sense of going against the norms of
non-interference and non-intervention that had underpinned their creation and early evolution. This is reflected in the security, economic, and
political agendas of regional groups.

Several developments contributed to a slow transition from a sovereignty-bound to a more intrusive regionalism. The first was the incre-
mental success of the Conference on Security and Co-operation in
Europe (CSCE, which later became an Organization, or OSCE). During
the 1980s, the CSCE developed and began to implement an extensive
menu of confidence- and security-building measures (CSBMs), including transparency and constraining measures and verification procedures
that crossed the bounds of non-interference in the internal affairs of
states. More importantly, the CSCE successfully incorporated human
rights issues into the regional confidence-building agenda, thereby setting norms that would regulate the internal as well as external political
behavior of states.[41] This aspect of the CSCE also distinguished it from
the other major regional groupings (such as the OAS, OAU, and the
Arab League) which, as mentioned earlier, had a minimal role in the
regulation of internal conflicts within their member states.

As the Cold War came to a close, the CSCE, then OSCE, acquired
greater legitimacy and appeal. Proposals for OSCE-style regional security mechanisms for Asia and the Middle East surfaced, although implementing these proposals proved to be difficult, because of the challenge
they posed to sovereignty concerns. But the ideas and norms behind
the OSCE could be localized in Asia and Africa, as could be seen from
the establishment of the ASEAN Regional Forum in 1995 and the creation of the African Union (AU) in 2000. Both organizations embraced
a broader agenda of security cooperation, including CSBMs and, in the
case of the AU, an agenda of human rights and humanitarian intervention. (See Table 6.1.)

A second factor explaining the erosion of sovereignty in regional
organizations was the impact of globalization, which led to an expansion
of their purpose and tasks. In contrast to the early post-Cold War period,
regionalism could no longer be associated with a set of relatively narrow security (whether as a dispute-settlement mechanism or as a framework for defense against a common threat in the inter-state system) and

---

[41] Philip Zelikow, "The New Concert of Europe," *Survival* 34, no. 2 (Summer 1992), 26.

Table 6.1. *Military interventions by African regional and sub-regional organizations, 1990–2013*

	Organization	No.	Year	Country intervened in	Intervention
A	Southern African Development Community (SADC)	1	1998–1999	Democratic Republic of the Congo (DRC)	Angola, Namibia, and Zimbabwe sent troops to the DRC following an earlier intervention in the region by Rwanda and Uganda.
		2	1998	Lesotho	Lesotho Highlands Water Project by Botswana and South Africa (to stabilize the country when violence erupted after the 1998 elections).
		3	2000–2009	Burundi	Mozambique and South Africa deployed troops alongside the AU and later UN hybrid missions.
		4	2010	Burundi	Peace support operations and military deployment.
		5	2013	Burundi	SSR activities as part of AU special task force (South Africa's involvement).
		6	2001	The Great Lakes (Burundi)	Arusha Accord, deployment of the South African Protection Service Detachment (SAPSD) in Oct. 2001. Mainly a South African intervention and initiative, but subsequently supported by SADC and the UN.

(cont.)

Table 6.1. (cont.)

	Organization	No.	Year	Country intervened in	Intervention
		7	1998	Democratic Republic of Congo (DRC)	Deployment requested by President Laurent Desire Kabila (when a rebel army threatened his regime). The force was mainly composed of Zimbabwean, Namibian, and Angolan troops (and sanctioned by SADC subsequently).
B	Economic Community of West African States (ECOWAS)	8	1990–1998, 2003	Liberia	Military intervention. Ceasefire Monitoring Group.
		9	1999, 2002	Sierra Leone	Military intervention.
		10	1999	Guinea-Bissau	Military intervention.
		11	2003	Côte d'Ivoire	Military intervention.
		12	(1990s)	Guinea	Military intervention.
		13	2013	Mali	Military intervention. Initially undertaken by France but subsequently taken over by ECOWAS.
C	Intergovernmental Authority on Development (IGAD)	14	2006–2009	Somalia	Military intervention. Initially undertaken by Ethiopia but subsequently endorsed by IGAD and taken over by the AU.

D	Organization of African Unity (later the African Union)	15	1981–1982	Chad	Military intervention (peacekeeping mission). Peacekeeping force was deployed to stabilize the civil war in Chad.
E	African Union (AU)	16	2004–2006, 2006–2013	Sudan	Military intervention (peacekeeping mission). Peacekeeping force was deployed in Darfur in Sudan (deployment was termed Africa Mission in Sudan [AMIS]). Initially the number of troops was 150 (in 2004), and later expanded to 6,000 (in 2006).
		17	2007–2013	Somalia	Military intervention. African Union Mission in Somalia (replaced and subsumed IGAD mission – see above).

trade liberalization goals. Regional groups have come to deal with an increasingly wider menu of issues, including the challenges posed by their debt burden, the crisis in the world trading regime, and environmental degradation. Doubts about the future of the liberal international economic order led to a revival of interest in regional economic integration in the Third World from the late 1980s. This included ASEAN's decision in 1992 to create a regional free trade area, and the emergence of two new trade groupings in South America (the Mercosur group including Argentina, Brazil, Paraguay, and Uruguay, created in 1991, and the Group of Three including Mexico, Venezuela, and Colombia, established in 1994).[42] While old problems associated with regional integration in the developing world remained, especially the difficulty of ensuring an equitable distribution of benefits, the advent of these new regional structures required a shift from a sovereignty-bound thinking and approach.

Moreover, the expanding scope of regionalist tasks entailed a corresponding broadening of regionalist actors. Intergovernmental policy coordination, the main traditional tool of sovereignty-bound regionalism, was being joined by a rapid proliferation of regionally based transnational social and cultural networks addressing human rights, democracy, environment, and social justice issues. In Latin America, Africa, and Southeast Asia, the emergence of nascent regional civil societies around the world was thus a further blow to sovereignty-bound regionalism. In the Western Hemisphere, the OAS significantly expanded its agenda of security to include democracy promotion with the adoption of the Inter-American Democratic Charter in 2001.

When it comes to sovereignty, there remain important variations among regional organizations in the developing world. African regionalism has become much less sovereignty-bound today than in Asia. African groups have embraced the R2P norm and peer review mechanisms, and have developed extensive security organs. The AU and ECOWAS have undertaken multiple collective interventions, with a humanitarian (although not entirely so) purpose (Table 6.2). In Asia, no regional organization has undertaken a collective intervention, humanitarian or otherwise. None has openly endorsed the R2P norm. ASEAN has a rudimentary economic peer review mechanism, which unlike Africa's is strictly about macro-economic policy alone.

[42] "NAFTA is Not Alone," *The Economist*, July 18, 1994, 47.

Table 6.2. *A normative view of the making of the Inter-American Democratic Charter*

Ideas	Democracy and human rights.
Regional cognitive prior	Promotion of democracy and human rights. Diluted sovereignty and non-interference.
Local agents	Peru
Contestation	Opposed by Venezuela (an authoritarian state which disagreed over the definition of democracy) and the Caribbean countries (out of deference to non-interference, which remains strong in that sub-region).
Prior norm	Non-recognition of regimes which came into power through coups.
Role of dominant powers or middle powers	The United States and Canada were relatively passive supporters.
Desired institutional outcome	Mechanisms that delegitimize not only regimes which come to power through coups, but also anti-democratic and unconstitutional "backsliding." Provides for both preventive and proactive measures as well as punitive or reactive measures.
Prospects	Relative success of norm diffusion.

The Diffusion of the EU "Model"

The spread of regionalism in the developing world shows that, although initially it represented a form of "subsidiarity" in the sense of asserting the autonomy of different regions from the universal organization represented by the UN while remaining within and supporting it, later trends conformed to "localization," especially of the norms and institutions (sometimes called a "model") which the EU itself has sought to diffuse. The EU's transition to a single market in 1992 was a major milestone in the long struggle against sovereignty-freeing regionalism in Europe. The expansion of the EU and NATO helped the diffusion of intrusive regionalism in Eastern Europe. By championing the "Western" concepts of market capitalism, human rights, and liberal democracy, NATO and the EU offered the post-communist states of Eastern Europe an irresistible chance to join, or "rejoin," the West by acquiring membership in them.[43] In this process, the aspiring members were made to accept, despite their occasional reluctance perhaps, norms of regional conduct specified by NATO and the EU which had become progressively less sovereignty-bound. Moreover,

[43] William Wallace, "Regionalism in Europe: Model or Exception?" in *Regionalism in World Politics*, ed. Louise Fawcett and Andrew Hurrell (Oxford University Press, 1996), 205.

the process of regional identity building around human rights and liberal democracy could not be meaningful unless the relevant regional groups also developed monitoring and enforcement mechanisms, be they political, economic, or military. In so doing, European regionalism assumed an increasingly intrusive character. This transformation was less visible outside Europe, however. In East Asia, regional integration resulted not from formal bureaucracy-driven trade liberalization, but from a "market-driven" process of transnational production, or what has been called *regionalization without regionalism*.[44] In Africa, regionalism was not limited to grand schemes such as the idea of an African Economic Community, but included transnational linkages in informal sectors. But they too did not, and could not, bypass state authority and regulation as entirely as initially expected by many observers. But the overall impact of these alternative forms of regionalism was to erode the importance of state sovereignty, and the EU served as an inspiration, if not a model.

To be sure, the EU's ideas and institutions have diffused to a number of regional groups with the active support of the EU itself as part of its "interregionalism" framework.[45] The EU's cooperation agreements with different regional bodies focus especially on developing stronger and more formal institutions.[46] These have led to some institutional similarities between these regions and the EU. For example, the EU has a long-standing cooperation initiative with ASEAN which has resulted in the ASEAN Charter, which was formally adopted in 2008, containing elements of the EU's institutional structure, such as the Committee on Permanent Representatives. The EU–Andean Community Political Dialogue and Cooperation Agreement of 2003[47] broadens cooperation between the two groups leading to the emulation of the major EU institutions by the Andean Community. Various agreements between the

---

[44] *Regionalization* differs from *regionalism*. The former refers to the emergence of transnational production structures within a given geographic area. In East Asia, regionalization has been defined as a form of "market-driven" regionalism in which the state only plays a facilitating role. Regionalism is a more political concept; it may or may not have a material basis in transnational production.

[45] Tanja A. Börzel and Thomas Risse, *Diffusing (Inter-) Regionalism*, Kolleg-Forschergruppe (KFG) Working Paper Series no. 7 (September 2009), 13; Reuben Wong, "Model Power or Reference Point? The EU and the ASEAN Charter," *Cambridge Review of International Affairs* 25, no. 4 (2012), 669–682.

[46] Börzel and Risse, *Diffusing (Inter-) Regionalism*, 11.

[47] European Commission, Joint Proposal for a Council Decision on the Conclusion of a Political Dialogue and Cooperation Agreement between the European Community and its Member States, of the One Part, and the Andean Community and its Member Countries (Bolivia, Colombia, Ecuador, Peru and Venezuela), of the Other Part, Brussels, February 3, 2016, http://eur-lex.europa.eu/legal-content/EN/TXT/?uri=CELEX%3A52016JC0004.

EU and Mercosur (1995 and 2000)[48] have also produced a degree of institutional emulation,[49] especially the strengthening of the Mercosur Secretariat and Mercosur Parliament.

But the extent of this diffusion needs to be qualified.[50] ASEAN's adoption of the EU's institutional model resisted the EU's formalism and supranationalism. To a large extent, ASEAN's approach has been a matter of localization, or selective, rather than wholesale, adoption of the EU model.[51] Similarly, the regional integration of the Andean Community has remained mainly at the intergovernmental level, instead of embracing the EU's supranationalism. States in the Andean Community emulate European Court of Justice (ECJ) practices "only when and to the extent they see ECJ practices as helpful to achieve their collective goals."[52] As Risse correctly notes, "regionalism in the Global South does not simply copy the European model."[53] The EU's role has been varied depending on the relative effect of each diffusion mechanism in the regional

[48] Joint Declaration on Political Dialogue between the European Union and Mercosur, December 15, 1995, https://eulacfoundation.org/en/system/files/Joint%20Declaration%20on%20political%20dialogue%20between%20the%20European%20Union%20and%20Mercosur%2C%20Madrid%2C%20December%2015%2C%201995.pdf.

[49] European Commissions Press Memo on Relations between the EU and Mercosur (memo/98/57), http://europa.eu/rapid/press-release_MEMO-98-57_en.htm.

[50] Philomena Murray, "The European Union and an Integration Entrepreneur in East Asia: Yardstick or Cautionary Tale?" Paper Presented to the Australian Political Studies Association Conference, University of Melbourne, September 27–29, 2010, accessed October 28, 2016, www.academia.edu/727404/THE_EUROPEAN_UNION_AS_AN_INTEGRATION_ENTREPRENEUR_IN_EAST_ASIA_YARDSTICK_OR_CAUTIONARY_TALE; Amitav Acharya, "Common Security With Asia: Changing Europe's Role from Model to Partner," *International Policy Analysis* (Berlin: Friedrich Ebert Stiftung, December 2012), http://library.fes.de/pdf-files/iez/09525.pdf.

[51] See Anja Jetschke, *Do Regional Organizations Travel? European Integration, Diffusion, and the Case of ASEAN*, KFG Working Paper no. 17 (Berlin: KFG "Transformative Power of Europe," Freie Universität Berlin, 2010); Anja Jetschke and T. Lenz, "Does Regionalism Diffuse? A New Research Agenda for the Study of Regional Organizations," *Journal of European Public Policy* 20 no. 4 (2013), 626–637; Reuben Wong, "Model Power or Reference Point? The EU and the ASEAN Charter," *Cambridge Review of International Affairs* 25, no. 4 (2012), 669–682.

[52] Karen Alter, Laurence Helfer, and Osvaldo Saldias, "Transplanting the European Court of Justice: The Experience of the Andean Tribunal of Justice," *Oñati Socio-Legal Series*, Oñati International Institute for the Sociology of Law, Antigua Universidad 1, no. 4 (2011), 4.

[53] Thomas Risse, "The Diffusion of Regionalism," in *The Oxford Handbook of Comparative Regionalism*, ed. Börzel and Risse, 93.

integration process: the EU's role is as a mentor[54], a referent point,[55] or a model.[56]

Interregional cooperation between the African Union (AU) and the EU, such as the Joint Africa–EU Strategy (JAES) of 2007, and initiatives such as the Pan-African Programme and African Peace Facility, have led the AU to emulate the EU in terms of its organizational design and policy framework. However, such emulation is limited, as the AU model is sometimes inspired by the United Nations' policy framework. The EEC/EU has been directly involved in promoting regionalism in West Africa from the very beginning of the West African regional projects.[57] Two sub-regional schemes of West Africa, the Economic Community of West African States (ECOWAS) and the West African Economic and Monetary Union (UEMOA), have developed institutions similar to the EU, such as the council of ministers, a commission, a court of justice, and a parliament. At the same time, however, ECOWAS and UEMOA deviate from the EU model, suffering a "syndrome of partial implemen-tation"[58] or a "decoupling between the nominal adoption of institutions and norms inspired by the EU-model and the everyday functioning of West African regionalism."[59] For example, no direct election has taken place to the ECOWAS parliament as provided under the 1994 Protocol, and the UEMOA parliament has not been inaugurated through election yet, contrary to the provisions of its amended treaty in 2003.[60]

The findings of a careful study of the EU's efforts to diffuse its form of regionalism undertaken at the Free University of Berlin, led by Tanja A. Börzel and Thomas Risse, are especially suggestive.[61] The study divides diffu-sion mechanisms into two broad categories: direct influence (supplier-driven, with the EU being the supplier), which includes coercion, manipulation of utility calculation, and social learning and persuasion, and indirect influence (recipient-driven), which consists of emulation, lesson-drawing, and mimicry. The study finds that the outcome of the EU's diffusion

[54] Toni Haastrup, "EU as Mentor? Promoting Regionalism as External Relations Practice in EU–Africa Relations," *Journal of European Integration* 35, no. 7 (2013), 785–800.
[55] Wong, "Model Power or Reference Point?"
[56] Jetschke, *Do Regional Organizations Travel?*
[57] Giulia Piccolino, *International Diffusion and the Puzzle of African Regionalism: Insights from West Africa*, UNU-CRIS Working Papers (2016), 13.
[58] Nicolas Van de Walle, *African Economies and the Politics of Permanent Crisis, 1979–1999* (Cambridge University Press, 2001).
[59] Piccolino, *International Diffusion and the Puzzle of African Regionalism*, 6.
[60] Ibid., 10.
[61] Börzel and Risse, *Diffusing (Inter-)Regionalism*; Thomas Risse, "The Diffusion of Regionalism, Regional Institutions, Regional Governance," Paper presented at the European Union Studies Association (EUSA) 2015 Conference, Boston, USA, March 5–7, 2015, https://eustudies.org/conference/papers/download/32.

efforts depends a lot on the type of diffusion mechanism employed. In particular, as one of the leaders of the project, Thomas Risse, notes, "the effects of direct influence and of inter-regionalism are rather mute,"[62] while "emulation appears to be the primary mechanism in the diffusion of institutional designs of ROs [regional organizations] that then triggers direct influence through persuasion and norms socialization via epistemic communities and other agents. Moreover, diffusion outcomes are mostly selective adaptation and transformation of institutional models, less so wholesale adoption. *Thus, localization matters hugely*" (emphasis added).[63]

In keeping with such research and debate, the literature on regions has become less Euro-centric, giving way to a growing and exciting body of work on comparative regionalism.[64] The new literature is more diverse and more cognizant of the variations among regional institutions and the different pathways to sovereignty, security, and development taken by different regions.

Participatory Regionalism

As noted in Chapter 2, agency in norm creation and diffusion (including localization and subsidiarity) can be undertaken not only by states but also by civil society groups and social movements. The engagement of social movements in the official regionalism of states may be best described as "participatory regionalism."[65] Such regionalism is distinguished by two key features. The first, at the level of official regionalism, is the acceptance by governments of a more relaxed view of state sovereignty and the attendant norm of non-interference in the internal affairs of states. This allows for more open discussion of, and action on, problems facing a region and creates more space for non-governmental actors in the decision-making process. A second feature of participatory regionalism is the development of a close nexus between governments and civil society in managing regional and transnational issues. This

---

[62] Tanja A. Börzel and Thomas Risse, "The EU and the Diffusion of Regionalism," in *Interregionalism and the European Union: A Post-Revisionist Approach*, ed., Mario Telò, Louise Fawcett, and Frederik Ponjaert (London: Routledge, 2015).

[63] Risse, "The Diffusion of Regionalism," 99.

[64] The best examples of such work include: Börzel and Risse, eds., *Oxford Handbook of Comparative Regionalism*; Fredrik Söderbaum, *Rethinking Regionalism* (London: Palgrave Macmillan, 2015); Mario Telò, Louise Fawcett, and Frederik Ponjaert, eds., *Interregionalism and the European Union: A Post-Revisionist Approach to Europe's Place in a Changing World* (Farnham, UK, and Burlington, VT: Ashgate, 2015).

[65] Amitav Acharya, "Democratisation and the Prospects for Participatory Regionalism in Southeast Asia," *Third World Quarterly* 24, no. 2 (2003), 375–390.

means not just greater cooperation among the social movements leading to the emergence of a regional civil society, but also closer and positive interaction between the latter and the official regionalism of states.

Mercosur/UNASUR and ASEAN offer two important, if differing, examples of participatory regionalism. In Latin America, new social movements emerged in response to the perceived and actual ills of globalization, such as increase in relative and absolute poverty (despite occasional growth periods), de-industrialization (evident in Argentina and Brazil), and environmental devastation.[66] These social movements have tried to organize their resistance at the regional level by seeking to influence the rules and principles of regional institutions such as Mercosur/UNASUR, as well as creating transregional alliances with NGOs and social movements in the North. Mercosur is a group of democratic states,[67] but has been derided as a creature of "diplomats and economists," born out of economic motives with little concern for citizen participation, reflecting a "historical social deficit" of the Latin American state. ASEAN too has been described as a club of elites.[68] The democratic systems of Mercosur members provide greater space for civil society actors. Some such networks can be found within the labor movement, whose regional orientation predates the establishment of Mercosur. Examples include the Worker's Council of the Southern Cone (founded in 1973) and the Southern Cone Syndical Coordinator (1986). Mercosur also has developed institutions which engage civil society (although the term is never used in official jargon, the standard reference being to "economic and social sectors") and address social issues. These organs, together with business representatives, played a central role in the creation in 1995 of the Economic and Social Consultative Forum (FCES), an official organ of Mercosur. Democratization in Mercosur led to the reemergence and expansion of "civic public spaces," and facilitated the emergence of transnational networks (including sub-regional, hemispheric, and global networks).

Compared with Mercosur, ASEAN has been less hospitable to transnational civil society actors. It rejected pressure from Western governments and transnational human rights advocacy groups to improve its human rights record and favored a relativist position, insisting that human rights should be defined and promoted with due consideration

---

[66] Heikki Patomaki, *Critical Responses to Globalisation in the Mercosur Region: Emergent Possibilities for Democratic Politics?*, NIGD Working Paper no. 1 (Helsinki: Network Institute for Global Democratisation, 2000), 14.

[67] Ibid., 27.

[68] Ibid., 20.

for the history, culture, and economic context of the ASEAN region and the ASEAN members. And it continued to support the military regime in Burma. But from the early 1990s at least, a group of Southeast Asian NGOs tried to persuade ASEAN to create a regional human rights mechanism. Although weakly organized due to lack of resources, it managed to articulate a clear alternative voice on human rights relative to the ASEAN governments. Groups like Forum Asia, Alternative ASEAN, and Asia-Pacific Conference on East Timor, and Focus on the Global South rejected cultural relativism and called for human rights universalism. In the late 1990s and 2000s, the ASEAN governments began to seriously explore the idea of creating a regional human rights mechanism. This shift was partly due to the democratic transition in Indonesia in 1998. Indonesia's leadership role in ASEAN helped to reorient ASEAN's stance on human rights. Moreover, ASEAN's doctrine of non-interference in the internal affairs of states, which was a major reason for its previous reluctance to support human rights promotion, had come under stress in the wake of the Asian financial crisis in 1997. The growing realization of the importance of human rights in the current world order gradually led ASEAN to set up two regional human rights mechanisms: the ASEAN Intergovernmental Commission on Human Rights (AICHR) in 2009 and the ASEAN Commission on the Rights of Women and Children (ACRWC) in 2010. This illustrates the proactive role of civil society in norm diffusion. As one study argues, "Non-governmental Organizations (NGOs) have been primarily responsible for lobbying for an ASEAN human rights mechanism, as part of the push for political liberalization and respect for human rights."[69] In a series of workshops on the idea of a regional human rights mechanism held since 2001, NGOs have participated and offered their suggestions to develop ASEAN's human rights institutions, although their suggestions were not always accepted.[70]

---

[69] Yvonne Mewengkang, *ASEAN Intergovernmental Commission on Human Rights (AICHR)*, Substantial Research Paper (SRP) (Washington, DC: School of International Service, American University, March 2012); Li-ann Thio, "Implementing Human Rights in ASEAN Countries: Promises to Keep and Miles to Go before I Sleep," *Yale Human Rights and Development Law Journal* 2, no. 1 (1999), 73.

[70] An example of this process was that the High Level Panel (HLP) of officials drafting the terms of reference of the AICHR invited "Civil society and human rights organizations in ASEAN Member States that wish to put forth their views about the TOR for the AHRB" to "get in touch with the HLP or meet with individual HLP Members." The HLP also held "dialogue with representatives of ASEAN civil society and other relevant stakeholders (the informal Working Group for an ASEAN Human Rights Mechanism (WG AHRM), the Network of Four National Human Rights Institutions (4 NHRIs), the Solidarity for Asian People's Advocacy (SAPA), and the Women's Caucus for the ASEAN Human Rights Body) in 2008." Termsak Chalermpalanupap, *10 Facts about ASEAN Human Rights Cooperation*, www.aseansec.org/HLP-OtherDoc-1.pdf.

But the ASEAN experience in AICHR shows that regional civil society groups matter in norm diffusion; they can work together to develop new institutions that can advance the human rights awareness and agenda.

There are growing indications of the emergence of a participatory regionalism in Africa. Engaging civil society is increasingly seen there as a critical aspect of the regional integration process in terms of democratization and good governance, which can overcome the democratic deficit inherent in the state-led neoliberal economic integration. This is seen in the moves to reform the AU institutional settings, particularly through the Constitutive Act of the African Union and the Abuja Treaty to build the African Economic Community. The AU has introduced new institutions such as the Economic, Social, and Cultural Council (ECOSOCC) as the official platform for civil society in the AU and created other channels through which civil society can contribute to the working of AU organs such as the Peace and Security Council (PSC). Civil society is also engaged in the implementation of the New Partnership for Africa's Development (NEPAD), the African Peer Review Mechanism (APRM), and the observer systems (the African Commission on Human and People's Rights (ACHPR)). Examples of civil society engagement can also be found in African sub-regions, such as the West African Community Court of Justice in ECOWAS and the East African Court of Justice. Civil society regional networks have established regional dialogue platforms with African sub-regional institutions as in the case of the West African Civil Society Forum (WACSOF), the East African Civil Society Forum (EACSOF), and the Southern Africa Development Community Council for NGOs (SADC-NGO). While civil society groups continue to face problems due to their limited capacity and resources in accessing information, platforms, and processes of the AU as well as sub-regional groups,[71] their engagement has shaped the content of continental norms and standards and the implementation of such norms.[72]

---

[71] The Centre for Citizens' Participation of the African Union (CCP-AU), *Dialogue on Civil Society Organizations Working with and/or on the African Union (AU) Organs and Institutions: Civil Society at the AU? What Impact?* (A report based on meetings held August 22–24, 2012, Nairobi, Kenya), 4; Marianne Millstein, *Regionalising African Civil Societies: Lessons, Opportunities and Constraints. Nordiska Afrikainstitutet* (Stockholm: The Nordic Africa Institute, Stockholms Universitet, 2015).

[72] CCP-AU, *Dialogue on Civil Society Organizations Working with and/or on the African Union (AU) Organs and Institutions*, 4.

Conclusion

Regionalism in its different forms and purposes has been a crucial site and source of agency in world politics. Despite variations in their institutional features and efficacy, demand for regionalism remains strong in the non-Western world.[73] Regionalism has been an important site for the diffusion of the norms and institutions of sovereignty and security that have underpinned the evolution of global order. Regionalism was a defender of sovereignty in the past, especially in the Third World. But lately it has become more intrusive, with new forms of regional identity built around intrusive regionalism signaling and catalyzing the transition to a post-Westphalian world order in the twenty-first century. Around the globe, intrusive regionalism is being practiced through a variety of means, ranging from new security architectures in Asia and Africa to developments of norms to promote human rights and democracy. While

---

[73] For a comparative study of changes to and the relative successes and failures of non-European regionalisms, see: Louise Fawcett, *Security Regionalisms: Lessons from around the World*, Working Paper 2013/62 (Florence: European University Institute, Robert Schuman Centre for Advanced Studies, 2013), accessed October 28, 2016, http:// cadmus.eui.eu/handle/1814/27701; Michael Bröning, "The End of the Arab League? What the Organization Can Learn from the African Union," *Foreign Affairs*, March 30, 2014, accessed October 28, 2016, www.foreignaffairs.com/articles/141077/michael-broening/the-end-of-the-arab-league; Tim Murithi, "The African Union's Transition from Non-Intervention to Non-Indifference: An Ad Hoc Approach to the Responsibility to Protect?" *IPG* 1 (2009), accessed October 28, 2016 http://library.fes.de/pdf-files/ipg/ipg-2009-1/08_a_murithi_us.pdf; Andrés Malamud and Gian Luca Gardini, "Has Regionalism Peaked? The Latin American Quagmire and its Lessons," *The International Spectator: Italian Journal of International Affairs* 47, no. 1 (2012), 116–133, accessed October 28, 2016, http://apps.eui.eu/Personal/Researchers/malamud/TIS_Peaking_Regionalism_Malamud-Gardini.pdf; Marco Pinfari, *Nothing But Failure? The Arab League and the Gulf Cooperation Council as Mediators in Middle Eastern Conflicts*, Working Paper (London: London School of Economics, Development Studies Institute, 2009), accessed October 28, 2016, www.lse.ac.uk/internationalDevelopment/research/crisisStates/download/wp/wpSeries2/WP452.pdf; Richard Weitz, "The Shanghai Cooperation Organization: A Fading Star?" *ASAN Forum*, August 11, 2014, accessed October 28, 2016, www.theasanforum.org/the-shanghai-cooperation-organization-a-fading-star/; Christopher Roberts, *ASEAN Regionalism: Co-operation, Values and Institutionalisation* (New York: Routledge, 2012); Mely Caballero-Anthony, *Regional Security in Southeast Asia: Beyond the ASEAN Way* (Singapore: Institute of Southeast Asian Studies, 2005); Hiro Katsumata, *ASEAN's Cooperative Security Enterprise: Norms and Interests in the ASEAN Regional Forum* (New York: Palgrave Macmillan, 2010); Tommy Koh, Rosario G. Manalo, and Walter Woon, eds., *The Making of the ASEAN Charter* (Singapore: World Scientific, 2009); Alice Ba, *(Re)Negotiating East and Southeast Asia: Region, Regionalism and the Association of Southeast Asian Nations* (Stanford University Press, 2009); Amitav Acharya, *Constructing a Security Community in Southeast Asia: ASEAN and the Problem of Regional Order*, 3rd edition (London and New York: Routledge, 2014); Z. S. Ahmed, *Regionalism and Regional Security in South Asia: The Role of SAARC* (Farnham: Ashgate, 2013); F. Mattheis, *New Regionalism in the South: Mercosur and SADC in a Comparative and Interregional Perspective* (Leipzig: Leipziger Universitätsverlag, 2014).

this remains far from complete, linear, or homogeneous, Asian, African, Middle Eastern, and Latin American regionalisms all have distinctive features and have made distinctive contributions to regional order, and through it, to global order. This may prove to be a crucial factor in the transition to a more pluralistic Multiplex World.

The literature on regions has progressively become less Euro-centric, both theoretically and empirically, producing a shift toward comparative regionalism. At the same time, a key question about the future of regionalism that has assumed greater importance is whether the new regionalism would complement or compete with global order with the decline of the American-led liberal international order. As noted at the outset, regionalism is not always seen as being compatible with global order. This was evident in the universalism–regionalism debate at the founding of the UN. Echoes of this debate persist to this day, with some proponents of the American-led liberal international order viewing regionalism as a "less desirable alternative" to that order.[74] In this view, regionalism is a signpost of the fragmentation of the global governance architecture that has underpinned the liberal international order of the post-war period. This harks back to the fear of regionalism harbored by the "universalists" during the drafting of the UN Charter, who similarly equated regionalism with nineteenth-century great power blocs.

But the nature and purpose of regionalism and regional orders have changed fundamentally since World War II. While the role of regional institutions in security (as well as development, trade, finance, ecology, human rights, humanitarian relief, refugees, pandemics, etc.) may be undertaken relatively independently of the UN system, in most cases it complements it.[75] Regionalism today is broader, more inclusive, open, and mutually interactive than in the nineteenth century and generally supportive of global multilateral regimes. In areas of human security, regional organizations have worked in tandem with the UN. In a recent study, Andrew Mack points out that regional organizations, along with non-governmental organizations and donor groups, have strengthened the role of an overstretched UN in managing conflicts around the world.[76] Regional human rights mechanisms, which have an important place in ensuring security and global order in its broader normative sense, have been especially important. Not only did a regional declaration on human

---

[74] G. John Ikenberry, *Liberal Leviathan: The Origins, Crisis and Transformation of the American World Order* (Princeton University Press, 2011), 32.

[75] For an extensive discussion of this issue, see *Why Govern? Rethinking Demand and Progress in Global Governance*, ed. Amitav Acharya (Cambridge University Press, 2016).

[76] Andrew Mack, "Security," in *Why Govern?*, ed. Acharya.

rights by Latin American countries precede the Universal Declaration of Human Rights, but subsequent specialized human rights governance arrangements, such as the Inter-American Commission and Court of Human Rights, have helped significantly in universalizing human rights norms and protection mechanisms.[77] The European Court of Human Rights and the OAS's Inter-American Democratic Charter provide examples of regional arrangements that are ahead of global institutions in the same areas. Crucial regional support for the R2P norm has come from the AU. Regional organizations can provide legitimacy to UN peace and security operations, as with the role of the Arab League in Libya. The growing trends towards interregionalism led by the EU but also featuring South–South mechanisms such as the Forum for East Asia–Latin America Cooperation (FEALAC) also keep regionalism more open and conducive to global order.[78] The African Union holds regular interactions with the EU, with China, and with India. A striking example of interregionalism can be found in Asia, where regional institutions are engaging not only the small and big players of Asia, but also those of the whole world. The membership of the ARF and the EAS, developed around and led by ASEAN, a grouping of weak or small states, includes all the major powers of the contemporary international system: the United States, China, Russia, India, Japan, and the EU (in the case of the ARF only). While the rise of regionalism could be at least partly attributed to the limitations and weaknesses of global institutions,[79] regionalisms around the world, with their similarities and variations, contribute to a more pluralistic world order. This does not necessarily point to a fragmented world of regional blocs.

---

[77] Kathryn Sikkink, "Human Rights," in *Why Govern?*, ed. Acharya.

[78] Jurgen Ruland, Heiner Hanggi, and Ralf Roloff, eds., *Interregionalism and International Relations* (Abingdon: Routledge, 2006).

[79] Ian Bremmer, "Decline of Global Institutions Means We Best Embrace Regionalism," *Financial Times*, January 27, 2012, http://blogs.ft.com/the-a-list/2012/01/27/decline-of-global-institutions-means-we-best-embrace-regionalism/.

7   Conclusion and Extensions

This book is centrally concerned with agency and change in global order. Chapter 1 examines various descriptive and normative conceptions of order. Following Bull, Hurrell, and Alagappa, among others, it conceives of order as limitation of violence and promotion of stability and cooperation through rule-governed interactions. But it lays particular emphasis on the representation and participation of the postcolonial countries to legitimize and transform the European-derived international order into a truly *global* order. Constructing global order involves challenging and changing some preexisting power configurations, institutional arrangements, and normative structures in world politics, and replacing them with more inclusive ideas, institutions, and practices. Agency lies in promoting and managing such change. Unlike some traditional conceptions of agency, which view it as a function of the material resources and capabilities of states, such as military and economic resources and power, this book adopts a broader notion of agency, paying special attention to the role of ideas and norms, and the variety of ways they produce change (Chapter 2). These forms of agency are illustrated in the subsequent chapters which deal with the expansion of universal sovereignty (Chapter 3), the emergence of responsible sovereignty (Chapter 4), the conception of human security as a challenge to national security (Chapter 5), and the crafting of regional institutions that not only seek a measure of autonomy from great powers and institutions dominated by them (like Cold War alliances or even the UN), but also offer different pathways to cooperation suited to their local contexts (Chapter 6).

Transforming Sovereignty and Security

The reconceptualization of agency in Chapter 1 and the discussion of different types of normative agency in Chapter 2 help to understand key transformations of sovereignty and security in world politics. Since sovereignty is generally regarded as the core norm of contemporary international relations, it was a good starting point for this book's investigation into the construction of global order. Indeed, the contemporary sovereignty regime is widely accepted as the global extension of the European-derived international order. But this view obscured a number of critical questions, such as how did non-intervention come to acquire such a prominence globally, especially in what came to be known as the Third World? *The simple attainment of sovereign statehood could not explain how this norm was operationalized into the foreign policy beliefs and practices of Third World states.* The norms of Westphalian sovereignty were not passively accepted by the new states, but actively debated, constructed, and even extended. The historical example of the Asia–Africa Conference in Bandung, Indonesia, in 1955, which was a turning point in the history of sovereignty, challenges those analyses of the diffusion of sovereignty norms in the international system which hold it to be an "essentially uncontested" process. As major differences emerged over the meaning of sovereignty norms and how to protect them from real and perceived challenges, in a major display of resistance-linked agency, which fits the concept of norm subsidiarity, a group of Asian and African countries meeting at Bandung sought to re/construct the Westphalian norms of sovereignty. These contestations and compromises delegitimized security frameworks under superpower patronage which some Third World leaders saw as a challenge to the sovereignty and autonomy of newly independent states. Moreover, these debates and interactions also demonstrated the positive agency of Third World states in developing a voice and influencing the making of the postwar global order. They shaped the nature of future regional cooperation and institution-building in other parts of the Third World.

One of the most ambitious efforts to redefine sovereignty, the doctrine of humanitarian intervention discussed in Chapter 4, shows the agency of non-Western countries. This chapter illustrates the multiple sources of R2P, including the African context of and contribution to the norm. As the international community struggled in separating the humanitarian imperative from the political and geopolitical constraints of great power caprice, it was in an African context, and largely through the advocacy of African leaders within the region and at the global level, that the doctrine of R2P was conceived. Africa's embrace of R2P occurred because of the existence of prior ideas of collective action, including intervention. These include pan-Africanism, one element of which was Nkrumah's call for an African intervention force. In Asia, there was no such precedent. While such agency was redefining the meaning of sovereignty, the hegemonic power, the United States, not only played a limited role in promoting R2P, but its own post-9/11 discourse of intervention conflated humanitarian intervention with the "war on terror" as an exercise in disorganized hypocrisy, overlooking the fact that different forms of violation of sovereignty may have differing degrees of legitimacy.

Like sovereignty, the idea and practices of security have been foundational in the evolution of post-World War II international relations. And like sovereignty, they have gone through a process of contestation and redefinition. Chapter 5 discusses the agency of non-Western actors and contexts in redefining national security. The concept of national security came to be challenged, not only by those who held it should be expanded to take into account non-military threats, but more importantly by those who believed that it should also explain the security predicament of Third World countries. This led to the questioning of the state as the main referent object of security, leading to the concept of human security. Just as the R2P norm had a pronounced African context and root, the idea of human security had a distinctive Asian context and root, although in both cases those origins and agency were blurred by the enthusiastic, and well-intentioned, "hijacking" of its underlying ideas ("responsible sovereignty" and "human development" respectively) by some Western champions. The construction of human security by Pakistan's Mahbub ul Haq and India's Amartya Sen exemplifies norm subsidiarity, as it demonstrates how an idea conceived in protest against the dominant approach to development and security thinking, and reflecting local realities in the developing world, can have global applicability.

The transformation of ideas about and approaches to sovereignty and security was also the outcome of contestations and constructions at the regional level, in which non-Western agency was clearly visible. One example would be the debate over whether regionalism could be best attained through the explicit backing or the "orbit" of great powers. Asia's rejection of hegemonic regionalism played a critical role in shaping the norms of many regional groups in the developing world. Another debate was between the universalists and regionalists, with the former seeking a virtual monopoly for the UN Security Council in matters of peace and security, while the latter argued for devolution of such authority. Latin America's advocacy of regionalism at the time of the drafting of the UN Charter is a major example of norm subsidiarity. It was clearly in response to the potential "tyranny" of a higher level institution, the UN. Faced with the Roosevelt administration's clear preference for a universal organization, Latin America states argued that placing the whole responsibility for international peace and security in the hands of the UN Security Council would compromise the autonomy of regional institutions such as their own inter-America system (the Organization of American States). Regional arrangements, of which the inter-American system was the oldest and most elaborate example, not only had a better understanding of local challenges to peace and security, they might also be in a better position to provide assistance and mediation in regional conflicts than a distant UN Security Council. Thanks mainly to Latin American advocacy, supported by Arab League member states, the Charter formally recognized the role of regional organizations as instruments of conflict control among member states. In other words, subsidiary norms embodied in regional conflict-control arrangements constituted a sub-systemic structure underpinning the framework of global norms embodied in the UN.

Yet another agency issue about regionalism has been over whether approaches to regional integration, indeed the very idea of integration (whether in sovereignty-eroding or sovereignty-pulling senses) itself, could apply outside Europe. Despite being a global dynamic, the ideal-type approaches to regionalism (backed by a powerful theoretical literature) initially remained very much inspired by and beholden to the EU's experience. Some diffusion of the EU's brand of regionalism did occur and stimulated the shape and functions of regionalisms elsewhere. But in many cases, the result was the localization rather than wholesale adoption of the EU model. In general, theories and approaches of regionalism derived from the EU did not travel well or fit the conditions in the non-Western world. This meant different understandings of and approaches to regionalism in the non-Western world also emerged and prevailed. Hence both the localizations of the EU models and constructions of new and different forms of regionalisms elsewhere (which can be better understood from a subsidiarity perspective) affirm non-Western agency in shaping the overall contribution of regionalism to global order.

Following the explication of a broader conception of agency in Chapters 1 and 2, Table 7.1 presents how the different forms of agency have worked in building global order.

The overall findings of Chapters 3–6 show that while ideas and norms about sovereignty, intervention, security, and regionalism have traveled between regions, the processes of their diffusion, especially localization and subsidiarity, also produce important variations among the regions with respect to them. Briefly stated, Asia led Africa in extending the norms of sovereignty (by extending the norm of non-intervention to cover multilateral military superpower-led alliances). But Africa led Asia in promoting the localized norm of inviolability of postcolonial frontiers. Latin America's application of the norms of sovereignty and non-intervention was much more legalistic than that of Asia, Africa, and the Middle East. In Latin American, the Europe-derived norm of non-intervention was stronger than in European practice (since in Europe, balance of power has a prior importance). In the post-Cold War era, Africa has moved ahead of Asia in championing humanitarian intervention, while Latin America has led Africa and Asia in advocating (at least in theory)

Table 7.1. *The analytic framework*

Chapter	Challenge	Agency	Outcome
Chapter 3	Localizing and expanding sovereignty to advance decolonization and limit outside (great power) intervention	Latin America's Calvo and Drago Doctrines; the Bandung injunction against Cold War pacts; postcolonial leaders in Asia (e.g. Nehru, Sukarno), the Middle East (Nasser), and Africa (Nkrumah)	Building subsidiary norms in Asia, Africa, Latin America, the Arab world; related but differing regional conceptions of sovereignty and non-intervention
Chapter 4	Transforming sovereignty to address humanitarian crises without inviting great power geopolitical intervention	African context, leaders, and diplomats (Nelson Mandela, Francis Deng, Kofi Annan, Mohamed Sahnoun), Brazil's "responsibility while protecting"	Contributing to the norms of humanitarian intervention and R2P; initial North–South disagreements over humanitarian intervention, but greater convergence on the R2P norm
Chapter 5	Redefining security to make it relevant to the security predicament of Third World countries where security of people is often threatened by governments	Development economists (Mahbub ul Haq, Amartya Sen), Third World (especially South Asian) context	Shaping the redefinition and broadening of "national security"; proposing ideas of "human development" and "human security"
Chapter 6	Ensuring a role for regionalism in the universal collective security system and developing a mode of regionalism relevant to stability and development (not the same as integration)	Latin American and Arab representatives at the San Francisco Conference; regionalist advocates and ideologies (pan-Americanism, pan-Africanism, pan-Arabism)	Challenging the exclusive role of the UN in conflict resolution, and the primacy of the EU model of economic integration; conceiving and diffusing other forms of regional institution-building

democracy promotion. The norm of human security was Asian in inspiration and context, whereas the R2P norm has an African pedigree. Regionalisms across the world, while remaining distinct from EU-style formalism, have also varied among themselves. In Asia regionalism in the economic arena (through market-driven production networks as well as in the formal intergovernmental ASEAN Economic Community) has progressed to a degree that has eluded Africa, Latin America, and their sub-regions, not to mention the Middle East. But Asian regionalism is facing a greater challenge to its ASEAN-centered normative core, because of its proximity to a materially rising China.

Extensions and Further Research

Human Rights

Although this book is concerned primarily with sovereignty and security, its conceptual approach opens up avenues for further research into agency in other areas. One such issue is human rights. The debate over human rights has often pitted the universalists of the Global North against the relativists of the Global South.[1] While Donnelly, among other scholars, rejects the view that the West's championing of human rights is due to some innate superiority of Western civilization, he also does not believe non-Western societies were capable of developing human rights norms of the kind that emerged in the West with the advent of capitalism.[2] Amartya Sen offers a more nuanced view:

> The idea of human rights as an entitlement of every human being, with an unqualified universal scope and highly articulated structure, is really a recent development; in this demanding form it is not an ancient idea either in the West or elsewhere. But there are limited and qualified defenses of freedom and tolerance, and general arguments against censorship, that can be found both in ancient traditions in the West and in cultures of non-Western societies.[3]

Aside from Sen's historical understanding of non-Western agency, recent work on the creation of global human rights covenants also points to a stronger advocacy of human rights by the postcolonial states than has been commonly assumed. The postcolonial states were especially crucial in resisting attempts by the leading Western powers to limit the scope of various human rights conventions to protect Western interests (including interest in preserving their dwindling colonial possessions).

---

[1] On relativism versus universalism in human rights, see Jack Donnelly, "Cultural Relativism and Universal Human Rights," *Human Rights Quarterly* 6, no. 4 (1984), 400–402; Alison Renteln, "Relativism and the Search for Human Rights," *American Anthropologist* 90, no. 1 (1988), 56–72; Christopher Tremewan, "Human Rights in Asia," *Pacific Review* 6, no. 1 (1993), 17–30.

[2] Jack Donnelly, "The Relativism of Universal Human Rights," *Human Rights Quarterly* 29, no. 2 (2007), 281–306. Donnelly thus associates human rights with capitalism, rather than culture.

[3] Amartya Sen, "Universal Truths: Human Rights and the Westernizing Illusion," *Harvard International Review* 20, no. 3 (Summer 1998), 42.

They also championed political rights and civil liberties, and not just economic and cultural rights, or the "right to development," as many narratives on human rights tend to assume. In a detailed study of the evolution of human rights, Reus-Smit observes:

> The standard account of the development of international human rights norms identifies three phases: the first addressing civil and political rights, the second economic and social rights, and the third collective rights. The West is credited with the first, the Soviet bloc with the second, and the developing world with the third. In reality, however, during the negotiation of the two Covenants newly independent states consistently stressed the primacy of civil and political rights, and they were the strongest advocates of robust enforcement mechanisms.[4]

Such findings, in keeping with the basic argument of this book, also warrant extending existing models for explaining human rights promotion. One of the most influential approaches to explaining the spread of human rights norms in the literature on international relations is the "boomerang" model. Briefly put, this model posits that human rights activists link up with transnational human rights groups and use their influence with their own national governments and international organizations to bring pressure to bear on their domestic oppressors.[5] The model has much merit, but can be seen as privileging the agency of the West, and presenting a generally top-down and adversarial approach to human rights norm diffusion. Moreover, the boomerang model in its original iteration was derived from the specific context of US–Latin America relations and the Eastern European experience. But as Hafner-Burton and Ron argue, research based on these frameworks on "Africa, Asia, or the Middle East may be barking up the wrong theoretical tree."[6] While the boomerang model recognizes the agency of domestic activists acting in concert with foreign governments and transnational NGOs, in reality the latter were mostly Western, while the former were mostly from the developing world. As Ron points out, this type of literature stressed the role of transnational actors and "paid far less attention to the

---

[4] Christian Reus-Smit, "Building the Liberal International Order: Locating American Agency," Paper Prepared for the Annual Meeting of the American Political Science Association, Washington, DC, August 28–31, 2014, 12–13. The paper is derived from his book, *Individual Rights and the Making of the International System* (Cambridge University Press, 2013). The covenants referred to are the International Covenant on Civil and Political Rights and the International Covenant on Economic, Social, and Cultural Rights, both adopted in 1966.

[5] On the boomerang model, see Margaret E. Keck and Kathryn Sikkink, *Activists Beyond Borders: Advocacy Networks in International Politics* (Ithaca: Cornell University Press, 1998).

[6] Emilie Hafner-Burton and James Ron, "Seeing Double: Human Rights Impact through Qualitative and Quantitative Eyes," *World Politics* 61, no. 2 (April 2009), 379.

local embodiments of human rights norms in the developing world."[7] He further adds that although in the Boomerang model local groups initi-ate "the process, their location, obscure language, and marginality have limited scholarly inquiry."[8] While "[t]ransnational NGOs and networks can monitor, inform, and advocate all they want, ... without serious investments of time and effort by local human rights champions, nothing much will change on the ground."[9]

A later model of human rights norm diffusion is the "spiral" model. It posits that governments may initially accept human rights norms for instrumental reasons, but gradually end up internalizing them due to moral pressure and accountability politics.[10] The spiral model is a further refinement and extension of the boomerang and gives much more play to domestic politics, and therefore to the agency of local actors in the oppressed countries. But external pressure and the advocacy and relative power positions of the abusers and the advocates still remain crucial to the success of norm diffusion.

Building on but looking beyond the boomerang and spiral models, I would call for a further pluralization of agency in human rights promo-tion. This would be in keeping with the realities of the global power shift and the growing influence of the emerging powers, which has weakened the leverage of Western powers and transnational groups in that it is key to the success of both the boomerang and spiral models. The role of social media, as demonstrated during the recent Arab uprisings, empow-ers local actors and permits a more horizontal mobilization among domestic activists than ever before. Hence local agents have less need for the boomerangs that travel internationally.

This book's framework suggests the need for greater emphasis on the role of local agents in an inclusive process of human rights promotion, which I call a "Banyan" approach.[11] Insights and findings from some of

---

[7] James Ron, "Legitimate or Alien? Human Rights Organizations in the Developing World," Paper circulated at the Workshops on Religion and Human Rights Pragmatism: Promoting Rights across Cultures, Columbia University, New York, September 24, 2011.

[8] Ibid.

[9] Ibid.

[10] On the spiral model and the difference between it and the boomerang model, see: Thomas Risse, Stephen C. Ropp, and Kathryn Sikkink, eds., *The Power of Human Rights: International Norms and Domestic Change* (Cambridge University Press, 1999); Thomas Risse, Stephen C. Ropp, and Kathryn Sikkink, eds., *The Persistent Power of Human Rights: From Commitment to Compliance* (Cambridge University Press, 2013).

[11] A Banyan tree is characterized by: (1) a large canopy that spreads out in all directions (representing the broadness of the meaning and scope of human rights); (2) its func-tion as a cultural symbol, as a place for festivals, ceremonies, worship; and (3) its role as a social institution or gathering place of diverse communities, under which dispute settlement and consensus-making in village life takes place. Furthermore, the aerial

the most recent work on human rights and transitional justice norms[12] support this view. In their study of faith-based organizations (FBOs), Boesenecker and Vinjamuri find that despite many transnational FBOs working closely with local civil society groups in the developing world, there are many instances where local civil society groups dissent from transnational human rights activists.[13] Moreover, the cultural beliefs (cognitive priors) and symbolic politics based on local culture may matter more than sanctions or accountability politics in promoting human rights. In Bolivia, Goldstein shows that traditional conceptions of community justice had to be "reconciled with ideas of human rights" promoted by transnational civil society groups.[14] In Cochabamba, Bolivia, indigenous communities sought recognition of community justice, their traditional form of law enforcement, as "being among the rights of citizens," even though transnational human rights groups generally opposed this practice. This necessitates a broadening of the scope and meaning

---

roots hanging down from the Banyan's branches illustrate *localization* (top-down), while these roots taking hold and supporting the branches and canopy illustrate *subsidiarity* (bottom-up). Just as a Banyan tree has multiple roots which collectively support the tree, a Banyan approach would stress the importance of basing human rights promotion on multiple constituencies rather than relying exclusively on specialized advocacy groups. It also underscores the importance of local (domestic and regional) ownership and entrepreneurship with a focus on "insider proponents," rather than relying mainly on transnational advocacy groups. A village Banyan tree shelters travelers, but as guests, not as residents. The travelers bring in new stories and ideas, but it is the locals who have to listen to them, accept them, and retell them. In a Banyan approach, regional mechanisms become especially important in human rights norm diffusion. The Banyan approach thus turns human rights promotion into an inclusive dialogue between local actors and outsider proponents rather than it being a matter of imposition by the latter through legalistic means and sanctions. Amitav Acharya, "From the Boomerang to the Banyan: The Diffusion of Human Rights Norms Reconsidered," Paper presented to the Workshop on Religion and Human Rights Pragmatism: Promoting Rights across Cultures, Columbia University, New York, September 24, 2011, and the Columbia University Human Rights Futures Conference, November 15, 2013. The relevance of the Banyan model has been discussed in Jonas Wolff and Lisbeth Zimmermann, "Between Banyans and Battle Scenes: Liberal Norms, Contestation and the Limits of Critique," *Review of International Studies* 24, no. 3 (2016), 513–534.

[12] Lisbeth Zimmermann, "Same Same or Different? Norm Diffusion between Resistance, Compliance, and Localization in Post-conflict States," *International Studies Perspectives* 17, no. 1 (2016), 98–115. Transitional justice and accountability norms, though different, are closely linked to human rights norms broadly conceived.

[13] Aaron P. Boesenecker and Leslie Vinjamuri, "Lost in Translation? Civil Society, Faith-Based Organizations and the Negotiation of International Norms," Paper presented at the Workshops on Religion and Human Rights Pragmatism: Promoting Rights across Cultures, Columbia University, New York, September 24, 2011.

[14] Daniel M. Goldstein, "Whose Vernacular? Translating Human Rights in Local Contexts," Paper presented at the Workshops on Religion and Human Rights Pragmatism: Promoting Rights across Cultures, Columbia University, New York, September 24, 2011, 7.

of human rights in the local context (which can be one result of localization). Such broadening was motivated by a sense of Bolivian culture, in which community justice figures prominently. Another example from Bolivia suggests creation of new rules in the local context (subsidiarity), this being the right to petition – or the right of each person "to formulate individual or collective petitions to state or communal authorities."[15] This meant alongside governments, community leaders and village authorities are brought into the purview of human rights.[16] Given that international NGOs are not present in many areas, and not interested in all issues, this leaves ample space for such local rule-making.[17]

The foregoing examples point to the need to at least supplement the boomerang/spiral model with a framework that incorporates the insights of the L-S-C framework, which not only captures the resistance to the so-called transnational "universal" human rights norms ironically by those who are victims of human rights abuses (as opposed to governments), but also the need to devise new more inclusive strategies for norm diffusion that are consistent with the prior beliefs of the local actors, including those who are in need of protection.

Global Governance

Although, as noted in Chapter 1, global governance is distinct from global order, the former sustains the latter by creating norms and mechanisms for legitimizing the exercise of power and authority and enabling the management of transnational threats and challenges.[18] Among the most interesting and urgent issues of global governance is climate change negotiations. These show the developing world's resistance to global norms that ignore their context and need (localization), and the emerging powers' agency (subsidiarity), in ensuring progress in such negotiations. Of particular relevance here is the "common but differentiated responsibility principle" (CBDR).[19] The CBDR challenges the principles

---

[15] Ibid., 6.
[16] Ibid., 7.
[17] Ibid., 6.
[18] For a detailed account of the agency of non-Western countries in global governance, see: Acharya, ed., *Why Govern?*
[19] Lavanya Rajamani, *Differential Treatment in International Environmental Law* (Oxford University Press, 2006); Paul G. Harris, "Common but Differentiated Responsibility: The Kyoto Protocol and United States Policy," *NYU Environmental Law Journal* 7, no. 1 (1999), 27–48; "Founex Report on Environment and Development," *International Conciliation* 586 (1972); Christopher Stone, "Common but Differentiated Responsibilities in International Law," *American Journal of International Law* 98, no. 2 (2004), 276–301.

of reciprocity and sovereign equality of states in earlier environmental negotiations and agreements. The norm assigns responsibility for dealing with climate change to the developed world because of their greater historic responsibility for global warming, as well as capacity to address the consequences of climate change. Enshrined first in the Framework Convention on Climate Change[20] and then in the Rio Declaration of 1992, it is now part of most environmental agreements.

The CBDR norm was clearly founded upon the Global South's long-standing common position on environmental degradation. Marc Williams has identified four aspects of that position: (1) that the industrialized countries bear the primary responsibility for the global environmental crisis; (2) that these countries should bear the major costs of environmental protection; (3) that the industrialized countries should ensure free transfer of technology to the South so that the latter can reduce its dependence on technologies damaging to the environment; and (4) that the industrialized countries should transfer additional resources to fund efforts by developing countries to ensure greater environmental protection.[21] The initial articulation of this principle can be traced to a group of Third World development economists, who, meeting in Founex, Switzerland, challenged the view that environmental pollution and damage was the outcome of development. Instead, their position held that poverty was the cause of pollution, whereas development was the solution, not the problem. The developed countries should not impose their standards on developing countries. Subsequently, the developing countries used their voting clout in the UN General Assembly to promote their view.

The CBDR principle not only reveals the importance of the agency of developing countries, it also upholds respect for local need and context, especially the particular circumstances and requirements of developing countries. The norm stipulates that international environmental agreements should consider the growth needs of developing countries, while developing countries would be subjected to less stringent standards, and they should receive assistance from developed countries.

---

[20] "The Parties should protect the climate system for the benefit of present and future generations of humankind, on the basis of equity and in accordance with their common but differentiated responsibilities and respective capabilities. Accordingly, the developed country Parties should take the lead in combating climate change and the adverse effects thereof." Article 3.1, Framework Convention on Climate Change, 1992.

[21] Marc Williams, "Re-articulating the Third World Coalition: The Role of the Environmental Agenda," *Third World Quarterly* 14, no. 1 (1993), 20–21. See also: Mitsuru Yamamoto, "Redefining the North–South Problem," *Japan Review of International Affairs* 7, no. 2 (Fall 1993), 263–281.

Increasingly, global climate negotiations, including those leading to the Paris Agreement of 2015, have shown the relevance of the CBDR norm.

Moreover, as Anne-Marie Slaughter argues, the Paris Agreement is by no means a return to old-fashioned multilateralism led by Western governments. It recognizes the role of a diversity of actors including civil society groups, business groups, and experts in managing the climate challenge. And the agreement was possible not only because of the work of transnational advocacy groups, but also owing to the consent of emerging powers, especially China. This is a sure signpost of the advent of a Multiplex World.

More striking, what Paris produced was not the formalism of a conventional treaty with fixed rules and binding commitments, but one that offers a more flexible approach, relying more on largely voluntary "non-adversarial and non-punitive" compliance mechanisms.[22] This is exactly the kind of negotiating style and outcome the ASEAN is known for. The ASEAN Way is known for its inclusivity, informality, pragmatism, expediency, consensus-building, and non-confrontational bargaining style, as contrasted with "the adversarial posturing and legalistic decision-making procedures in Western multilateral negotiations."[23] So what was evident in Paris was not just the agency of relatively powerful non-Western actors such as China, but also the normative relevance of the negotiating process of a regional grouping of weaker nations that differs markedly from the EU's legalistic approach to regionalism.

Global governance, including its various issue areas, is thus an important arena to consider when rethinking agency in world politics. There is an emerging body of work on the agency of the Global South that challenges the orthodox views of the origins of global norms and multilateral institutions.[24] Sikkink urges "scholars of international norms to pay greater attention to the potential 'protagonist' role of states outside the Global North despite important structural inequality in the international

---

[22] Anne-Marie Slaughter, "The Paris Approach to Global Governance," Project Syndicate, December 28, 2015, www.project-syndicate.org/commentary/paris-agreement-model-for-global-governance-by-anne-marie-slaughter-2015-12.

[23] Amitav Acharya, "Ideas, Identity and Institution-Building: From the 'ASEAN Way' to the 'Asia Pacific Way,'" *The Pacific Review* 10, no. 3 (1997), 329.

[24] "Principles from the Periphery: The Neglected Southern Sources of Global Norms," special section of *Global Governance* 20, no. 3 (2014). This section includes contributions by Eric Helleiner (international development), Kathryn Sikkink (human rights), Martha Finnemore and Michelle Jurovitch (universal participation), and this author (normative impact of the 1955 Asia–Africa Conference in Bandung on human rights, sovereignty, disarmament, and the UN). See also the essays in "The UN and the Global South, 1945 and 2015: Past as Prelude?" special issue of *Third World Quarterly* 37, no. 7 (2016). This author has contributed to both the collections.

system. Southern protagonism arguably increases the global legitimacy of global governance projects including the human rights project."[25] Thakur points out that support for the "Responsibility to Protect" idea (R2P) came not just from the West, but also from the victims of atrocities (especially in Africa) as well as non-governmental organizations and the UN. He describes the R2P as "a distinctively African response that spoke to a distinctively African need."[26] The drafting of the United Nations Convention on the Law of the Sea (UNCLOS) shows a substantial role by non-Western countries, including Southeast Asian lawyers.[27] Analyzing the origins of international development cooperation, Eric Helleiner contests the commonly held view that the norm of international development originated with a speech in 1949 by US President Harry Truman. He credits the norm to the thinking of nationalist Chinese leader Sun Yat-sen dating back to 1918. In the 1930s, Latin American countries developed ideas about development which influenced the US official initiative in the 1940s to develop the International Bank for Reconstruction and Development (World Bank).[28] Trends in global security governance suggest that the developing countries are increasing their share of UN peacekeeping operations, with all the top ten contributing countries in 2013 coming from the developing world, compared with the situation in 1990 when seven of the top ten were from the developed world.[29] More work is needed to fully uncover and appreciate the critical role played by non-Western actors in various aspects of global order-building; and this constitutes a productive and promising area of further research in developing a global discipline of international relations.

---

[25] Kathryn Sikkink, "Latin American Countries as Norm Protagonists of the Idea of International Human Rights," *Global Governance* 20, no. 3 (2014), 389–404, 390. One of the key figures in developing both the boomerang and spiral models, Sikkink's work has increasingly acknowledged and dealt with local agency. She also argues that such agency matters in strengthening the legitimacy of human rights arrangements. See also: Kathryn Sikkink, "Human Rights," in *Why Govern?* ed. Acharya, 121–137.

[26] Ramesh Thakur, "Atrocity Crimes," in *Why Govern?*, ed., Acharya, 145.

[27] Amitav Acharya, ed., *The Quest for World Order: Perspectives of a Pragmatic Idealist* (Singapore: Times Academic Press, 1997). This is a collection of the speeches and writings of Ambassador Tommy Koh, who, as the President of the Third UNCLOS (1980–1982) and the Chairman of the Main Committee of the UN Conference on Environment and Development (1990–1992), played an instrumental role in the conclusion of UNCLOS and Agenda 21 of the Rio Summit.

[28] Eric Helleiner, "Southern Pioneers of International Development," *Global Governance* 20, no. 3 (2014), 375–388. This article is based on his book, Eric Helleiner, *The Forgotten Foundations of Bretton Woods: International Development and the Making of the Postwar Order* (Ithaca: Cornell University Press, 2014).

[29] Mack, "Conflicts and Security," in *Why Govern?*, 101.

Agency and Order-building in a Pluralistic World

The election of Donald Trump as US President has cast a shadow over the future of the global order.[30] Many of his stated policy platforms suggest a retreat from liberal internationalism, and its replacement with a nationalist, inward-looking US approach to foreign policy. His stated views on trade, the environment, and US alliances will undermine the global norms and institutions that underpin the liberal order, such as the WTO and the UN as well as global climate change negotiations.

But Trump may be the consequence, rather than the cause, of the decline of the existing US-dominated liberal international order. Many of the signs of and reasons behind this crisis were already evident,[31] and Trump was able to exploit it to his electoral advantage. His case for presidency, as could be surmised from his electoral slogan of "Make America great again," was essentially a narrative about America's relative decline, which may be viewed as the erosion of America's primacy and agency in the global order. Hence his ascent to power has important implications for the question of agency in world politics. While Trump may or may not revive America's national power, he is unlikely to revive US primacy and agency, the causes of the decline of which predate his rise as a political actor and have to do with a continuing global power shift.

One aspect of this is the rise of non-Western countries such as China and India. In 2001, the GDP of the United States was 8 times that of China, whereas by 2015, it was only 1.6 times. The US share of the global economy fell from 31.6% in 2001 to 22.2% in 2014, while China's share grew from 4% to 13.4% over the same period.[32] The European Union Institute of Security Studies (EUISS) estimates that by 2030, China and India could account for more than 34% of the global economy.[33] Another estimate puts China and India as the top two economies of the world by 2050, followed by the United States, Indonesia, Brazil, Mexico, Japan, Russia, Nigeria, and Germany. This means seven of the top ten economies of the world would be non-Western (six if Japan is considered Western). The same report suggests that of thirty-two leading economies in the world by purchasing power parity (PPP) terms, twenty-one (including Japan) will be from the non-Western world by

---

[30] Joseph S. Nye, "Will the Liberal Order Survive?" *Foreign Affairs* (January/February 2017), www.foreignaffairs.com/articles/2016-12-12/will-liberal-order-survive.

[31] For a detailed discussion, see Amitav Acharya, *The End of American World Order* (Cambridge, UK: Polity Press, 2014).

[32] Malcolm Scott and Cedric Sam, "China and the United States: Tale of Two Giant Economies" May 12, 2016, www.bloomberg.com/graphics/2016-us-vs-china-economy/.

[33] *Global Trends 2030: Citizens in an Interconnected and Polycentric World* (Paris: The European Union Institute for Security Studies, May 2012).

2050.[34] But the global power shift is brought about not just by the rise of a handful of emerging powers alone. There is also a more general "rise of the Rest" phenomenon. The Global South's share of global GDP rose from 33% in 1980 to 45% in 2010. During the same period, their share of world merchandise trade rose from 25% to 47%.[35] There has also been a marked success in extreme poverty reduction (below $1.25 per day): the overall figures for the world fell from 43.1% in 1990 to 22.4% in 2008. In individual countries, the figures are: Brazil, from 17.2% in 1990 to 6.1% in 2009; China, from 60.2% in 1990 to 13.1% in 2008; and India, from 49.4% in 1990 to 32.7% in 2010.[36] The OECD estimates that the Global South could account for 57% of global GDP by 2060.[37] While the growth of some of the emerging powers has slowed down in recent years, much of the shift has already occurred and will continue to redefine the global environment. "The global economic power shift away from the established advanced economies in North America, Western Europe and Japan will continue over the next 35 years."[38] Another aspect of this global power-shift is South–South trade, the volume of which is increasing relative to North–South or North–North trade. South–South merchandise trade rose from less than 8% in 2008 to more than 26% in 2011.[39] This could mean a future in which globalization is driven more by South–South linkages than by North–North or North-South linkages.[40]

While these trends do not necessarily mean a post-Western world, they will give further impetus to non-Western agency in world politics. To understand this, I return to the idea of a Multiplex World already introduced in Chapter 1. Some clarifications, already provided in Chapter 1, are worth repeating. First, a Multiplex World is not a multipolar world. Whereas the traditional conception of multipolarity (derived from

---

[34] PricewaterhouseCoopers, *The World in 2050: Will the Shift in Global Economic Power Continue?*, (February 2015), 3, http://www.pwc.com/gx/en/issues/economy/the-world-in-2050.html

[35] United Nations Development Program, *Human Development Report 2013. The Rise of the South: Human Progress in a Diverse World* (New York: United Nations Development Program, 2013), 2.

[36] Ibid., 13.

[37] "Developing Economies to Eclipse West by 2060, OECD Forecasts," *The Guardian Datablog*, available at www.guardian.co.uk/global-development/datablog/2012/nov/09/developing-economies-overtake-west-2050-oecd-forecasts (accessed June 5, 2013); *Future State 2030: The Global Megatrends Shaping Governments* (KPMG International, 2014), 34, https://home.kpmg.com/xx/en/home/insights/2015/03/future-state-2030.html.

[38] PricewaterhouseCoopers, *The World in 2050*, 1.

[39] United Nations Development Program, *Human Development Report 2013*, 2.

[40] Amitav Acharya, "Donald Trump as President: Does It Mark a Rise of Illiberal Globalism?" *YaleGlobal*, January 22, 2017, http://yaleglobal.yale.edu/content/donald-trump-president-does-it-mark-rise-illiberal-globalism.

Europe) assumed the primacy of the great powers, actors (or agents) in a Multiplex World are not limited to being great powers or indeed states (both Western and non-Western), but also include international institutions, non-governmental organizations, multinational corporations, and transnational networks (good and bad). As with a multiplex cinema, or living room variants such as streaming and Netflix, a multiplex world gives audiences a wider choice of plots, actors, producers, and directors. A Multiplex World is marked by complex global linkages that include not just trade but also finance and transnational production networks, which were scarce in pre-World War European economic interdependence. While that interdependence was mostly intra-European, with the rest of the world being in a dependent (colonial) relationship with Europe and the United States, today's interdependence is truly global and increasingly reciprocal. It binds players all around the world, as exemplified by G20 membership, a product of global financial interdependence. Moreover, interdependence today goes beyond economics and also covers many other issue areas, such as the environment, disease, human rights, and social media.

Though not a multipolar world, a Multiplex World is a decentered world. Its defining feature is absence of hegemony, although not the disappearance of power inequalities and hierarchies. Such a world results from the waning of the American-dominated world order. This does not necessarily mean the United States is in decline – the jury is still out on that issue. While America may remain as a "first among equals," it is no longer in a position to create the rules and dominate the institutions of global order in the manner it did for much of the post-World War II period. And while elements of the old liberal order survive, they will have to accommodate new actors and approaches that do not play to America's commands and preferences.

A Multiplex World has multiple layers of governance, including global, interregional, regional, domestic, and sub-state. Regionalism is a key part of this, but regionalism today is open and overlapping, a far cry from the imperial blocs of the nineteenth century. Twentieth-century regionalism has been a more open and broader phenomenon encompassing a variety of purposes, approaches, and outcomes. The EU-centrism of the earlier theories of regionalism had already been questioned even before the Brexit referendum vote, and given way to a comparative regionalism framework which takes into account the diversity among regional cooperation contexts and initiatives.

A key message of this book is that non-Western agency is not just a negative phenomenon, in the sense of being substantially limited to resisting and challenging the existing international order and its norms.

To be sure, as outlined in Chapter 1, agency often begins with challenge and resistance. This was especially true of non-Western agency in the early postcolonial period. As a latecomer to a Europe-derived international system with scant material resources, non-Western agency had a visibly rebellious disposition. It was seen as a spoiler of, rather than a contributor to, the existing global order. Hence, many early accounts of the role of the Third World in world politics focused on its "revolt against the West" (to use Bull's term)[41] and the North–South "structural conflict" (Krasner's phrase).[42]

But this has not been a constant. Dissatisfaction with and challenge to the existing Western-dominated international order has also been accompanied by attempts to develop new approaches that are more inclusive and representative of the larger segment of states and societies. As Chapters 3–6 have shown, many instances of non-Western agency are "positive" and proactive, aimed at addressing the current order's deficiencies, and introducing new and potentially transformative ideas and norms, such as human security, responsible sovereignty, and various regionalist approaches, to strengthen global order, even as it seeks to modify and reform some aspects of that order. Indeed, the very idea of norm subsidiarity captures this dual role: "challenging/resisting" and "supportive/subordinating," as discussed in Chapter 2. I share Ayoob's earlier notion of "schizophrenia," in which the Third World actors simultaneously challenge and adapt to the international system.[43] But this book also highlights the constitutive role of the Third World in the global order. In short, non-Western agency is moving from "revolt" to adaptation, and then to positive and proactive contribution. And it will probably continue to do so in a Multiplex World. While new forms of dissent and rebellion will emerge, this will occur in the more complex context of an increasing blurring of North–South boundaries. Indicative of this is the willingness of China and India to defend globalization, a key element of the liberal order, from the challenge posed by Trump's policies, even if China does not accept the liberal values associated with Western-led globalization.[44]

---

[41] Hedley Bull, "The Revolt against the West," in *The Expansion of International Society*, ed. Hedley Bull and Adam Watson (Oxford: Clarendon Press, 1984), 239–254.

[42] Stephen D. Krasner, *Structural Conflict: The Third World against Global Liberalism* (Berkeley: University of California Press, 1985).

[43] Mohammed Ayoob, "The Third World in the System of States: Acute Schizophrenia or Growing Pains?" *International Studies Quarterly* 33 (1989), 67–79.

[44] Amitav Acharya, "Emerging Powers Can Be Saviours of the Global Liberal Order," *Financial Times*, January 19, 2017, 12, www.ft.com/content/f175b378-dd79-11e6-86ac-f253db7791c6.

The victory of Donald Trump in the 2016 US presidential election has sparked a frenzy of concern about the future of the liberal international order. But the crisis and decline have been forewarned for some time,[45] although many of the liberal order's proponents were slow to acknowledge it. Until Trump, it was generally assumed that the main challenge to the liberal order would come especially from the rising powers led by China. Hence, the debate over world order had focused mainly on the global power shift. But the liberal order is also imploding. Trump's victory and Brexit suggest that the main challenge is also from within, especially from the citizenry in the West dissatisfied and disillusioned with globalization. This is certainly true of the United Kingdom and the United States, but also potentially in other Western countries. But one should not forget that part of the reason for that disillusionment had to do with economic shifts associated with the Rise of the Rest.

Trump's victory compounds the ongoing challenges to the liberal order on several fronts. One is to international trade. The Trump administration has withdrawn from the Trans-Pacific Partnership (TPP) and threatens to do the same with NAFTA unless its terms are renegotiated to the advantage of US workers. It is placing greater stress on bilateral deals based on a stricter and direct reciprocity rather than multilateralism. Trump statements have also raised serious questions about US alliance commitments, especially toward NATO.

Furthermore, Trump has unleashed a new populism in Europe and encouraged anti-democratic leaders throughout the world, such as Putin in Russia, Erdogan in Turkey, Duterte in the Philippines, and Orban in Hungary, as well as far-right movements in Europe. Trump's platform and persona represent a powerful challenge to liberal values and norms. As Volker Perthes, Director of the German Institute of International and Security Affairs, put it, Trump's victory "represents a hard knock for the West's normative bedrock of liberalism."[46]

It is by no means clear as yet how far Trump will go in carrying out his campaign promises related to alliances, institutions, and trade. But even if the changes are less far reaching than his electoral platform and campaign rhetoric suggested, the United States would still face a credibility problem in rebuilding the liberal order. After witnessing Trump's

---

[45] Acharya, *The End of American World Order.* See also: "The End of American World Order," *The Diplomat,* November 10, 2016, http://thediplomat.com/2016/11/the-end-of-american-world-order/.

[46] Volker Perthes, "President Trump and International Relations," Point of View, Stiftung Wissenschaft und Politik (German Institute for International and Security Affairs, SWP), November 18, 2016, www.swp-berlin.org/en/point-of-view/president-trump-and-international-relations/.

immediate and total repudiation of a free trade agreement (TPP) negotiated painstakingly over many years, how many countries will trust an
American president when he promises a new international agreement,
whether over trade or security?

While Trump has promised to "Make America great again," he is
unlikely to reverse the decline of the American-led liberal international
order. On the contrary, Trump's election platform and statements on
trade, alliances, and immigration, if carried to their logical conclusion,
will speed up the breakdown of the liberal order. More importantly,
Trump's victory will hasten the arrival of a Multiplex World. As discussed in Chapter 1 and elsewhere, a Multiplex World is defined as a
world which no single power or ideology dominates globally, which is
culturally and politically diverse yet deeply interconnected and interdependent, and whose main players – both the makers and breakers of
order – are not just states and the great powers, but also international
and regional bodies, non-state groups, corporations, and people's movements and networks.

Many pundits see the decline of the United States and the Western-
dominated liberal order as a return to pre-World War multipolarity. But this
is misleading. The world today is very different from the multipolar world,
especially of the pre-World War II European kind. For one thing, today's
key players in international politics are not just great or rising powers. They
include international institutions, non-state actors, regional powers and
organizations, and multinational corporations. European interdependence before World War II, based narrowly on trade, was undermined by
dynastic squabbles, balance-of-power politics, and a bloodthirsty rivalry
for overseas colonies. The major nations of the world today are bound by
much broader and complex forms of interdependence comprising trade,
finance, and production networks as well as shared vulnerability to transnational challenges such as terrorism and climate change.

One of the main consequences of the effects of Trump will be a further
diffusion of agency in world politics. One dimension of this, as already
noted, could be seen in the future direction of globalization. The United
States under Trump is unlikely to reverse globalization, but it might
hasten the advent of a new kind. While the benefits of globalization are
questioned in the West, China and India have benefited from it too much
to abandon it. As noted above, China has defended economic globalization, even if it does not accept the liberal political values associated with
the hitherto Western-led globalization.[47] So instead of seeing the "end" of

[47] Acharya, "Emerging Powers Can Be Saviours of the Global Liberal Order."

globalization, the world might witness the transition to a new form of globalization. The new globalization is likely to be led more by the East than by the West, by the emerging powers such as China and India than by the established powers, and built more around South–South linkages than around North–South ones.

In a Multiplex World, demand for global governance will remain robust, but we should expect a further fragmentation of its architecture and agency. The big post-war multilaterals such as the IMF, the World Bank, and the WTO will be joined by new bodies such as the Asian Infrastructure Investment Bank (AIIB) and other initiatives launched by China and the emerging powers. Multilateralism is becoming a complex patchwork of separate and overlapping multitudes of global, plurilateral, regional institutions and networks, private sector initiatives, civil society movements, and public–private partnerships.[48] This will redefine agency in global governance.

The emerging powers will assume a greater role in managing and shaping world order and will not allow a precipitate collapse of the liberal order. While China and India do not seek to displace the liberal order, it would also be a mistake to assume that they and other emerging powers would have the same stake in the West's interest in preserving the liberal order in the long term. Without concrete progress in meeting their demands for reform of the existing international institutions to give them more voice and influence, they will be suspicious of accepting any new schema devised in the West for preserving the liberal order. The West has to negotiate accommodation with them in order to salvage aspects of the liberal order. This will contribute further to non-Western agency in global order-building and accelerate the shift toward a Multiplex World.

In a Multiplex World liberal internationalism will not disappear. But it has to compete with other forms and forces. The liberal international order would be one of the multiple, but cross-cutting systems alongside other ideas and approaches in a world of growing complexity and interconnectedness. The stability of a Multiplex World would require other Western nations shedding their free-riding on the United States and accepting shared leadership with the rising and regional powers. It would require greater partnership between global and regional bodies, public, private, and civil society groups. It would require a reformed system of global governance that accords genuine recognition to the voices and aspirations of the Rest.

---

[48] Acharya, *Why Govern?*

Thus, a Multiplex World is likely to witness a further diffusion and pluralization of agency in world politics. To be sure, the United States and Western agency in global order will remain important, even critical. But its salience will decline relative to non-Western agency. This broadening of agency will include not just the rising powers such as China, India, Brazil, South Africa, etc., but also other regional actors and institutions. Their agency will focus on reforming the existing institutions of governance, security, and development and more generally seeking representation and participation in global order-building.[49] This may create tensions and conflict, but also new opportunities for bridging the West–Rest divide. To this end, institutions such as the G20 and the AIIB, which bring together both Western and non-Western players, and multilateral agreements such as the Paris Climate Agreement, in which the emerging powers played a critical role side-by-side with the Western leaders, might assume a greater salience.

Summing Up

To sum up, the standard view of the post-World War II global order has been that it was constituted by the universalization of the principles and institutions of the European international society, albeit modified and managed by the power and purpose of the United States. But this view does not fully account for the contribution of non-Western actors in global order. Although many governing ideas and institutions of the global order did originate from a specific European and American milieu, in reality they have been and continue to be contested and redefined to fit the larger milieu of a pluralistic world. This has especially been the case with sovereignty and security, the two core themes of this book. For example, while sovereignty at its origin was a European (Westphalian) construct, security, especially the prevailing idea of national security, is American in origin. While often assumed to be universal, their meaning and application have been marked by significant contestations and contributions when applied to the non-Western world. These have opened the space for other actors to put forward alternative, sometimes localized, ideas and institutions that also support global order-building.

Understanding the complex, varied, and multiple contributions to the making of global order requires a broader conception of agency.

---

[49] Andrew F. Cooper, "Labels Matter: Interpreting Rising Powers through Acronyms," in *Rising States, Rising Institutions*, ed. Alan S. Alexandroff and Andrew F. Cooper (Waterloo, Ontario, Canada and Washington DC: The Center for International Governance Innovation and The Brookings Institution, 2010).

But agency cannot be limited to the material domain alone. Normative agency matters much. When it comes to normative agency, the role of non-Western actors is simply not a matter of passive acceptance of Western principles and approaches to sovereignty and security. The global sovereignty regime, the foundation of the modern world polity, came about not just through the passive inheritance of Westphalian principles by newly decolonized states. The latter also actively constructed these principles and translated the abstract notion of sovereignty into rules of conduct. The process was marked by local initiative and adaptation in the non-Western world. The same can be said about the idea of security, whose meaning has changed through distinctive constructions in non-Western contexts, but construction with wider global relevance and applicability.

The pluralization of agency has driven and will continue to drive the transformation of global order. It is opening the door to a Multiplex World, which is in essence a multi-agentic world. By advancing a pluralistic conception of agency, this book allows for a greater acknowledgement of the agency of non-Western actors in the global order. If the analysis of this book is accurate, then it portends the narrowing, if not the end, of the West–Rest divide and makes it possible to imagine the possibility of a truly global order.

Index

Abdulghani, Roeslan, 77, 79
adaptation, 45
Afghanistan, 74
Africa
    regionalism, 157, 182
    response to R2P, 121–3
    sovereignty, 93–5
African National Congress (ANC), 74
African Union (AU), 121, 170, 174
    EU and, 178
agency, 12–23, 186, 189, 206
    challenge and contestation, 14–16
    non-Western, 202
    pluralization, 207
        global order and, 28–34
        subjective elements, 17–18
    weaker actors, 18–20
Agent Orange, 151
Agip, 101
Alagappa, Muthiah, 4, 11
Algeria, 162
Ali, Mohammed, 80
Amoco, 101
Annan, Kofi, 102, 104, 106
apartheid, 94
Arab League, 127, 156, 160
Argentina, 61
Asia
    human security, 145
    regionalism, 180–2
    response to R2P, 122–3
    security doctrines, 136–7
    sovereignty and regionalism, 85–90
Asia Pacific Conference on East Timor, 181
Asian financial crisis, 181
Asian Infrastructure Investment Bank (AIIB), 205–6,
Asian Relations Conferences, 74–7
Association of Southeast Asian Nations (ASEAN), 89, 123, 136, 142, 162, 164, 165, 170, 180–2, 197
    adoption of EU model, 177–8

ASEAN Way, 64, 197
    Charter, 176
    Commission on the Rights of Women and Children (ACRWC), 181
    Intergovernmental Commission on Human Rights (AICHR), 181
    Plus institutions, 62
    Regional Forum (ARF), 62, 123
Aung Sang Suu Kyi, 156
Axworthy, Lloyd, 97, 106, 142
Ayoob, Mohammed, 131

Balkan conflict, 106
Ban Ki Moon, 121
Bandung Conference, 16, 68–9, 72, 74, 75, 92, 93, 122, 187
    principles, 81–2
Bangkok Declaration, 84
Banyan approach, 193
Barnett, Michael, 91
Bellamy, Alex, 124
Berbera, 101
Blyden, Edward Wilmot, 157
Boesenecker, Aaron P., 194
Bolívar, Simón, 156
Bolivia, 194
boomerang model, 192
Börzel, Tanja, 178
Bosnia, 114
Boutros-Ghali, Boutros, 101, 106, 109
Brazil, 159, 200
Brexit, 201, 203
BRICS countries, 29, 126
Buhe Commission, 107
Bull, Hedley, 5
Burma, 74, 77, 83, 120, 181
Burundi, 109, 162
Bush, George W., 26, 50, 110
Buzan, Barry, 12

Calvo, Carlos, 91
Calvo Doctrine, 63, 91, 158
Cambodia, 74